SKATE LIFE

TECHNOLOGIES OF THE IMAGINATION NEW MEDIA IN EVERYDAY LIFE

Ellen Seiter and Mimi Ito, Series Editors

This book series showcases the best ethnographic research today on engagement with digital and convergent media. Taking up in-depth portraits of different aspects of living and growing up in a media-saturated era, the series takes an innovative approach to the genre of the ethnographic monograph. Through detailed case studies, the books explore practices at the forefront of media change through vivid description analyzed in relation to social, cultural, and historical context. New media practice is embedded in the routines, rituals, and institutions—both public and domestic—of everyday life. The books portray both average and exceptional practices but all grounded in a descriptive frame that renders even exotic practices understandable. Rather than taking media content or technology as determining, the books focus on the productive dimensions of everyday media practice, particularly of children and youth. The emphasis is on how specific communities make meanings in their engagement with convergent media in the context of everyday life, focusing on how media is a site of agency rather than passivity. This ethnographic approach means that the subject matter is accessible and engaging for a curious layperson, as well as providing rich empirical material for an interdisciplinary scholarly community examining new media.

Ellen Seiter is Professor of Critical Studies and Stephen K. Nenno Chair in Television Studies, School of Cinematic Arts, University of Southern California. Her many publications include *The Internet Playground: Children's Access, Entertainment, and Mis-Education; Television and New Media Audiences;* and *Sold Separately: Children and Parents in Consumer Culture.*

Mimi Ito is Research Scientist, Department of Informatics, University of California, Irvine, and Visiting Associate Professor at the Graduate School of Media and Governance of Keio University, Kanagawa, Japan. She has published widely on new media and youth and led a recently completed three-year project, Kids' Informal Learning with Digital Media, an ethnographic study of digital youth funded by the MacArthur Foundation.

TITLES IN THE SERIES
Skate Life: Re-Imagining White Masculinity by Emily Chivers Yochim

DIGITALCULTUREBOOKS is a collaborative imprint of the University of Michigan Press and the University of Michigan Library dedicated to publishing innovative and accessible work exploring new media and their impact on society, culture, and scholarly communication.

SKATE LIFE

Re-Imagining White Masculinity

Emily Chivers Yochim

THE UNIVERSITY OF MICHIGAN PRESS AND
THE UNIVERSITY OF MICHIGAN LIBRARY
ANN ARBOR

Published in the United States of America by
The University of Michigan Press and
The University of Michigan Library
Manufactured in the United States of America

♾ Printed on acid-free paper

2013   2012   2011   2010   4   3   2   1

A CIP catalog record for this book is available from the British Library

Library of Congress Cataloging-in-Publication Data
Yochim, Emily Chivers
    Skate life : re-imagining white masculinity / by Emily Chivers Yochim.
        p.   cm.
    Includes bibliographical references.
    ISBN 978-0-472-07080-0 (cloth : alk. paper) — ISBN 978-0-472-05080-2
(pbk. : alk. paper)
    1. Skateboarding—Social aspects.   2. Masculinity in sports.
3. Men, White—United States—Attitudes.   I. Title.
GV859.8.Y64   2009
796.22—dc22   2009033066

    ISBN13 978-0-472-02660-9 (electronic)

To my boys, my loves
Christopher Yochim and
Elliot Colin Yochim

And in loving memory of
Colin Matthew Chivers
(1982–2004)

Acknowledgments

Skate Life has been accompanied by and ushered through great joys and great sorrows, and I have many friends, colleagues, mentors, and family members to thank for seeing it and me through. The words throughout this book are punctuated by many lives, and it is my hope that the following paragraphs can convey my deep appreciation for their contributions.

In the course of writing, I have developed friendships and professional relationships with many thoughtful, passionate, and smart people. It was an honor and a pleasure to work with Susan Douglas, whose *Where the Girls Are* suggested to my undergraduate self that academic work could be both smart and a delight to read. As my graduate cochair, Susan provided sage and pragmatic writing advice, modeled dedicated and energetic engagement in academe, and offered clear and sharp comments that always shepherded my thinking. Bambi Haggins, from my first steps into graduate school, demonstrated dedication, love, and creativity, which allowed me to write with confidence and joy. Bambi's rigorous commitment to the significance of pop culture, her venerable writing and editing, and her nuanced understanding of theory and practice have made my work more dynamic and complex. I'll never forget sketching out my first-year research project with her and hearing her exclaim, "This is a book!" Derek Vaillant's keen enthusiasm for theoretical debate and discussion and his willingness to work through the multiple layers of theory that accompany interdisciplinarity have both challenged and inspired me. Robin Means Coleman's lively and sagacious approach to research is a consummate model, and her pointed and supportive critiques brought new energy to this project and made my work more rigorous.

My new colleagues in the Communication Arts Department at Allegheny College have been enormously welcoming and kind. As the department chair, Dan Crozier wisely guided me through the first year of teaching, and he carefully advised me as I worked to finish the book, teach my students, and maintain my sanity. It has been a great pleasure to work with and get to know Courtney Bailey, River Branch, Mark Cosdon, Meg Coyle, Mike Keeley, Michael Mehler, Vesta Silva, Ishita Sinha Roy, Jim Strickler, Beth Watkins, and Jon Wiebel. Jan Mailliard was both helpful and generous as we both worked our way through new jobs. It is truly a joy to work in this department, and I thank these individuals for that.

Many thanks to the folks at the University of Michigan Press who have brought this project to life. Alison Mackeen, Tom Dwyer, and Alexa Ducsay have been wonderful and have adeptly guided me through the process of publishing. As reviewers, Ellen Seiter and Joellen Fisherkeller both boosted my confidence and asked meaningful questions that added to this book. The anonymous third reviewer provided me with a great list of academic accounts of extreme sports and asked important theoretical questions that moved my analysis along.

I've also been granted a great deal of institutional support that gave me the time necessary to complete this ethnographic, historical, and textual analysis. The University of Michigan's Rackham Regents Fellowship and Rackham One-Term Dissertation Writing Fellowship each provided time off from teaching so that I could focus on research and writing. I was also fully supported by the Department of Communication Studies at the University of Michigan, which provided a Winthrop Chamberlain Research Award and a Dissertation Research Award. I am grateful to the Institute for Research on Women and Gender at the University of Michigan for the opportunity to be a part of its Community of Scholars program, which provided me both the funding and the community necessary to usher this project along.

My friends and colleagues Megan Biddinger, Sarah Crymble, Kamille Gentles, and Debra Burns Melican brought their vastly impressive brains to my work, reading countless drafts, listening to too many presentations, and talking through theoretical quandaries that reminded me how exciting research can be. More important, each of these women has been a trusty confidante and supportive ally through the peaks and valleys of, well, life. Megan, always creative and passionate as she grapples with theoretical and social problems, has inspired me to demand more of myself and society, and together she and I are absolute writing dynamos. Sarah's thoughtful and empathic wisdom has ushered me through much and served as a model for staying true to oneself and others. Her theoretical prowess and dedication to her work are exemplary. I am ever grateful for my friendship with Kamille and the phone calls that have sustained our relationship. Time and time again, her compassion, humor, and astute questions and comments about my work reinvigorated and inspired me. Debbie's energy, courage, and style move me to cull as much I can from all of my experiences. She read over 100 pages of my work at a moment of last-minute desperation and gave me astute, clear, and invaluable feedback. Each of these women has touched my work in many ways, but, more important, they have enriched my life.

I am lucky to have had the opportunity to study, write, and work with a number of other creative, vibrant, and loyal individuals who have deepened my love for teaching and research. Pete Simonson is the reason I went to graduate school. His mind is vast, and as my undergraduate mentor he constantly pushed me to ask new questions of theory and to find joy and new knowledge in the nuances and quirks of everyday life. Pete has remained a steady and supportive friend and mentor, and I am always moved by his continued engagement in my work and my life. Catherine Squires was a steady presence through graduate school, and her skillful and fiery commitment to theory and practice is exemplary. Roei Davidson's smarts, energy, and wide-ranging knowledge widened my own experiences. Brad Taylor's thoughtful and dedicated approach to teaching served as a reminder of its pleasures. Since Phil Hallman amassed a host of surfing movies for me years ago, his vast knowledge of the mediated world and his interest in my work have been invaluable. Rachel Kennett, Stephanie Wooten, Emily Dalton, and Alexandra Coury, my intrepid research assistants, have contributed an enormous amount of frequently mind-numbing labor to this book with patience and humor. I'm lucky to know them. Alex deserves special thanks for coming in at the end with unparalleled excitement, energy, and verve. Thanks also to Brian V. Smith, whose great graphic design abilities pale in comparison to his humor and generosity.

This volume truly would not exist were it not for the skateboarders.

More than willing participants in my research, these young men have come to represent hope, passion, youthful vigor, and humor, and I deeply value their friendship. All of the boys happily provided thoughtful responses to my questions in exchange for a bit of food, but Mason, Andrew, Marcus, Sikander, Davidson, and Eric went above and beyond, welcoming me into their lives, guiding me through skate culture, and providing a humorous and hip respite from schoolwork. I am glad to call them friends.

Butch Thomas's love, support, and constant interest in the challenges of schoolwork sustained me through many professional challenges, and his firm belief in my physical power has followed me through all aspects of my life. Cindy Anders has been a model partner, inspiring me with her energy and dedication. The humor, perseverance, and friendship I found at Z-Force Fitness were irreplaceable during my solitary days of writing, and the willingness of the Lighthouse coffee shop in Milan, Michigan, to allow me to commandeer their back booth for hours at a time was crucial to the completion of this book. Providing coffee and good conversation, the Lighthouse was an ideal space in which to write about popular culture and everyday politics. In these places, I've had the opportunity to engage in many dynamic conversations about local skateboarding policies; skateboarders' reputations in school, church, and home; and individuals' opinions and attitudes about teenage boys in general and skateboarders in particular.

Great big thanks to all those who knew me before. My close friends Bethany Lewis, Nicole Conrad, Maria File, and Timilee Vaughn have been steadfast in their support, celebrating my accomplishments along with me and keeping my head above water when I was about to drown in work. The Yochim family's cheerful love and creative humor are always comforting, and their resolute love and commitment to Elliot have been both invaluable and touching. I thank them for this and their countless hours of child care, without which this book would never have been completed. The Chivers family has been supportive in many, many ways. My mom, Mary Chivers, listened to regular end-of-semester breakdowns and cheered me through every accomplishment. I have been especially lucky to have her since I became a mother. The hours and energy she has given to help me through the challenges of parenting are priceless, and I'm happy to be able to share the joys of parenting with her as well. She, too, has offered hours of child care for which I am fantastically thankful. My mom is a model of grace and generosity, and I will never be able to adequately thank her. My dad, David Chivers, has encouraged me in my professional endeavors and offered a sympathetic ear as I talked about the challenges of work. He is a model in his humor, charisma, and work ethic, and I thank him for that. My brothers, John and Tim Chivers, are steady in their love and steady in their teasing. Always willing to help with whatever I need, they are worthy, worthy allies, and I'm grateful to have them.

When it comes down to it, we all study what we know and worry about, and I have known and worried about many men. My men past and present inspire and drive my work, and this book is dedicated to them. I lost my brother Colin, too suddenly and too soon, in 2004, and I forever miss his tender love and mocking humor. Baby Elliot motivated me to finish my work in a way that no one else could. His quiet joy, thoughtful curiosity, sweet demeanor, and warm love give me great pleasure, and he just makes me an enormously proud mama. And, of course, Chris Yochim, my longtime love, best friend, and partner, has offered irreplaceable support, encouragement, and love through the demands of research, teaching, and writing. The model skateboarder, Chris's sensitivity, gentleness, and creativity have shown me that men can get it right. He always brought me back to earth, reminding me of the absurdity of hegemony, problematics, and theory in the face of true love, friendships, and the everyday joys of regular life. I thank him forever.

Contents

Introduction

Regarding Skate Life

"Pay attention to what he's saying, because he's a skate legend. He's saying how he lived in a small town and skating saved his life. Listen to what he's saying," 15-year-old skateboarder Braden told me as I sat with him in his mother's living room watching a skateboarding video. I had met Braden on a sidewalk several months earlier. He was carrying a skateboard, and I was looking for skateboarders to interview. He and I had gotten to know one another during a lunchtime interview, and he had eagerly responded to my interest in skate culture, allowing me to tag along during skate sessions in Ann Arbor, Detroit, and Toledo; introducing me to his parents; and inviting me to participate in both his everyday life and special events such as his high school graduation party. On this particular day, Braden and his close friend, 16-year-old Jack, who are both white, middle-class, suburban boys, were taking me on a tour through their media lives, waving books, magazines, and videos in front of me and defining themselves via their media habits.

By the time Braden told me to "Listen to what he's saying," we were watching excerpts from a number of their favorite skateboarding videos. In my time with Braden, I had come to realize that he was a teenager with big dreams, a willing student who was often in awe of the people he met and their varied accomplishments. The only son of divorced artists, Braden saw the world as a site of possibility, but he also was easily frustrated with himself and sometimes expressed disgust with his peers and their seemingly lazy and sole interest in partying. So when he directed me to listen to the skater on the screen it was immediately clear that he was telling me, "This is what skating is all about for me. Skating has saved *my* life." It had expanded his peer group, opened his eyes to new ways of thinking, and provided him with a social space in which he could hone his strategies of self-expression. For Braden, skateboarding media served as a reflection and projection of himself, his values, and his aspirations. Although I did not know Braden's friend Jack as well as I knew Braden, Jack was far more explicit in making the same claim, noting at one point, "Brian [the professional skater featured on the video] says it very well. This is how I think." Skateboarding videos comprise just one element in a vast network of texts that make up Jack and Braden's highly mediated culture, and the pleasure they take in finding themselves through niche skateboarding media is complicated by their knowledge and consumption of the mainstream media that construct skate life in ways sometimes antithetical to—and sometimes aligned with—the boys' self-constructions.

In 2006, FedEx released an ad proclaiming its value to corporations' bottom line as well as its hip sensibilities. Aired during NBC's *The Office*, the latest incarnation of a slew of media texts mocking the banality of the corporate workplace, the ad features three company folks standing in a cubicle farm. A gray-haired, white male exec wearing a dark suit notes the time that FedEx has been saving the company and wonders, "So why aren't we getting more done?" The three pause for a beat, thinking, and then a white, middle-aged woman wearing a brown suit deadpans, "Maybe we should get rid of the half pipe." The camera follows the group's glance and settles on a medium shot of a half pipe (a large ramp shaped like a letter *U* [half of a pipe] on which skateboarders perform their tricks) crowded into a space at the edge of the cubicles. Two skaters ride the half pipe (some falling) as five others look on. The camera cuts back to the corporate folks, and the executive decides, "No. The half pipe stays," to which the woman replies, "Gotta keep the half pipe." Drawing on skateboarding's cultural cachet to represent its own hip sensibilities, this commercial constructs skateboarders as slackers while at the same time representing an aversion to the mundane, buttoned-up world of corporate America and the constrained images of white masculinity that accompany it. Although the ad does not explicitly reframe skateboarding in a manner antithetical to skateboarders' principles, its mere presence on network television might cause some skateboarders pause. FedEx's appropriation of skate life is just one of many co-optations that more and less successfully represent the values espoused by many skaters.

Skateboarders are surrounded by and ensconced in a media culture that locates them on the cool side of mainstream, and they are also devoted to and take great pleasure in niche media that appeal to them exclusively as skateboarders and often inspire or supply dominant media outlets with their representations of skateboarders.[1] Videos and magazines produced by skateboarding companies and available for purchase in skate shops communicate the styles, locations, heroes, and values of the culture. Skateboarders avidly consume these media and say that they provoke pleasurable moments of escape and inspiration. They also produce local, independent videos modeled on niche skate videos.

The practice of skateboarding has been read, variously, as an innocuous childhood pastime, a lazy pursuit of teenage slacker/stoners, destructive rebellion, and cultural critique. Scholars have generally examined either skateboarders' relationship to urban space or the gender politics of skate culture. Iain Borden's insightful analysis suggests that skateboarders rework city space as a sight of pleasure rather than a location of commerce.[2] Ocean Howell's work updates Borden's, arguing that skateboarders can now be understood as members of the "creative class" who "produc[e] surplus value by leading the reclamation of [city] space."[3] Kyle Kusz understands skate culture to be part of a white male backlash against the perceived slights of feminism, gay rights, and civil rights.[4] More broadly, Belinda Wheaton reports that

> the central question lifestyle sport researchers have sought to answer is whether these newer non-traditional sports offer *different* and potentially more *transformatory* scripts for male and female physicality, than the hegemonic masculinities and femininities characteristic of traditional sports cultures and identities.[5]

Skate Life builds on this work to develop an analysis of the identity politics of skate culture and the media related to it.

Defining themselves in, through, and around multiple representations of skate life, skateboarders comprise what I call a "corresponding culture" that is always in the process of developing and responding to critiques of dominant masculinities that never fully challenge the power of straight, white, middle-class American men. Instructing me to "listen" because "this is how I think," Braden and Jack were initiating me into the norms of skate media consumption, showing me that their personal notions of identity were being constructed in correspondence with the texts of skate culture specifically and popular culture more generally. By referring to skateboarders as a corresponding culture, I am defining them as a culture that both is in constant conversation (or correspondence) with a wide array of mainstream, niche, and local media forms and finds various affinities (or corresponds) with these forms' ideologies. Continuously in motion, a corresponding culture is a group organized around a particular lifestyle or activity that interacts with various levels of media—niche, mainstream, and local—and variously agrees or disagrees with those media's espoused ideas. Skateboarding media and skateboarders, as I will demonstrate, frequently center these correspondences on nascent critiques of dominant masculinities that manage, at the same time, to maintain the power of white, middle-class, heterosexual American men.

"Modern Marketing's Mother Lode": White Male Teenagers, Alternative Masculinities, and Consumer Culture

As a white teenage girl, I became, I must admit, enamored with a group of white skateboarders who positioned themselves as different from, and superior to, "typical" high school boys. These skaters spent their time listening to punk and indie music that was not on the radio, going to "shows" (small concerts featuring local and national bands), and skateboarding. Their quirky sense of humor, seeming disdain for high school hierarchies, and knowing sense of irony about life in general operated as an apparent foil to the macho displays, ego-driven drug use, and boring preoccupation with "cool" typical of most of my fellow high schoolers, and I quickly began to spend most of my free time with this crowd. I went to shows, the beach, and house parties with these boys, watched their bands practice, hung out with them while they skated idly around convenience store parking lots, and spent my fair share of time sitting around, bored, while they watched skateboarding videos with just as much enthusiasm as the skateboarders in the current study.

In 1995, at age 17, I began to date one of the skateboarders, and in 1999, as an undergraduate communication arts major, I produced a documentary featuring skaters in my college town who were working with the local government to develop a skate park.[6] My senior thesis explored the hardcore music community in Erie, Pennsylvania, a community with which my high school friends were periodically engaged. At 24, I married the skateboarder I had begun to date at 17, and my relationship with him has helped me to maintain my ties to my high school peers, as has my younger brothers' interest in skateboarding and BMXing.[7] My youngest brother, Tim, who is 8 years my junior, has turned an outbuilding on our family farm into an indoor BMX and skate park, and his ramps have been featured in a national BMX magazine with several professional BMXers. He has also served as an intern for Quiksilver, a national skate and surf apparel brand, working to design portable ramps as part of a community outreach program in Los Angeles.

Despite my 14-year involvement with the skateboarding and BMXing communities, I remain a relative outsider. I am loath to admit that I operate in this community principally as an observer. I have set foot on skateboards more often than many people, but I can only coast tentatively on very, very smooth surfaces. I don't play in the bands; I watch the bands. I am not "in" on all of the boys' jokes, I continue to be invited along primarily as a heterosexual partner, and I have little agency within the group. The boys know me well enough to ask me about my life, to chuckle at my wry observations about their culture, and to ask about my family. They have attended the major events in my life, and they count me as a friend. And I do, truly, appreciate their friendships. But it is clearly *their* world, a culture in which men remain at the center and carry much of the day-to-day power.

My experience as a female outsider in skateboarding culture is not unique. As Deirdre M. Kelly and her colleagues make clear in their study of female skateboarders, despite skateboarding's "association with non-conformity and anti-mainstream values, it has been oddly traditional in its membership, dominated by boys and men."[8] Becky Beal and Charlene Wilson explain that skateboard culture's overvaluation of risk taking, paired with many male skaters' belief that women seek to avoid pain and injury, places women on the outskirts of the culture. Moreover, stories about talented female skateboarders have been relegated to the mainstream press (deemed inauthentic by skaters) because niche skateboarding publications (deemed authentic) have refused to print them.[9] Even programs purportedly aimed toward including female extreme sports athletes manage to maintain men as the standard-bearers in extreme sports culture, Michele K. Donnelly observes.[10] Although I never defined myself as a skateboarder within this culture, my gender still pushed me to the sidelines.

I have carried the relationships from my youth into my relationships with Michigan skateboarders, and, though I have known many of the boys for five years, I still find myself hanging out on the margins, watching as they act, laughing along with jokes I don't find particularly funny, and shyly asking them to explain the context of particular comments. At the same time, I have been invited to their graduation parties, gone to dinner with them, kept in touch via the Internet, and spent afternoons watching them skateboard with and without my husband. I am an insider watching from the outside, an outsider with a history of peering in. My position on the borders of this community—a borderland constructed primarily through my gender and secondarily through my age and position as a researcher—has been a privileged location for an ethnographer, a location affording me an insider's access, through my history and my husband's skate culture cachet, to both the community and knowledge of its norms and the outsider's insight into the peculiarity of those norms.

In the beginning years of my friendship with skater boys, skateboarding's relationship to popular culture began to shift. In 1995, when the television sports network ESPN launched *The Extreme Games*, later branded *The X Games*, the age of extreme began. Tony Hawk, who was already well known to skateboarders in the 1980s, became the mainstream face of skateboarding, and the practice began its journey (some might say descent) into a culture of cool.[11] During the late 1980s or early 1990s, my friends had seen Tony Hawk up close and in person during a skateboarding demo (demonstration) in a McDonald's parking lot in Erie, Pennsylvania. They had been called "skater fags" throughout their middle school years in the late 1980s and early 1990s, and some endured such treatment into their high school years. In 1993, a self-proclaimed jock brutally beat one of our friends after school one day; the victim was an extremely talented skateboarder, swimmer, and artist who occasionally had the audacity to wear skirts to school. The skateboarding, swimming, artistry, and skirts were all clearly tied together as part and parcel of our friend's *seemingly* and *supposedly* feminized and sexually ambiguous identity. For committing these "crimes," the jock broke our friend's back. He was taken to a hospital in Pittsburgh, where he was put on life support and deemed paralyzed. With much hard work, determination, and luck, he now walks with a walker. Clearly, for this group of heterosexual, middle-class, white boys gathered loosely around skateboarding and punk music, their identities placed them on the outside of the mainstream, and the outside was not always comfortable or safe. But the introduction of *The Extreme Games* and skateboarding's attendant popularity were also vaguely troubling.

Since 1999, the business and advertising press have been reporting major increases in participation in extreme sports generally and skateboarding more particularly. In 2000, Fuse Sports Marketing, a self-described "youth culture marketing agency,"[12] reported a 35 percent increase in extreme sports participation since 1995.[13] American Sports Data noted that participation in snowboarding increased by 51 percent between 1999 and 2000, to 7 million participants, while participation in skateboarding increased by 49 percent, to 12 million participants.[14] In comparison, by 2000, baseball, basketball, volleyball, and softball had all experienced falling numbers, with baseball participation dropping to 10.9 million individuals.[15] In 2004, the Sporting Goods Manufacturing Association reported 19.23 million Rollerbladers, 11.09 million skateboarders, 7.82 million snowboarders, and 3.37 million BMXers.[16]

This marked shift in American sporting practices from organized team sports to more individualistic "extreme" or "action" sports prompted, and was perhaps influenced by, new trends in youth marketing. *The Extreme Games*, ESPN's weeklong alternative to the Olympics, featured nine extreme sports: BMXing, bungee jumping, barefoot water-ski jumping, inline skating, mountain biking, skysurfing, street luge, windsurfing, and skateboarding. The broadcasts were sponsored by Taco Bell, Advil, Chevrolet trucks, Mountain Dew, Nike, AT&T, and Miller beer.[17] By 1996, both Nike and Adidas were developing skateboarding shoes,[18] and in 1999 *Fortune* reported that the IEG Sponsorship Report had noted a 500 percent increase since 1993 in "revenue for alternative sports sponsorships" to 135 million dollars.[19] Wheaton reported that by 1999 the surf and skate retailer Quiksilver was selling over 450 million dollars' worth of surfing-related products annually.[20]

By the turn of the century, it seemed that everyone had jumped on the extreme bandwagon. *Advertising Age* proclaimed, "Everything from cheeseburgers to jeans is being dubbed 'Xtreme,' as marketers use 'X' to get to Y—Generation Y, that is," and went on to list Right Guard's Xtreme Sport deodorant, Schick's Xtreme III razor, Clairol's Xtreme FX hair color, and Burger King's X-Treme double cheeseburger. The "U.S. Patent and Trademark Directory," the magazine reported, listed 296 brands and products using the word *Xtreme*.[21] Indeed, less than a year later the magazine noted, "Extreme sports have become so popular they no longer seem extreme," and reported that ESPN had begun calling this same group of activities action sports.[22]

Despite industry fears that "extreme" had gone too mainstream, the business press indicated that the extreme marketing strategies continued to be successful. Eight weeks after its sponsorship of the 2000 Winter X Games, for example, Heinz's Bagel Bites posted a 20 percent increase in sales and noted, "Action sports is a sport that embodies the lifestyle and personality of the Bagel Bites consumer."[23] Similarly, Dave DeCecco of PepsiCo suggested that until its 1992 "Do the Dew" campaign Mountain Dew was regarded as a "hillbilly drink." With its new marketing strategy tied directly to extreme sports, Mountain Dew became the fastest-growing soft drink of the 1990s.[24] By 2004, Tony Hawk, spokesman for the snack foods Bagel Bites and Doritos and the name behind Activision's Tony Hawk line of video games, was earning approximately 9 million dollars a year, reported *Forbes*, and his own brand had pulled in 300 million in sales of apparel, skateboards, tours, and video games.[25] According to Belinda Wheaton, a May 2002 marketing report indicated that "Hawk was voted the 'coolest big time athlete,'" besting such big-name stars as "Michael Jordan and Tiger Woods."[26]

The extreme marketing trend stems not only from the sports' rising popularity but also from their perceived affinity to teens more generally. Julie Halpin, a youth marketer, contends, "Teens are naturally impelled to test limits. Something extreme pushes the pre-existing boundaries and appeals to that part of a teen who fancies him or herself on the very edge of what the rest of the world considers normal."[27] Others have reported extreme sports' success in reaching the notoriously elusive 14- to 30-year-old male; both the U.S. Marines and the Air Force have sponsored extreme sports events and used extreme sports in their marketing campaigns. Lt. Col. Ismael Ortiz, assistant chief of staff advertising, noted the Marines' "inclusive" attitude, writing that extreme sports events "reach our target audience, the 18-to-24-year-old. . . . We don't let the color of their hair or how they wear their clothes take away from who they are." Laura Petrecca of *Advertising Age* has suggested that the Marines' involvement in extreme sports could have been the reason for their recruiting success.[28]

Extreme sports were certainly a successful appeal for white males aged 12 to 34. In 2001, the *Gravity Games* (NBC's answer to ESPN's *X Games*) boasted a 1.7 rating for males aged 12 to 17 (approximately 200,000 young men) and a 1.2 rating for males aged 12 to 24 (320,000). In the same year, the *Summer X Games* reached about 178,000 males aged 12 to 17 and 330,000 aged 18 to 34. In comparison, the median age of baseball's audience is 46.4, and ESPN's "total-day median age" is 40.7. Brad Adgate, an executive with Horizon Media, called this a "demographic sweet spot."[29] In 1999, *Fortune* reported that corporate interest in extreme athletes resulted from the fact that "They sit smack in the middle of modern marketing's mother lode, the 17-year-old-male demographic and its $650 billion in annual spending power."[30]

Beyond their use as a marketing tool, extreme sports, and skateboarding in particular, have played a role in the rise of the market for "alternative" clothing. Styles and brands originally marketed to niche outlets such as skate shops have made their way into suburban malls. In its 2008 "Size of Skateboarding Market Trend Report," the market research company Board-Trac predicted annual sales of 4.78 billion dollars. This includes spending on both skateboarding equipment (wheels, axles, decks [boards without wheels attached]) and apparel (shoes, shirts, sunglasses, watches, jeans, and shorts) and takes into account sales at both "core" (niche) and mainstream retailers.[31] Hot Topic, an in-mall chain retailer that sells "alternative" apparel and accessories, was founded in 1989 and by 1999 was earning over 100 million dollars annually.[32] In 2006, *Forbes* listed the store as one of its top 100 places to work.[33] The surf- and skatewear retailer Pacific Sunwear doubled its earnings in 2004, earning 15 million dollars in the first quarter.[34] Tony Hawk's line of menswear retails at the department store Kohl's, and niche skate shoe brands Vans, Es, Etnies, and DC, formerly sold only in catalogs and skate shops, are now sold by major retailers. My 18-month-old child wears a pair of baby Vans that we bought at JCPenney.

Within a culture generally inundated with extreme sports, skateboarding has become particularly resonant both as a referent within popular culture that produces particular ideologies of race, gender, and youth and as a material practice that inspires civic debate about young people's use of public space. Skateboarders have been central in the television network MTV's contemporary lineup (in *Jackass*, *Viva La Bam*, *Wildboyz*, *Rob and Big*, *The Life of Ryan*, and *Scarred*) and appeared in an episode of *Made*.[35] They have also appeared in numerous music videos, including those for Will Smith's "Switch," the Pussycat Dolls' "Don't Cha" with Busta Rhymes, Pharrell Williams's "Can I Have It Like That" with Gwen Stefani, and Lupe Fiasco's "Skate/Push." The comedian Dave Chappelle often adopts a style associated with skateboarding, and MTV's Tom Green is closely associated with the professional skateboarder Tony Hawk; Tom Green is sponsored by Hawk's skateboarding company, Birdhouse Skateboards, and Hawk has appeared on Green's MTV show, *The Tom Green Show*. Skateboarders are also the focus of many advertisements in extreme marketing campaigns, including commercials for Doritos, Hot Pockets, McDonald's, Coca-Cola, Right Guard, and Mountain Dew. Finally, skateboarding was the subject of two nationally released documentaries (*Dogtown and Z-Boys* and *Stoked: The Rise and Fall of Gator*) and two fictional movies (*Grind* and *Lords of Dogtown*) between 2002 and 2005. Tony Hawk, with his extensive *ProSkater* and *Underground* Activision video games and numerous appearances in popular culture venues, including on the TV shows *CSI: Miami* and *The Simpsons*, is arguably the most recognizable extreme athlete in contemporary culture. Clearly, in the plethora of practices labeled "extreme," skateboarding is the figurehead.

Moreover, skateboarders have become the subject of rigorous debate in communities throughout the United States. Unlike surfing, snowboarding, or motocross, skateboarding can be practiced virtually anywhere with relatively small entry fees. A skateboard costs between 20 and 120 dollars, requires no special clothing, and can be practiced on any paved street, sidewalk, or driveway. American communities have spent considerable time debating the legality of skateboarding in public spaces and the necessity of establishing public skate parks open for community use. City councils

Tony Hawk, professional skateboarder, all-American family man, and the height of mainstream cool. (Courtesy PhotoFest.)

and citizens routinely voice concerns about skateboarders' safety,[36] pedestrians' safety in the path of skateboarders,[37] and skateboarders' destruction of public space and disruption of civil society (e.g., through vulgar language, loud and rowdy behavior, the destruction of property via both the practice of skateboarding and graffiti, and general disrespect toward elders).[38] While marketers celebrate teenage boys' spending power and the cultural appeal of skateboarding, parents, teachers, local politicians, and law enforcement officers sometimes revile these practices in their own locales and dismiss teenage boys' behavior as immature and irresponsible.

It is crucial to note that skateboarders are not wholeheartedly despised by the majority of adults. Their presence is the subject of debate, and many reports indicate that some adults, concerned with the criminalization of this youth activity, do come to skateboarders' defense in city meetings, noting that skaters are simply looking for a place to practice their sport.[39] In fact, many American cities have developed public skate parks in order to give

Hawk battles Homer for Bart's affections in *The Simpsons*. Homer is trying to show Bart that he is, indeed, hip. (Courtesy PhotoFest.)

skateboarders an alternative to skating on streets and sidewalks. Heidi Lemmon, director of the Skatepark Association, a California nonprofit organization, told the *New York Times* in 2005 that there are approximately 2,000 parks in the United States, with about 1,000 more in development, and indicated that cities manage most of the parks.[40] As I've noted, despite their ubiquity, skate parks are fraught with debate within skateboarding communities about the relative containment of skate parks and the rules that often accompany them.

Skateboarders, clearly, are a significant element of both popular culture and everyday life. Their culture and style have become principle elements in popular appeals to young men, and their increased presence in everyday life has given way to the development of both legal restrictions on the sport and sanctioned spaces for its practice. Skateboarders' ever-shifting location within mainstream youth culture—celebrated yet debated, popular but edgy—suggests that they strike a chord with Americans (parents, advertisers, and youths more generally) working to define the boundaries of youth identity, and as such it positions them as indicators of the contemporary status of American youths and their encounters with the media.

Identity Politics in Youth Cultures of Cool

Taking skateboarders as a case study, *Skate Life* contributes to our understanding of youth consumer culture and the pleasure and politics of its consumption by discussing the ways in which white masculinity is presented in youth media and by elaborating young men's reactions to these portrayals. Arguing that male skateboarders are dissatisfied with the norms of adult white masculinity but do not challenge the power that white men hold in our society, I suggest that media representations of white male youths present alternative masculinities that rely on both dominant American values and the mockery of nonwhites, homosexuals, and women to maintain men's power in this culture of cool.[41] Finally, I contend that skate culture creates a space in which young men can experience the mental and emotional pleasures of escape and self-expression, an experience often denied young men in a dominant culture that expects them to be emotionally reticent and in control.

Youth culture is a particularly interesting place in which to investigate identity because the rhetoric of youth is so frequently used as a symbol for the desires of an aging population; for the anxieties about new ways of being, current ideologies, and the state of the nation; for hopes for the future, particularly with respect to the nation; and for the possibilities of resistance. Although (and perhaps because) they so strongly engage the fears, hopes, and desires of the nation and its adults, youths are often the site of moral panic. Viewed as simultaneously *in* trouble and *causing* trouble, youths are highly scrutinized, surveilled, and controlled. Their symbolic resonance also makes them ideal emblems in consumer culture; more than existing as willing and able shoppers, youths—and the discourse of youth—are regularly used in advertising appeals.

As Mike Davies argues, "youth has become such a regulated, curfewed and controlled social group in the late twentieth century, that 'the only legal activity . . . is to consume.'"[42] Robert E. Rinehart suggests that the so-called millennial generation, or Generation Y, "is the first generation to be totally immersed in branding,"[43] which, as opposed to advertising, links consumer objects to a way of life or an attitude. What's more, drawing on N. Howe and W. Strauss, he points out that this generation, born in the 1980s, has a collective spending power of "$140 billion in total . . . or $4,500 per teenager per year."[44] Still, Michael D. Giardina and Michele K. Donnelly argue that

> the last 20 years of rapidly expanding commercial forays into youth culture have been paralleled by a concomitant, government-sanctioned slashing of educational funding . . . the increased surveillance and restriction of the civil liberties of youth in schools and public venues, the rise in disciplinary mechanisms of control, and the rapidly expanding psychotropic medicalization of youth who are deemed to be "different" or "at risk" because of their association with particular forms of popular cultural attitudes or expressions.[45]

Simultaneously, as the authors point out, youths are held responsible "for the collapse of urban—and occasionally suburban—environments into pseudo war-zones."[46]

Despite the overwhelming focus on surveillance and consumption in youth culture, affective pleasure is a key aspect of youthful experience that should be examined, particularly when considering youths' leisure activities. Belinda Wheaton draws on M. Atkinson and B. Wilson to suggest that lifestyle sports encourage participants to experience freedom from normative feelings of bodily discipline and "emphasize the creative, aesthetic, and performative expressions of their activities."[47] She observes that for participants in lifestyle sports pleasure is paramount, and pleasure is derived from a loss of the self, "the standing still of time."[48] What's more, this focus on immediacy and feeling counters "the commodified, aestheticized, and disciplined body that many describe as symptomatic and expressive of contemporary consumer culture."[49] As I discuss in the third chapter, "Freedom on four wheels," this type of pleasure is central to skateboarders' experience and is one avenue through which they contest dominant norms of white middle-class masculinity.

The dialectics of youth, as a site of anxiety and hope, fear and desire, control and freedom, and consumption and political engagement, present an ideal lens through which we can examine the possibilities for political engagement in a consumption-oriented world as well as a crucial site for considering the production of ideologies of identity. In other words, because youths occupy such a central place in the American imagination, through them we can shed some light on how race, gender, class, and sexuality inform and are informed by national identity as well as enlivening and expanding our definitions of political work.[50] Youths, then, can help us to reimagine the relationship among pleasure, politics, and identity so that we can provide more opportunities for their engagement in the larger world.

Much work has been done on the role of youth in the development of national identity as well as the production of identity within youth cultures. Most recently, Sunaina Maira and Elisabeth Soep have proposed the notion of a youthscape, drawing on Arjun Appadurai's theorization of globalization, which uses the idea of "scapes" to connote the uneven, conflicted, varied terrain on which social and political power are contested. By utilizing youthscapes, we can keep firmly in mind the dialectics of youth, the contradictions, complexities, and fluidity of a group that operates both in material culture and in discourse to define our hopes and dreams.[51]

Maira and Soep draw on Garcia Canclini, contending that

> we need to be more attuned to the new forms that citizenship takes in an era where relations of social belonging are "steeped in consumption," acknowledging the ways in which young people, among other social actors, may express political motivations or aspirations through their use of the media rather than assuming, a priori, that the space of consumption is opposed to that of citizenship.[52]

This project contends that skateboarding culture, which is steeped in consumption, is also a space of citizenship in which young men produce a politics of identity. The fluidity of this concept is quite useful for summarizing the scope of the book, which approaches skateboarders as members of a dynamic group whose conceptions of identity are produced through and within media designed to facilitate consumption and whose identity is tied to broader notions of white American masculinity. The notion of youth-scape also takes into account the various discourses, texts, institutions, and individuals that cross over, define, and interact with skateboarders, and as such it reinforces the fluid understanding of identity production that *Skate Life* develops.

Consumption, Politics, and Pleasure in Youth Culture

Many of this book's premises about media, consumption, and politics draw on subcultural theory. Stuart Hall and his colleagues at the Birmingham Centre for Contemporary Cultural Studies (CCCS) have posited that youth subcultures resist dominant ideologies by rearticulating signs of consumer culture with resistant ideas. Perhaps most influential is Dick Hebdige's *Sub-culture: The Meaning of Style*, which argues that subcultures use bricolage to imbue banal mainstream objects (such as safety pins in punk culture) with new meanings that mainstream culture can, in turn, reincorporate, causing them to lose their resistant undertones. Subcultural symbols, for Hebdige, are continually in jeopardy of being repackaged and resold to mainstream consumer culture, and so subcultural politics are always doomed.[53] That is, these ideological, symbolic resistances are only

> *attempts at a solution* to that problematic experience: a resolution which, because pitched largely at the symbolic level, was fated to fail. The problem-atic of a subordinate class experience can be "lived through," negotiated or resisted; but it cannot be *resolved* at that level or by those means.[54]

As Ken Gelder contends, there was "a familiar narrative at the Birming-ham Centre, that subcultural empowerment is empowerment without a future."[55]

Contemporary scholars, characterized by David Muggleton and Rupert Weinzierl somewhat problematically as "post-subcultural theorists,"[56] have produced several key critiques of the CCCS's "heroic" analyses of subcul-tures.[57] While the CCCS's work postulates that subcultural styles are a uni-fied reaction to dominant but contradictory demands of class relations, post-subcultural theory characterizes subcultures as dynamic and contradictory groups whose relationship to mainstream culture in highly contested and flexible. More specifically, these theorists question the political nature of subcultures;[58] the strict binary between subculture and mainstream; the theorists' sole and limited focus on class relations to the exclusion of gender, race, nation, and sexuality;[59] and their dependence on semiological methods to interpret subcultural style while ignoring subcultural practice (e.g., producing music or making zines). This work rightly disrupts heroic subcultural theory and more accurately describes various subcultural practices, demonstrating the ways in which subcultures can provide a space in which disempowered groups can vie for discursive power.[60]

However, post-subcultural theorists have fully evaluated neither subcultures' interactions with mainstream media nor the ways in which subcultures and the mainstream influence one another in their portrayals of race, gender, class, sexuality, and nation in youth culture. Belinda Wheaton points out that "the mainstream is a perpetually omnipresent yet absent 'other' that defies definition" in subcultural theory.[61] Furthermore, while subcultural practices are undoubtedly crucial to our understanding of subcultural politics, post-subcultural theorists, claiming that traditional subcultural theory limits "subcultural practices to a narrow notion of spectacle,"[62] make the reactionary mistake of focusing on practice to the detriment of an understanding of subcultural symbols or, more broadly, the discursive meaning of subcultures throughout popular culture. This omission ignores youth subcultures' contributions to changing or static identity norms and mainstream media stabilization, disruption, and appropriation of subcultural critiques of and resistances to these norms. It is only by considering subcultural practices, values, and discourses in conversation with one another and with mainstream practices, values, and discourses that we can see how the layers of subcultures can critique and maintain power relations.

Sarah Thornton's highly influential discussion of the role of media in British "club cultures" in the late 1980s and early 1990s provides some inroads into the intersections between mainstream media and subcultures. Beyond making crystal clear the false binary between subculture and mainstream, Thornton rightfully contends that media are "a network crucial to the definition and distribution of cultural knowledge" in subcultures.[63] Furthermore, she highlights the specific roles various media play in youth cultures: "micro-media," such as homemade flyers, serve to organize youths into identifiable groups; "niche media," such as magazines, further solidify these groups' standings as a subculture; and mainstream media can elevate subcultures' status to that of movements.[64]

Thornton's work deserves to be extended and revisited. Unfortunately, researchers have done little more than pay lip service to the intersecting nature of global media flows and local subcultural action. Treating this intersection only theoretically, some have discussed globalization and its relation to both homogenization and difference.[65] Others, seeking to illustrate the fallacy of the subculture-mainstream binary, have introduced new terms to replace *subculture*, including, for example, *neotribe*,[66] but few have explicitly considered the relationship between subcultures and mainstream cultures.[67] This relationship is crucial for, as Wheaton and Beal suggest, "In our postmodern image culture, media culture in all its forms provides many of the resources for identity, how we come to understand ourselves."[68]

Even a cursory examination of skateboarders' media engagement reveals the difficulty in parsing *mainstream* and *subculture;* the videos of which the boys are such keen fans are produced by niche skateboarding companies as a means of marketing their wares. The skateboarders obviously think of these videos as part and parcel of "their" culture despite their commercial intent. Such engagement between *subculture* and *mainstream* seems to be typical of lifestyle sports such as skateboarding, snowboarding, and windsurfing, as Belinda Wheaton makes clear. Members of these cultures "are not simply victims of commercialism but mould and transform the identities and meanings circulated by consumer culture."[69] Where do niche products fall in the dichotomy between subculture and mainstream? What constitutes "authentic" subcultural fare? In his discussion of *The X Games*, Robert E. Rinehart argues that "there is a continuum of choices within the ranges of opposition and co-option,"[70] but he doesn't fully explicate how this continuum operates in terms of the politics of skate life. Wheaton and Beal suggest that "rather than imagining an opposition between hegemonic incorporation and resistance . . . research needs to examine how the cultural commodities provided by these cultural/media industries are made meaningful in specific acts of consumption, in particular time and spaces."[71] And Beal and Wilson argue that skateboarders' "identities are partially constituted through mainstream commercial processes which provide some of the raw materials as well as the discourses from which skaters can draw."[72] By thinking about skateboarders as a "corresponding culture," my work addresses these questions and the relationships between subculture and mainstream.

For subcultural theorists, questions about "authenticity" implicitly draw on concerns about cultural power and individual free thought, that is, such questions are founded on a frequently unstated assumption that mass culture is concerned *only* with the demands of capitalism and operates in a political void. The other assumption on which these questions rest is the notion that small pockets of individuals are capable of developing their own concerns outside of the ideologies of capitalism. But, as Stuart Hall reminds us:

> The notion that our heads are full of false ideas which can, however, be totally dispersed when we throw ourselves open to "the real" as a moment of absolute authentication, is probably the most ideological conception of all. . . . When we contrast ideology to experience, or illusion to authentic truth, we are failing to recognize that there is no way of experiencing the "real relations" of a particular society outside of its cultural and ideological categories.[73]

Although Muggleton and other theorists of post-subcultures certainly understand mass culture and ideology in all their complexities, their work fails to explain the relationships between what might be deemed mainstream culture and subculture, and they never adequately discuss the politics of these relationships. Muggleton concludes that subcultures are "liminal," "fragmented," and "individualistic" and suggests that they operate as "manifestations of self-expression, individual autonomy and cultural diversity."[74] Although my time with the skateboarders has certainly demonstrated that individuality is a key value for all of them, I'd like to push our understanding of youth cultures beyond this to better explain how they develop particular affinities for various "subcultures" and how these affinities are aligned with political concerns such as mediated limitations on expressions of identity, the movement of capitalist and patriarchal ideologies, and youths' capacity to critique and reimagine everyday cultural mores. Throughout the course of this book, I examine the appeals that skate life holds for youths and the ways in which it aligns with their identities and produces possibilities for new articulations of identity. In short, I ask, what might youthful pleasure tell us about youthful politics?

Both youthful pleasure and youthful politics are undoubtedly tied to youths' experiences as members of particular identity groups, but subcultural theory has not adequately accounted for identity's role in politics. Although scholars have noted that the Birmingham Centre's theorization of subcultural politics is limited by its empirical focus on working-class youth cultures, they have specified neither the ways in which class might operate differently in the new millennium than in the 1970s nor the differences between British and American conceptions of class. Although class clearly contributes to American youths' varying experiences, in the contemporary context its role is frequently downplayed because the United States is supposedly a "classless" society.[75] Furthermore, middle classness, like other dominant identities (such as masculinity and whiteness), is largely invisible in its normative status,[76] and clear lines between the working and middle classes do not seem to exist; virtually all Americans, that is, seem to be able to deem themselves middle class.

Despite such invisibility and the absence of overt discussions of class from many explanations of identity politics, class does play a role in the construction of particular modes of masculinity and conceptualizations of race. *White trash* is a derogation that makes whiteness visible via class,[77] and working-class masculinity and its attendant physicality and gruff demeanor are imagined to be clearly distinct from middle-class masculinity's association with office work and gentility. Moreover, although working-class men may experience oppression via class, their association with physically dominant masculinity may produce moments when they feel some power over or superiority to middle-class men. Class, in other words, intersects with other axes of identity not only in the construction of identity but also in individual experiences with power and oppression.

Although, as I have noted, masculinity operated as the primary point of identification and politics for Ann Arbor skateboarders, the role of class in this culture should not be ignored. Skateboarding is largely imagined as a suburban, middle-class pursuit, but the skateboarders in my study hailed from a wide range of class backgrounds. In large part because of the invisibility of class in American culture, I found it very difficult to ask the boys directly about their class backgrounds; however, my time with them revealed that several of my respondents lived in trailer parks, others were the children of divorced parents living in distinctly middle-class neighborhoods, and still others were the children of upper-middle-class parents working in the professional world of college professors, engineers, and doctors. The wide range of ages in this group also complicated any specification of class; although some of the 20- and 30-somethings may have grown up in middle-class families, they were now almost completely independent and relying on their own working-class incomes. Clearly, skateboarding is not a "class culture"—it is not a group organized primarily around class identification—but various class backgrounds may play a role in the production of multiple masculinities represented in skateboarding culture.

Despite the relationship between particular expressions of masculinity and class, and regardless of the differing levels of opportunity afforded to middle- and working-class skateboarders, masculinity was consistently the salient identity around which skateboarders were organized. As such, when skaters produced critiques of dominant society they focused not on class and the capitalist system but on masculinity and patriarchal norms. This distinction does not mean to deny the very real relationship between capitalism and patriarchy, but it does mean to suggest that in the everyday experiences of skateboarders gender is significant and visible while class is secondary and less visible. While capitalist appropriation may have threatened the integrity of the working-class subcultures examined by the Birmingham Centre, such appropriation does little to threaten skateboarding culture's critique of dominant masculinities.

By introducing the notion of "corresponding cultures" to the discussion of youth cultures and politics, I am able to discuss the multiple ways in which skateboarders interact with various media forms and their many inflections of young white masculinity. "Corresponding," as a concept, offers two meanings, which, when taken together, successfully explain the ways in which skateboarders come together as a community around the shared culture of skateboarding. First, the values attendant on skateboarding—individualism, cooperation, artistry, independence, and self-expression—align with, or *correspond to*, the skateboarders' values. Second, the importance of these values to skateboarding is communicated via numerous forms of mediated and in-person *corresponding*, including skateboarding videos, magazines, and television shows as well as competitions, informal gatherings, and even style.

Skateboarders, I would argue, have an affinity toward both the core values expressed through the culture and the various accoutrements of the culture. These affinities inspire multiple forms of engagement with other skateboarders and skateboarding media—and they also allow for continued discussion of, or corresponding about, the core values and their relationship to everyday life. Furthermore, the notion of corresponding allows us to consider that which does not correspond to the needs, desires, or values of skateboarders, and, as I discuss, they usually locate such discord in a stereotypical "jock." Finally, the idea of corresponding opens up space for examining the culture's relationship to—or correspondence with—various media lines, including those produced by niche marketers, local skateboarders, and national television networks.

In its underlying reliance on notions of taste, communication, alliance, and affinity, corresponding provides the flexibility for a more complete examination of a group that previously might have been deemed a subculture (with its focus on resistance), taste culture (with its focus on cultural capital), community (with its focus on relationships among members), or public sphere (with its focus on overtly political engagement). The term *corresponding cultures* aligns in some ways with Pierre Bourdieu's conceptualization of "fields," which he presents as an analytic tool (rather than an empirical object) for discussing social bodies. Joanne Kay and Suzanne Laberge define *field* as "a social arena, simultaneously a space of conflict and competition, within which struggles take place for the accumulation of the resources valued in it."[78] For Bourdieu, fields encourage researchers to consider the relationships between various social spaces.

Although a social fields analysis following Bourdieu's conceptualization would usefully discuss the connections between a variety of fields and highlight the primary "stakes and interests" in the field of study, the field as a construct is limited in its explanatory capabilities.[79] While it highlights "struggle" as the mode of relating between various fields, the concept does not fully conceptualize the ways in which differing fields relate to one another. In this capacity, *corresponding cultures* is specific: various "scapes" (e.g., mainstream media and skateboarders) correspond with and to one another for a variety of reasons. The notion of struggle is also, perhaps, too forceful to adequately describe on-the-ground reality for youth cultures, which sometimes relate to and with the dominant culture in a manner that is less thought out than the idea of struggle suggests. Finally, the active nature of the word *corresponding* serves as a reminder that youth cultures are always moving in relationship with dominant conceptions of youth, current norms of identity, and contemporary appeals to youth. *Corresponding culture* allows me to examine the many elements of skateboarding while maintaining a spotlight on the relationship between individuals and the media.

Within this culture, the skateboarders' subscription to a generalized notion of individuality allows different groups within this culture to express an affinity to various expressions of masculine identity. Put more simply, the value placed on individuality allows skateboarding culture a degree of heterogeneity. Although almost all skateboarders suggested that their desire for a space of freedom, cooperation, and self-expression corresponded fully with skateboarding culture, they also imagined such self-expression via various styles. For example, consider the difference between what 21-year-old Jeff called "hesh" and "fresh."

> Hesh, hessian, would be more of the tight clothes, studded belts, bandannas. Just a more form-fitting style with probably more gnarly things! (*Laughs*) Uh, but the fresh thing would be a cleaner cut, the clothes look really good, crisp, the shoes look really good. The shoes are bigger, puffier tongues, uh, rap music, just generally you know, it doesn't have to be, people can pull off different kinds of music, but if someone's listening to rap music, their style's generally gonna reflect that.

Hesh and *fresh* refer to two styles within this culture that suggest, respectively, a more aggressive approach and a more stylistic, precise approach to skateboarding. Both hesh and fresh skaters can express themselves, both can cooperate with one another, and both feel that skateboarding moves them away from the perceived competitiveness and institutionalization of the traditional sporting world. Both, in other words, correspond with the culture's more general critique of dominant norms of masculinity; however, each also corresponds to skaters' various stylistic affinities.

Skate Life considers how and why a group of mostly white, mostly middle-class, mostly heterosexual young men might purposefully set themselves apart, that is, how and why they might adopt a type of willful otherness. It is crucial to note that this otherness is highly contingent; skateboarders are not throwing off their social privileges, nor are they adopting a highly radical way of approaching the world. Rather, they are expressing an affinity with a culture that seems somehow different from most institutionalized youth cultures, particularly those centered on sports or physical activity. I argue throughout that skateboarders' particular expressions of masculinity serve as a nascent critique, a not fully formed sense of dissatisfaction with what they perceive to be expected of their masculinity. This burgeoning critique relies on continued expressions of heterosexuality, dominance over nonwhite "others" and women, and traditional American norms of freedom and independence. Using my framework, skate culture easily corresponds with such expressions of dominance while at the same time aligning itself with an expressive, artistic, cooperative masculinity. It is this degree of correspondence—with both alternative and dominant norms—that allows skateboarding to maintain itself as both subculture and mainstream and provides skaters with space in which to question dominant norms while maintaining their own dominance.

Skate Life traces skate culture's multiple images of dominant and alternative white masculinities in mainstream, niche, and local media outlets, taking care to discuss skateboarders' responses to these images. The next chapter, "'The mix of sunshine and rebellion is really intoxicating': American Mythologies, Rebellious Boys, and the Multiple Appeals of Skateboarding's Corresponding Culture, 1950–2006," traces skateboarding's discursive history in the mainstream press to demonstrate the correspondence between skate culture and dominant American values such as independence, exploration, and conquest. It explores the multiple moments during which skateboarding emerged into dominant culture and discusses the contemporary branding of the practice as both rebellious and mainstream.

This history provides the context for the third chapter, "'Freedom on four wheels': Individuality, Self-Expression, and Authentic Masculinity in a Skateboarding Community," an ethnographic examination of southeastern Michigan skateboarding culture that demonstrates the ways in which media are interwoven into the construction of skateboarders' identities. The chapter argues that skateboarders see skate culture as a space in which they can perform alternative masculinities centered on self-expression and cooperation rather than competition and physical dominance. The chapter also contends that skaters' alternative masculinities rely on the high value they place on individuality and freedom and that in this reliance they produce a not necessarily antipatriarchal critique of patriarchy.

The fourth chapter, "'Why is it the things that make you a man tend to be such dumb things to do?': Never-Ending Adolescence and the (De)stabilization of White Masculine Power on MTV," argues that mainstream representations of skate culture, particularly MTV's *Jackass*, *Viva La Bam*, and *Wildboyz*, also develop critiques of dominant masculinities that nevertheless maintain the power of white masculinity. Presenting alternative masculinities and mocking masculinity as a construct, these shows ensure their white male stars' power by constantly making fun of nonwhite, nonmale, nonheterosexual others.

The fifth chapter, "'It's just what's possible': Imagining Alternative Masculinities and Performing White Male Dominance in Niche Skateboarding Videos," evaluates niche skate videos and skateboarders' independently produced videos to discuss the corresponding nature of mass, niche, and local media outlets, as well as to argue that niche and local skate media reject dominant formulations of adult white masculinity. Further, this chapter suggests, the videos only imagine alternative masculinities by overvaluing individuality. That is, rather than imagining new social formations that would produce radical notions of masculinity, these videos simply suggest that skateboarders can perform any type of masculinity they wish as long as it is decidedly heterosexual. Taken together, these four chapters situate skateboarding as a culture in correspondence with dominant ideologies that nonetheless operates as a space in which young men can develop nascent critiques of dominant masculinity and explore strategies for taking on alternative identities.

The sixth chapter, "'You do it together, and everyone just does it in their own way': Corresponding Cultures and (Anti)patriarchal Masculinity," both explicates the ways in which the construct "corresponding culture" can contribute to cultural theorists' explanations of youth culture, identity, and the media and highlights the manner in which skateboarders reinscribe and redefine masculinity and its attendant powers. In this chapter, I call for further theorization of identity and power relations, noting that changes in the construction of identity do not necessarily alter or eliminate the power tied up with masculinity, whiteness, middle-classness, and heterosexuality.

Finally, I draw attention to several more recent developments associated with skate life and contemporary race and masculinity, including the "skate pimp" and the "beta male," in order to discuss the ways in which these new constructs might re-imagine white masculinity.

As I watched skateboarders watch TV, listened to them speak about the pleasures of skate life's practices and portrayals, and followed them through multiple corners of skate life, they introduced me to their constantly changing and complex processes of identity construction. Skateboarding culture's multiple locations—in local skate shops, on network and cable television, in marketers' appeals to both young men and aging hipsters, in skateboarding magazines and videos, and on local streets and sidewalks—operate in correspondence with one another to establish the many-layered and dynamic norms of skate life. The mainstream press, MTV, and niche skateboarding companies produce a variety of representations of skate life that speak to its principles of identity—masculinity, whiteness, youth, and so on—in various and sometimes contradictory ways. In their everyday lives, skateboarders are in constant negotiation with these representational layers, and their conversations about and responses to skate media serve to indoctrinate them and others into skate life's possibilities for identity. In the community of southeastern Michigan skateboarders, these negotiations tend to center on masculinity; conversations about race, as I will demonstrate, are comparatively tentative and uncomfortable. Skaters in a different group may focus on other issues, but the contours of skate media suggest that discussions of masculinity pervade skate culture. In its many corners, skate life produces and celebrates alternative masculinities that never fully challenge patriarchal power relations; they express dissatisfaction with the demands of masculinity and create spaces in which they may transcend those demands. Watching their heroes skate on TV, practicing their craft on the sidewalk, talking with one another while watching videos, and articulating their reasons for skating to a curious researcher, the skateboarders announced, "This is how we think." It is my hope that the following chapters adequately articulate the intersections and correspondences between skate media and skate life and accurately transcribe and interpret what skateboarders mean when they point to the media and say, "This is how I think."

"The mix of sunshine and rebellion is really intoxicating"

American Mythologies, Rebellious Boys, and the Multiple Appeals of Skateboarding's Corresponding Culture, 1950–2006

First commercially released as a toy in 1959, the skateboard has "rolled in and out of the public's consciousness" over the course of almost five decades.[1] Several popular histories of skateboarding suggest that the first skateboards were born of youthful imagination in the early twentieth century when children made milk crate scooters from two-by-fours and old roller skate wheels.[2] The skateboard quickly grew into a popular childhood toy that would later be remembered, with both nostalgia and derision, as a fad akin to hula hoops and yo-yos.[3]

More than a simple fad, by 1995 skateboarding had come to be a key discursive marker of white male youth. That is, throughout the 1990s and into the new millennium, extreme sports—and skateboarding in particular—became a powerful marketing tool, the go-to lifestyle for appeals to white male teenagers, who by 1995 comprised the largest group of adolescents in history.[4] During its many moments of popularity in each of the decades since 1959, layers of mythology have been built into skateboarding's practice and portrayal. By considering the articulation of these mythologies, as well as their particular connections to ideologies of gender, race, class, and nation, we can begin to understand both the relationship between youth subculture and mainstream culture and skateboarding's contemporary symbolization of white male youth.

Michele K. Donnelly rightly contends that academic discussions of skateboarding have relied on the idea that the practice was at one time an "authentic" subculture rooted in resistance to the mainstream.[5] While most contemporary accounts ground themselves in the myth of skateboarding's subcultural origins, skateboarding's earliest roots in the nostalgically remembered children's culture of suburban postwar America provide it with a distinctly *mainstream* origin myth. Remembered either as a childhood creation or a commercial toy enjoyed by white, middle-class kids, skateboards sometimes represent a more carefree time when the streets were safe and children could go out alone. This early history associates skateboards with the conformist but simple Middle America of the 1950s and thus with dominant society.

These roots have certainly been eclipsed of late, as skateboarding has come to represent "extreme youth" via media texts such as MTV's *Jackass*, *Viva la Bam*, and *Wildboyz*, which each feature skateboarders' gross-out humor, and the award-winning documentary *Dogtown and Z-Boys*, which rewrites skateboarding's beginnings as the product of working-class teenage boys' energetic rebellion.[6] Skateboarding, in short, has experienced a discursive evolution from innocuous childhood game to rebellious youth subculture.

The contours of this evolution—the various moments at which particular mythologies of the skateboarding culture are solidified and disrupted—demonstrate skateboarding's flexibility as both a discourse and a practice built into and outside of mainstream culture. Skateboarding traverses mediascapes[7] and youthscapes,[8] moving in and out of—and accepting and rejecting—a host of cultural locations that define it, variously, as a diverse and dangerous subculture, a mainstream marketing mechanism, a childhood toy, and a creative enterprise. This discursive flexibility, I argue, allows skateboarding fans to imagine themselves as both inside and outside of dominant culture and consequently as both resistant to and in possession of dominant modes of power. That is, skateboarding's multiple locations of engagement—or correspondence—with both dominant ideologies and images of resistance situate skate culture as a corresponding culture in which notions of resistance are fluid.

By tracing the movement of the key ideas, heroes, and innovations of skateboarding into and out of mainstream media, I highlight the ways in which enduring ideas associated with skateboarding—enterprise, innovation, individuality, and creativity—correspond with values embedded in American origin myths and associated with white masculinity. Despite these associations, however, skateboarding maintains its status as a culture on the edges of mainstream American life. By mapping these seeming contradictions, this chapter accomplishes three goals: (1) expand the boundaries of subculture theory to make clear the ways in which American subcultural values may interlock with key values of American mainstream culture; (2) illuminate the specific ways in which subcultural and mainstream media overlap and correspond with one another, highlighting mainstream media's use of skateboarding's multiple performances and portrayals of masculinity and whiteness; and (3) explain the scope of skateboarding discourses with which contemporary skateboarders contend, thereby locating my analysis of a skateboarding community's proclaimed pleasures and politics in the current discursive moment.

Throughout this chapter, I argue that many of the values associated with skateboarding ally themselves with fundamental tropes of American origin myths produced in stories of the Pilgrims, the Puritans, the pioneers, and the American frontier. These stories construct the foundation of the United States as a fight for freedom from religious persecution and as a quest for independence. Almost needless to say, these are the myths of white male America that completely ignore or whitewash the genocide of Native Americans, slavery, the denial of women's rights, and the destruction of land that accompanied white American men's pursuit of "liberty." In his analysis of late 1990s popular news stories about extreme sports, Kyle Kusz notes that extreme sports are aligned with "a set of traditional American masculine values and pursuits: rugged individualism, conquering new frontiers, and achieving individual progress."[9] More, he argues, because it is white men who are depicted as participating in extreme sports, these stories "represent whiteness as American-ness" and thus further deny the multicultural history of the country.[10] As such, Kusz rightly contends, the extreme athlete as frontiersman trope reinscribed white male dominance during a moment when that dominance was being challenged by feminism, civil rights, gay and lesbian rights, and economic decline. Not insignificantly, the rise of the powerful, white, male extreme athlete coincided with and responded to rising fears about the role of white men in sports. *Sports Illustrated* published an article in 1997 titled "Whatever Happened to the White Athlete?" Kusz characterizes the article as "a panic-driven news story focusing on the increasing absence of the white athlete in contemporary American professional sports."[11]

Beyond assuaging fears of white male decline, the change in extreme sports' image—from the domain of Gen X slackers to that of mainstream, white male adventurers—was, as Kusz suggests, marketers' response to the newfound buying power of Generation X ("$700 billion in individual and familial spending power per year").[12] While extreme sports' new image was undoubtedly a marketing ploy, it was also a move made in the context of mythologies that from the beginning have moved back and forth between mainstream America and subcultural rebellion.

Moreover, it is important to note the ways in which America's foundational myths privilege rebellion and populism. In many ways, these myths present the United States as a land of subculturalists, a country founded on the backs of brave and independent-minded individuals fighting for nothing less than the freedom to live their lives as they wish. The Pilgrims and the Puritans, in other words, were "sticking it to" the man of all men, the Church of England. Contemporary discourse frequently locates American discomfort with sexuality in our Puritan roots, but we must also consider the ways in which these stories might contribute to a particularly American mode of engaging with subcultures. While individual subcultures may produce specific ideologies that directly confront a variety of American mores, arguably their broader appeals to individuality and freedom align closely with values learned in kindergarten. American subcultures, then, may correspond quite easily with dominant culture while at the same time critiquing it in specific and subtle ways. In the case of skateboarding, enthusiasts regularly refer to the freedom and independence that it allows them while also producing a nascent critique of dominant norms of white teenage masculinity.

In the American context, then, it makes sense for a subculture, or a corresponding culture, to find itself in advertisements, on television shows, and in the movies, for subcultural stories can be refashioned as stories of the American spirit. What's more, in this refashioning the fundamental claims of that subculture need not necessarily be forfeited or even reworked. As Angela McRobbie notes, much subcultural practice is entrepreneurial,[13] and even when it is not explicitly market based, I argue, it is about the creation of a culture and the production of cultural codes, modes of communication, gathering places, and so on. These independent productions can find their roots in stories of the development of the American colonies, and entrepreneurs can surely place themselves in the context of the American dream. As such, the correspondence between American subcultures and American mainstream cultures may take on a different shape or tendency than that in other cultural contexts. This chapter takes the specificities of American identity into account, keeping firmly in mind the ways in which the values of the subculture parallel those of the mainstream.

In tracing the evolution of skateboarding discourse, this chapter sheds light on the dynamics of corresponding cultures, noting the moments at which they converge and diverge. It will also serve to characterize the cultural moment in which current skateboarders exist, elucidating their ideas about resistance and subcultural identity and their relationship to dominant cultural ideas and institutions. Most broadly, this discursive history should showcase the ways in which institutions imbued with economic and discursive power open up and close down spaces in which individuals and institutions with less power formulate ideas about whiteness, masculinity, and youth.

Boyhood Creativity: Skateboarding Pre-1959

Popular accounts of skateboarding's early history locate its origins in the hands of creative and enterprising male youths looking for entertainment in the mundane world of the neighborhood. From the early 1900s through World War II, the stories suggest, restless young boys borrowed the wheels from their "sister's rollerskates" and worked with "backyard mechanics (dads)" to fashion milk crate scooters.[14] Recollected distinctly as a boys' culture, the practice in which youths tinker with found objects to build their own skateboards is highly reminiscent of other boy-dominated subcultures.[15] Such nostalgic accounts, laden with myths of a better time when children didn't turn into zombies in front of the television and fathers were available to their sons, belie the exclusionary and homophobic undertones of such cultures. For example, skateboarding fan Bob Schmidt remembered building skateboards with his group of friends in the 1950s: "We tried painting them, then we found out the girls liked 'em that way, so decided that was for sissies and we soaked off the paint and left them plain. But the girls got mad, mostly because it was usually one of their skates we were using!"[16] While Schmidt's use of the word *sissies* is surely meant to evoke the simplicity and innocence of childhood, it also points to the way girls are excluded from discourses of early skateboarding and the creativity and hard work that these discourses are meant to conjure.

More than just male, these memories are almost exclusively white. While skateboarding's earliest history as a homemade toy can be located in urban neighborhoods, its commercial and more mainstream history is located in a space explicitly denied to African Americans through redlining practices: the suburb. The skateboarding magazine *Thrasher*'s book-length retrospective includes a two-page, black-and-white photo from 1952 featuring an "'anything on wheels' derby" in New York City.[17] This photo portrays white girls in bloomers, mothers pushing strollers, and both white and black boys pushing milk crate scooters. The photo's city scene, set in front of the Children's Aid Society on New York's East Side, connotes working-class simplicity and childlike lightheartedness.

This urban image of easy diversity is overshadowed by most nostalgic accounts. The skateboard's early incarnation as a milk crate scooter in urban neighborhoods is located only in industry retrospectives, and in most accounts its most significant origins are situated alongside other images of white youth rebellion in the 1960s. That is not to say, however, that images of skateboarding in the 1960s evoke the counterculture. In fact, 1960s skateboarding oscillated uncomfortably between, first, being defined as a harmless childhood game and a dangerous and annoying teenage craze, and, second, being associated with suburban childhood and California teen surf culture. As *Thrasher* asserts, "Product development and skating styles coincided with the invention and perfection of two other modern American postwar activities: Surfing and suburban sprawl," and "The dawn of skateboarding coincided with the realization of the industrial revolution in America and the increase in cheaper mass-production of steel products for car parts, tools, and toys."[18] As it moved to the world of the suburbs and California, skateboarding also became distinctly white, as the availability of leisure time and access to the relative quiet and space of suburban streets and sidewalks were distinct to whites. At the same time, however, its surfing roots in both Polynesia and California and its relative danger, as well as its association with the burgeoning teen culture, lent skateboarding a rebellious and even exotic edge.

Suburban Roots/California Myths, 1959–66

Skateboarding emerged at a moment in U.S. history when the figure of the youth rebel was gaining prominence. Leerom Medovoi argues that figures such as James Dean, the beats, and Holden Caufield all served to shore up the cold war image of America as "antiauthoritarian [and] democratic."[19] That is, in order to present itself as the better alternative to communism, the United States had to demonstrate that it would welcome rebellious characters in the context of its homogeneous middle-class suburbs. Medovoi's genealogy of identity and identity politics demonstrates the ways in which countercultural symbols are a fundamental part of the imaginary of American myths. Along with images of middle-class America, they demonstrate that the United States offers the freedom and security to "be all that you can be."

Skateboarding, however, did not emerge into this context as a fully formed symbol of suburban youth rebellion. Rather, its location in a moment when youth rebellion was moving to the forefront of public consciousness, as well as its seemingly simultaneous existence as a commodity toy and a new symbol of California surf culture, set skateboarding up to take on a number of dualities that have followed it through its history and make possible the particular culture surrounding it today.[20]

Shot through the contours of skateboarding's early history are two quintessential images of idyllic America: the postwar suburb and California surf culture. More than situated within such nostalgic American places, skateboarding in this moment is tied closely to suburban (white) children—mostly boys—and California surfers—mostly male teenagers. The ideas and values associated with skateboarding in its many guises, then, bespeak America's youthful identity. As I noted earlier, images of youth are tied strongly to American myths, and the United States is imagined as a youthful nation replete with the energy, desires, and modern ways of thinking of the young. *Thrasher*'s retrospective comments, "Skateboarding has a rich history charged with youthful intensity and adventurous spirit."[21] "Youthful intensity" and "adventurous spirit" quite easily evoke notions of American inventiveness and vigor, and skateboarding's origin narratives certainly call these traits to mind.[22]

By 1959, surfers and suburban kids seem to have found skateboarding virtually simultaneously, and its suburban origins overlap and interlock with its location in California surf culture. While Michael Brooke's *The Concrete Wave* makes no mention of surfers until after the development of a commercial toy skateboard, both *Thrasher* and James Davis contend that surfers discovered homemade skateboards in the late 1940s and early 1950s before a toy board was produced. The particular sequence of events is relatively inconsequential to contemporary narratives of skateboarding, for it is the overlap that allows for its multiple meanings. What matters, in other words, is that both surfers and commercial interests play a central role in the early days of the skateboard, and the tension and cooperation between "independent" youth culture and consumer culture traverses the remainder of skateboarding's history.

Surely, the overlap between the technologies (i.e., the boards) used for surfing and skateboarding cemented the connection between the two practices. What is more telling, however, is the way in which mainstream media picked up on skateboarding's suburban appeal and surfer style. Constructing skateboarding initially as a craze among kids "who have gone land-surfing berserk" and subsequently as the latest menace to children's safety, the media served to make skateboarding decidedly suburban and subcultural.[23] In other words, by simultaneously playing up a rather nonthreatening practice as a fad (and therefore short-lived, simplistic, and superficial), linking it to the strange and nonmainstream counterculture of California surfing, and asserting its inherent danger, mainstream media in the 1960s laid the foundation for skateboarding's current discursive/cultural location as a practice wherein white male youths can imagine themselves as outside the mainstream and actively critiquing particular modes of masculinity while concurrently asserting traditional forms of masculine power.

As early as 1959, the *Los Angeles Times* was reporting efforts to outlaw skateboarding. On June 14, 1959, it reported, "Students comprising the Pasadena Youth Council board of officers" asked the city of Pasadena to outlaw skateboarding because of the number of injuries it caused. It further reported that more than six teens had been hurt riding skateboards the previous month.[24] Only a month later it published a story about a teenage boy who had to have his arm amputated after a skateboarding accident.[25] Not yet regarded as a subculture, a commercial toy, or even a central part of youth culture, skateboarding was deemed dangerous (by students, no less!) and therefore the business of city councils.

The *Los Angeles Times* did not discuss skateboarding again until 1962, but in just three years the practice had been transformed from simply a dangerous pastime to a distinctly rebellious and masculine fad. Reporting on a growing movement to ban skateboarding throughout Los Angeles County, the paper enthused:

> Skateboarding, to the uninformed, is one of the latest rages of the teen-age set. Most of the demons either are roller-skating enthusiasts with a yen for high adventure or surfboard novices who feel they can acquire additional practice. . . . Others are just roller rebels without straps. . . . You don't need an expensive surfboard. Junior just grabs a length of 2 x 4 from the wood pile, tears apart his sister's roller skates and nails them to the board.[26]

Skateboarding, the paper reported, was "such a nuisance" that schools were prohibiting it, and coaches of both high schoolers and younger children were upset about the loss of players in other sports to skateboarding injuries.[27]

In 1963, a commercial skateboard associated with surfing was developed. *Surf Guide* publisher Larry Stevenson began producing skateboards through his company, Makaha, and as a promotional device he organized a team to participate in skateboarding competitions, the first of which Makaha sponsored in 1963 in Hermosa, California. In May 1964, the Santa Monica Civic Auditorium showed Bruce Brown's movie *Surf Crazy*, and the screening included a live demonstration by Makaha's skate team.[28] Zody's, a local store, began to advertise the Champion "sidewalk surf board" as "Exciting healthful, safe fun!" and public debate about skateboards' safety heightened. The *Los Angeles Times* asked, "Skateboards—are they a menace to life and limb or one of the greatest boons to childhood since the printing of the first comic book?" According to the paper, public debate was favoring the skateboarders. One citizen bemoaned, "A child nowadays has a hard time being a child," and another celebrated the "skill" required for "this healthy sport."[29]

Noticeable in these debates is their focus on children's safety and the absence of a more fraught argument about teen rebellion or boys with attitude. While such rebellion was a more general concern during this era, skateboarding had not yet been broadly associated with such rebellion in public debates about its safety.[30] In other words, skateboarding was troubling because it appeared to put children at risk for accidents and injuries, particularly given the poor materials used in their construction, not because it was tied to adolescent misbehavior.

Between 1964 and 1966, the mainstream media spent a significant amount of time warning of these dangers. The *Los Angeles Times* published several letters to the editor warning of the dangers of skateboarding in 1964.[31] In 1965, the California Medical Association deemed skateboarding "a new medical menace," and the national media paid attention despite the association's lack of statistics and dependence on doctors' reports. One auto insurance company dubbed skateboarding a "new traffic menace."[32] *Good Housekeeping* offered safety rules provided by the National Safety Council, warning of the possibility of facial fractures, permanent damage to growing bones, and even death.[33] Doctors at Children's Hospital in Washington, DC, blamed skateboards for doubling the number of fractures they treated in one summer, and the chief of radiology there told the *Washington Post*, "The skateboard should be outlawed."[34] So dire, and so numerous, were such warnings that by November the latest issue of *Changing Times* commented, "The ski season is at hand, at least for you lucky few who survived skateboards."[35]

Beyond being dangerous for children, skateboarding was perceived as a growing nuisance to pedestrians, especially women and the elderly. The city of Arcadia's citizens worried that a sidewalk planned for students walking to school "would become a 'juvenile freeway' with skateboards, wagons and bikes,"[36] and the editor of *Consumer Bulletin* reported, "Shopping centers find skateboarding a nuisance because women with arms full of bundles find it difficult to get out of the way in time to avoid a swift collision."[37] The July 27, 1965, *Nancy* cartoon portrayed a mailman falling and spilling all of his mail after tripping on a skateboard.[38] Some city officials also began to speak of the property damage skateboarders might cause.[39] Skateboarding was so annoying that the *Wall Street Journal*'s "Pepper . . . and Salt" column joked, "The scientists who unlocked atomic energy for industry are now seeking a peaceful use for the skateboard."[40]

The tension between images of skateboarders as children in need of protection and as teenagers who posed a threat to adults came to a head in Jerry Doernberg's *Los Angeles Times* article "Skateboarders Near Thin Ice." The head of the West Arcadia Business and Professional Association told the city council that 50 teenagers were hanging out in front of the shopping center. "Sixty per cent of these kids have skateboards," he wrote, "and they terrify older women. These are good kids. But there's a real danger of runaway skateboards seriously hurting people."[41] Others noted problems with enforcing skateboarding laws. "We have enough trouble with 'public relations' as it is without six-foot cops handing out tickets right and left to 8-year-old kids," one police officer said. Others were not as forgiving. The police chief in Bountiful, Utah, "was confiscating all visible skateboards, calling them a common public nuisance," and Chattanooga, Tennessee, also banned the boards.[42]

The media focused on characterizing this new sport as a wild new youth fad that they hoped would soon die out. The new laws prohibiting skateboarding were upsetting to skateboarders, *Newsweek* lamented, "But with such a fad, there has to be a break in it somewhere."[43] In claiming that skateboarding was a fad, the 1960s media deemed it passing and thus less threatening. However, the media also characterized the popularity of skateboarding as a "craze," suggesting that its fans might, in fact, be crazy. A 1966 *New York Times* article discussing children's safety quotes a pediatrician who proclaimed skateboarding at once a serious danger and a passing trend.

> "Skateboards are treacherous," he says, "and should be absolutely prohibited. It's wise, in general, to beware the fad of the moment, which always seems to involve some sort of danger. We used to get a lot of dislocated bones from hula hoops [!], and next year something equally hazardous will come along."[44]

Some adults, including parents, community leaders, and industry spokespeople, did take skateboarding seriously, characterizing it as childhood fun or healthful exercise. Skateboard manufacturers, in particular, tried to reverse the negative press their product had been receiving. One manufacturer began printing safety rules on its boards,[45] and SAFE, the Skateboard Association for Education, was established, urging skateboarders to wear helmets, participating in campaigns to advocate for safety rules, and providing awards to organizations promoting safe skateboarding.[46] Even those adults who enforced bans sometimes did so with reservations, most often because they perceived skateboarding to be a healthy childhood activity. One city leader explained, "I've been for the kids and skateboarding looks like a lot of good, clean fun. But lack of supervision or control creates problems."[47] In order to create control, some cities began to sponsor skateboarding competitions and exhibitions.[48]

While media reports of these competitions indicated that they included girls' divisions, boys generally seem to have been the default sex on which most stories relied. When they included images, advertisements for skateboards usually showcased boys, who were always white. Only one advertisement in the 1960s used a female image. Stern Brothers Children's World advertised a "Tite 'n top set switched on for the skateboard crowd." This advertisement is for clothing, not a skateboard, and it uses an image of a young girl with her foot on a beach ball, rather than skateboarding.[49] Perhaps the most logical conclusion to be derived from this ad is that the outfit was meant to attract members of the male skateboarding crowd, not to be worn by them.

Most feature stories used masculine pronouns. For example, the *Los Angeles Times* reported that a skateboarding competition in the Covina City Park had achieved a "separation of 'men' from boys," and contest judge Hobie Alter, a professional skateboarder and the namesake of a popular brand of skateboards, told the paper that the skills acquired while skateboarding could help to "train a boy to become an expert surfer or skier."[50] It is important to note that the *Los Angeles Times* did sometimes run photographs of the winners of the girls' division at various contests. In fact, skateboarders Colleen Boyd and Wendy Bearer appeared in the newspaper several times, apparently the best—or the only—girls competing in many of these contests.[51] Still, very few articles about contests listed the winners of both the boys' and girls' divisions.[52]

The only space where girls are relatively regularly featured is in human interest photos presenting skateboarding as an interesting new children's hobby. Many of these show preteen girls with their dogs or parks and recreation officials.[53] Far from a nuisance, danger, or craze, skateboarding in these photos is portrayed as cute and interesting. Female skateboarders are represented as competitive only when they are included in listings of contest winners, but in most media depictions, female skateboarders are not to be taken seriously.

By 1965, skateboarding had been banned in 20 cities, and companies that had been working hard to fill holiday orders suddenly found themselves overstocked, victims of numerous canceled orders.[54] Still, the practice was the subject of *Skaterdater* (1965), an Oscar-nominated short film and winner of the 1966 Cannes International Film Festival's Grand Prix for Best Short,[55] and the magazine *Quarterly Skateboard*. The national press praised *Skaterdater*.[56] Kevin Thomas of *The Los Angeles Times* called it "delightful" and enthused that it "skims across the screen with style and verve."[57]

In 1966, skateboarding simultaneously became a part of everyday culture and a diminishing trend. Several articles wondered if it was becoming less popular. "Is the skateboard going the way of the hula hoop?" asked Charles R. Donaldson of the *Los Angeles Times*. Studio City recreation administrators suggested that skateboarders' interest in competitions was on the wane, though children were still interested in skateboarding recreationally. At the same time, a member of the Studio City Recreation and Parks Department claimed, "To our knowledge, nobody is manufacturing skateboards any more," noting that they are durable and parents were bothered by their noise.[58]

Not quite a waning trend, skateboarding became an easy symbol for youths in 1966 and the mass media spent far less time defining the practice or discussing its origins and dangers. The *New York Times* discussed British and French Samsonite commercials featuring mannequins on skateboards.[59] Another article invoked the free feeling "plebes" at the U.S. Military Academy felt while their older classmates were gone, describing "a young cadet . . . rolling down the tiled corridor on a skateboard [who] went winging around a corner with a swift and beautiful grace."[60] Johnny Carson joked that an NBC vice president was angry with General Motors because "a wheel has broken off his skateboard."[61] Skateboards, in short, seemed to have become part of the fabric of everyday life.

Skateboarding Disappears, 1967–74

By 1967, skateboarding had lost its hold on both mainstream media's and mainstream youths' attention. Michael Brooke attributes the decline in popularity to manufacturers' inability to produce a high-quality product, writing that "skateboarders were faced with poor technology (that is, clay wheels) and concerns about safety."[62] While the clay wheels certainly were rickety and unreliable, the media's coverage of skateboards as "a new medical menace" and skateboarders as a nuisance surely contributed to the practice's decreasing popularity. However, I also want to note that this dramatic disappearance occurred at a moment of clear strife for young people. With the Tet Offensive in Vietnam in 1968, war protests escalated. In this same period, the country was rocked by urban riots, civil rights protests, and the assassinations of Martin Luther King Jr. and Robert Kennedy. The end of this moment also coincides with the Watergate scandal. Perhaps the dramatic nature of this moment—as well as youth culture's explicit engagement in and reaction against a well-defined establishment—rendered discussions of skateboarding's rebellious nature rather banal.

Over the course of the seven years between 1967 and 1974, skateboarding was scarcely mentioned in the mainstream media. Periodically, the news outlets would note a municipality's decision to ban it or include it in a list of dangerous toys or California fads, but not a single report features an in-depth discussion of the practice. In 1968, the *Washington Post* declared motorized minibikes the "successor to the skateboard."[63] Although skateboarding did not entirely disappear from public discourse, its presence decreased dramatically, though it did continue to be defined as a risky childhood endeavor and an interesting California fad.

Technology and Daredeviltry, 1975–79

Stacy Peralta's film *Dogtown and Z-Boys* (2001) remembers skateboarding's 1970s resurgence as distinctly working class. For Peralta, the famed Zephyr Skateboarding team from Santa Monica, California, was a group of aggressive and energetic boys with little to lose who gave skateboarding their all and shunned the contemporary norms of the sport. The winner of the Sundance Film Festival's Audience Award and Director's Award, the documentary positions its protagonists as products of "the last great seaside slum." The story begins with a tour of Dogtown, the California coastal communities of Venice and Santa Monica. Narrator Sean Penn intones, "There is a place where America's Manifest Destiny collides into the Pacific

Ocean. A place where the fabled Route 66, the roadway of America's dreams, terminates. This is Dogtown." Juxtaposing the American dream and economic and social hardship, Penn guides us through Dogtown and the wreckage of its myriad amusement parks, including the Pacific Ocean Park, which one skater describes as a "dead wonderland." This narration suggests that by growing up in this run-down, formerly utopic place, the (mostly) white boys of Dogtown developed the raw, creative, independent ways of thinking that produced and pushed forward the practice of skateboarding. In advancing this argument, the documentary aligns American mores of independence, freedom, and adventure with working-class, white masculinity.

The film consolidates these values through archival footage of California in the 1960s and 1970s that contrasts sunny beaches inhabited by lily-white surfers with run-down, gritty, working-class towns. As white, bourgeois beach culture collides with racially diverse, working-class beach culture, *Dogtown and Z-Boys* envisions a distinct group of "raw," authentic, white teenage boys. The mythology of California as a utopic site of possibility haunted by racial and economic divides serves as a central trope accounting for the particularities of white adolescent masculinity. Because *Dogtown and Z-Boys* functions as a foundational myth explaining skateboarding circa 1970 and guiding contemporary skateboarding, I argue, its portrayal of white masculinity reverberates in current visions of this identity.

While *Dogtown and Z-Boys* illuminates a key element of skateboarding's history, it does not tell the whole story. In fact, while skateboarding did take on a distinctly masculine tinge and was regarded by some as rebellious, it also opened doors for women's participation and became a far more expensive—and thus middle class—pursuit. Erupting in 1975 as a major moneymaking industry, skateboarding came to be defined as a daring and graceful sport requiring a particular set of skills rather than a fleeting childhood fad. Skateboarders, in turn, were represented as both risk-taking and rebellious teenagers and expressive young athletes and artists. As this newly defined sport/art evolved, its expense pushed it farther into middle- and upper-middle-class enclaves, and its multiple definitions invited girls' involvement. Most crucially, the varied and contradictory ways in which skateboarding was defined during this moment of popularity made the sport and its culture a discursive space—a youthscape—in which it was possible to envision multiple modes of masculinity.

Inventing the Wheel: Technology, Innovation, and Entrepreneurship

As I have noted, skateboarding's rapid demise in 1966 is most often attributed to the dangers that clay and metal wheels presented. But by 1975 the popular press was heralding the "rebirth of the boards,"[64] crediting skateboarding's newfound popularity to the triumph of male ingenuity and technological innovation. Several publications recounted the story of Frank Nasworthy, a Virginia Polytechnic Institute student who was suspended for participating in a political demonstration in 1970, and one proclaimed that "in the annals of skateboarding" Nasworthy would "go down as the man who invented the wheel."[65] The myth has Nasworthy hanging out in a Virginia plastics factory that made polyurethane wheels for roller skates. While roller skaters often complained about the slow speed of these wheels, Nasworthy realized that they would work for skateboards, and in 1973 he opened a California-based business, the Cadillac Wheels Company. Virtually overnight, these articles suggest, skateboarding became popular again.[66]

Nasworthy's story highlights several key values that follow skateboarding throughout its history. Having been kicked out of college for going to a political demonstration, he represents the 1960s counterculture and brings rebellion to mind. More than a rebel, though, he became successful because of his creative approach to the relatively new plastics industry and his entrepreneurial spirit. The *Los Angeles Times* called him a "visionary."[67] While he lost access to the educational institution, he found success independently and in the process revitalized the practice of skateboarding. Nasworthy's story is, in essence, the American dream. This myth's centrality to popular accounts of skateboarding carries through the various veins of a discourse that allows skateboarders to be perceived (and perceive themselves) as subcultural and mainstream at the same time. Skateboarders can reject certain institutions (in Nasworthy's case, higher education) and creatively, independently, innovatively participate in mainstream culture—like Nasworthy did.

While Frank Nasworthy did not take center stage in all accounts of skateboarding's resurgence, the reinvention of the wheel certainly did.[68] The development of urethane wheels serves as an origin myth even in contemporary accounts of skateboarding. *Dogtown and Z-Boys* attributes the 1970s evolution of skateboarding to these wheels. Urethane wheels were more stable and softer than clay and metal wheels, and so small obstructions in the skateboard's path did not so easily cause it to skid or stop short. The *Los Angeles Times* described the new wheel almost lovingly: "It is translucent, often amber in color, softer than the old wheel."[69] In fact, the article implies, use of the new wheels might have saved 18-year-old James Robert McClenahan, who died on May 4, 1975, after falling off his skateboard and hitting his head. An innovation in safety, urethane wheels also allowed enthusiasts to progress athletically and provided them the freedom to experiment with daring new tricks.

Technological ingenuity brought more than a safer wheel to skateboarding. The mid-1970s skateboard was completely redesigned. Decks (the board) could now be constructed of wood or fiberglass, and the trucks (axles) on which the wheels are mounted had been redesigned to be steadier and allow for greater ease in turning.[70] The *New York Times* enthused that the new skateboards were being marketed "with a space-age supersell that points out superwide, supergrip and superspeed features, including such things as unidirectional fiberglass deck, aerospace locking nuts, aircraft aluminum fittings, hand-laminated super-flex board, alloy steel axles and so on."[71] The discussions of skateboarding's new technology were so intense that in 1976 the paper joked:

> Somewhere in this country—maybe a small garage, maybe in a large factory—someone who understands the American marketplace is building the ultimate skateboard. It will come equipped with radial tires, a rear heel defogger, a citizen band radio and air-conditioning. It will sell for $1000, local tax and dealer prep not included. And there will be lines around the block to buy it.[72]

Despite the joking, this celebration of technology legitimized skateboarding as a wholly American and masculine sport, an activity to be taken seriously rather than a forgettable fad. Indeed, William Knowlton Zinsser of *Sports Illustrated* noted, "American technology in its relentless push solved the various problems" of skateboards.[73]

"Hotdogging of a High Order": Skateboarding Redefined

These technophilic descriptions suggest that the skateboard had become far too complicated for any backyard mechanic to produce with his young son. With new technology, skateboarding changed in several ways. First, the skateboard became far more expensive; second, skateboarders were able to develop new tricks; and, third, skateboarding was elevated from a fad or pastime to a sport. In this evolution, skateboarding became simultaneously more grown up, and thus the domain of teenagers and adolescents rather than children; more feminine, as the new tricks could be classified alongside those of gymnastics and dance; and more masculine, as the new technology allowed greater speed and specialization. As an adolescent sport, skateboarding also took on two contradictory qualities. It could be associated closely with teenagers and juvenile delinquency while at the same time being legitimized as a sport fit for televised contests and marketing campaigns, and these multiple meanings carry through to the present moment.

Skateboarding simultaneously became a daring new masculine teen culture and a newly sophisticated sport through which young men and women could develop athletic skills and grace. Grown up and more daring, skateboarders were portrayed as risk takers. Far from young boys hammering together two-by-fours and roller skate wheels with their dads—or even neighborhood children getting in the way of shoppers on city sidewalks—skateboarders in 1975 were tackling empty swimming pools, where they skated up and down the sides of the pool walls "like the steel ball in a roulette wheel."[74] At the same time, *Sports Illustrated* characterized pool riding as "breathtaking" and noted the "grace" of 1970s skateboarding more generally.[75] *Newsweek* described "solos and couples do[ing] graceful figure-skating routines as well as acrobatic backbends and handstands" and "Skateboard hotdoggers look[ing] for exotic sites to conquer."[76] The *Washington Post* captured the duality of skateboarding succinctly in its description of a skateboarder who "duels with disaster, the semisoft wheels making sighing sounds on the hard asphalt. It is hotdogging of a high order, beautiful and dangerous and done for the pure pleasure of it, performed not because but in spite of the onlooker."[77]

The dialectic of grace and aggression that exists in 1970s discourses about skateboarding provides a space in which young boys can be reimagined or redefined. In other words, in this dialectical space, skateboarding boys can be graceful and creative while simultaneously conquering space and participating in a sport that encourages an ever more athletic progression in skill. William Knowlton Zinsser of *Sports Illustrated* commented, after observing his son and others at a skate park, "I felt that I was watching a random ballet. In a society that suspects the worst of its teenage males, I would rather have a skateboard park as my neighbor than a grown man with power tools."[78] Zinsser's comment implies that skateboarding attracts or produces a different type of masculine performance, one that is expressive and stylish.

Dangerous, Annoying, Criminal—and Legitimized

The burgeoning interest in skateboarding caused worry, as the practice was still considered to be very dangerous. *Newsweek* announced, "In the Midwest, [skateboarding] is causing parents more terror than Junior's first time out with the car."[79] Several articles reported on injuries to skateboarders,[80] and medical reports indicated that 27,000 injuries in 1975 were due to skateboarding.[81] *Family Health* warned that with the new technology young skateboarders would be pressured by their peer groups to try risky moves as "a cult glamorizing both risk and pain is rapidly developing around the sport. According to the code, if you haven't been badly hurt at least once, you haven't attempted a really difficult trick."[82] Still, others noted that the new equipment was far safer,[83] and officials from the U.S. Skateboarding Association insisted that the sport was safe as long as enthusiasts didn't try to do more than they were prepared to do.[84] Mary McHugh of the *New York Times* reported that the U.S. Product Safety Commission had found skateboarding to be relatively safe, ranking it twenty-fifth in a list of dangerous sports, which bicycling topped.[85] But in November 1975 the Consumer Product Safety Commission noted skateboarding's role in an increase in toy-related accidents.[86] In the same year the Consumer Affairs Committee of Americans for Democratic Action warned consumers that skateboards were dangerous and suggested that they buy cheaper models, which were not as fast and did not "have streamlined and lethal points in front."[87]

Some, as in the 1960s, complained of speeding youths and the nuisance and danger they presented to pedestrians and adults more generally. The California Highway Patrol began to ticket skateboarders, "some of whom have been clocked zooming downhill at speeds up to about 30 m.p.h.," because they were hazardous to pedestrians.[88] Reader Patricia Bayley grumbled in a letter to the *Los Angeles Times*, "[A]ny lives or limbs endangered should be those of the skateboarders, alone, not some innocent pedestrian's." She went on, criticizing another letter that suggested that people should accept a modicum of risk in the quest for accomplishment, "Try to tell a mother who has just miscarried because of an irresponsible youth on a skateboard about a fair trade-off. . . . Set up daredevil courses for skateboarders in neighborhood parks where they can maim themselves, but not the rest of us."[89] Bayley's letter puts in sharp relief a perceived disconnect between responsible (female) adults and reckless (male) youths.

Skateboarders also came to be associated with a variety of crimes. Though few articles suggested that they committed crimes (aside from skateboarding) more than other groups of young people, several articles did mention that juveniles had been in possession of skateboards while committing their crimes. For example, the *Los Angeles Times* reported that a ten-year-old boy had escaped on his skateboard after stealing $2.68 from an ice cream shop,[90] and a mall Santa reported that he "got his quota of smart comments from older boys riding down the mall on skateboards."[91] A report of a "street melee" featured a photo of three young men in handcuffs, "one holding a skateboard and another standing on one."[92] As interest in skateboarding in swimming pools mushroomed, skateboarders also began to trespass on properties with empty pools.[93] As the promoter Bill Riordan, manager of the tennis star Jimmy Connors, described skateboarding, "It's clandestine—the kids have all these secret riding spots. It's got speed and danger. It's got its own language. It's got a mystique."[94]

While Riordan found skateboarding's "mystique" to be ripe for marketing, other adults were less than enthused. As in the 1960s, many cities responded to the perceived dangers and nuisances of skateboarding by banning it.[95] Safety clinics at schools and shopping centers were another solution to the problem of skateboarding.[96] The Pro-Am Skateboarder Racers Association teamed up with communities, police, and schools to develop safe skateboarding guidelines and programs.[97] This organization supported the creation of skateboarding "areas" or parks in the vein of other public recreational facilities such as baseball diamonds. Seeking to legitimize the practice, one spokesman enthused, "Skateboarding is a beautiful way to develop poise and self-confidence."[98] The International Skateboard Association (ISA), an organization of 12 skateboarding companies, was founded in 1976 to advance the sport. The ISA also staged safety clinics and competitions.[99] The city of Glendora even decided to make ticketed skateboarders and bicyclists attend safety lectures on Saturday mornings.[100] These clinics served to normalize skateboarding, as did the development of skate parks, which exploded in the mid-1970s.

Municipalities nationwide began to respond to skateboarders' needs with skate parks in 1975. The *New York Times* listed "California, Texas, Florida, Maryland, Chiba Beach, Japan, the town and shire of Albany, Western Australia, and Huntington, Long Island" as having opened skate parks in 1975–76. [101] Skate parks required their patrons to wear safety gear, including helmets, elbow pads, and knee pads, and effectively negated the danger of a skateboarder being hit by a car. In fact, in 1977 the Consumer Product Safety Commission reported that skateboarding in parks was significantly less risky than doing it elsewhere and that skateboarding had risen from the twenty-fifth riskiest sport to the second (after bicycling),[102] having caused at least 188,000 injuries in 1976.[103] Skate parks also became a prime source of revenue, and their owners opened "pro shops" near their parks and sponsored lessons and contests. Skateboard World in Torrance, California, wooed customers with music, an arcade, closed circuit television (which allowed skateboarders to review their skills), and a concession stand.[104]

"A Real Sport": Skateboarding Contests as a Legitimizing Tool

With the development of the urethane wheel, Frank Nasworthy proclaimed skateboarding "a real sport."[105] As marketers and promoters began to notice the success of the industry, they developed contests and exhibitions to further promote skateboarding and gain monetarily from it. These contests, in turn, worked to shore up skateboarding's status as a sport.

Of course, not all contests were sponsored by big industry players, and various California locales held competitions beginning in the summer of 1975. Most of them included slalom races and "freestyle" events that tested skateboarders' ability to perform gymnastic or acrobatic tricks, such as handstands, on their boards. Skateboards were also included in parades,[106] Young Men's Christian Association (YMCA) holiday events,[107] and charity events.[108] These contests and events were not new, particularly to the Los Angeles area, as they were held throughout skateboarding's boom in the 1960s. However, as more people proclaimed the activity a true sport, television began to take notice, and in 1976 the ABC network broadcast the World Skateboard Championships.[109]

In June 1976, National Skateboard Shows, Inc., a new production company, spent 250,000 dollars to develop the Skateboarding World Masters Invitational, and the World Professional Skateboard Championships Invitational was held in California in September. Wholly developed by industry organizations, the titles of these contests are meant to instill skateboarding with cosmopolitanism as well as an aura of tradition. These contests feature "professionals" and "masters," invited by a legitimizing organization to exhibit their skills. In reality, the *New York Times* scoffed, "the main floor of the arena . . . looked rather amateurish for what was billed as the World Professional Skateboard Championship."[110] While supposedly world events, the contests were always located in the United States, and the World Masters Invitational was only "worldly" in that some of its contestants came from Hawaii.[111] In this context, rumors also began to circulate that skateboarding would be a part of the 1980 Olympic Games in Moscow.[112]

Manufacturers hoped to further legitimize skateboarding by paying to promote it widely and raise it to the level of a popular family sport enjoyed even by nonparticipants. "With a second lease on life," the *New York Times* reported, "skateboard companies are sending 'teams' on nationwide tours to push skateboarding as the new family sport."[113] Manufacturers began to pay skateboarders up to 30,000 dollars to demonstrate skateboarding at exhibitions around the country and on television,[114] and between sponsorships and prize money skateboarders such as Russ Howell, who told the *Los Angeles Times* that he had been in "seven or eight movies, written two books and won 18 major championships,"[115] made 60,000 dollars.[116] Although *Dogtown and Z-Boys* positions the Zephyr Skateboard team as distinct from the larger culture of skateboarding in the 1970s, team member Tony Alva did indeed reach the mainstream press. He told the *Los Angeles Times* that other professional skateboarders are "sportsmen and health freaks. They're people just having fun."[117]

Bill Riordan started to manage skateboarder Ty Page and endorsed a skateboarding tournament to be held in Long Beach, California. "'Anything that generates $300 million in annual sales,' Riordan said, 'can't be all bad.'"[118] He also developed a children's show featuring skateboarding for the television network CBS with former American Basketball Association commissioner Jack Dolph.

Riordan's discussions about promoting Ty Page capture some of the many layers of discourse that have accumulated on skateboarding and its culture. He told the *New York Times:*

> To make this sport viable in America . . . you need to create national heroes to sustain it. Ty is a super athlete, he jumps off Oceanside cliffs, he was the national boys' surfing champ at age 12 . . . and his image is apple pie and ice cream. He's clean-cut, wears proper safety equipment, and everyone wants to mother him. Jimmy Connors came up in the age of the anti-hero. It was easy to make a rascal out of him. Those days are over.

Describing Ty Page elsewhere as "a Huckleberry Finn in a blond Afro," Riordan represents Page as an all-American boy with a twist.[119] That is to say, he was white, childlike, adventurous, and good spirited while at the same time stunning audiences with his daring skateboarding ability and perhaps even his hair. His father claimed that before his son became a professional skateboarder he was interested only in "surfing, skateboarding, and girls" and was "a ne'er-do-well in the making."[120] Not only all-American, Page was decidedly heterosexual and possessed at least the potential to be a rebel. Riordan, at least by his own account, was certainly successful in making Page a star; he estimated that Page would earn between 75,000 and 100,000 dollars in 1977.[121]

In 1976, the *New York Times* declared, "[P]eople are getting rich on skateboards. . . . [Skateboarding] has gone Hollywood. And everybody who is anybody wants a piece of the action."[122] With the development of new technology, the price of skateboards rose from approximately 10 dollars in 1965 to as much as 125 in 1976. The newspaper claimed, "Though many of the early boarders were kids who couldn't afford two roller skates, today skateboarding is not a sport for the poor. Like stereo freaks, the stoked often buy components and assemble them themselves."[123] By 1977, sales had risen approximately 25 to 35 percent to 550 to 650 million dollars,[124] and skateboard manufacturer Hobie Alter was selling his boards through JCPenney and Sears.[125] Toy maker Mattell Corporation launched its Magnum Skateboard Division in 1977 as well, and its marketing manager said, "We do see permanence to the sport. The outlaw nature of it is changing, and skateparks are providing an anchor to the sport. It has become less faddish, and a more year-round sport."[126]

More than an industry, skateboarding was perceived to be part of a new youth culture along with rock music and surfing. Skateboarders began to be featured elsewhere in the media besides in televised contests. In 1977, Ty Page reported doing four television commercials.[127] As the *Los Angeles Times* listed skateboarding's reach into popular culture, "Six national TV commercials (Pepsi, RC Cola, Three Musketeers, Master Charge, Orange Plus and MG) use skateboarding in their pitch. Three slick new magazines have been devoted to the subject, each full color and filled with expensive ad lineage. Universal will soon distribute a feature film titled 'Skateboard.'"[128]

At least part of this youth culture was focused on "authenticity." Some professional skaters made it a point to proclaim that they were not participating in skateboarding for financial gain. "The thing is" one said, "they could be giving away lollipops at this meet and it would have the same importance as if they were giving away thousands and thousands of dollars."[129] Still, even Bill Riordan's all-American skateboarders began to demand compensation. A "cheerful little tyke," 13-year-old professional skateboarder Bobby (Casper) Boyden, when asked what he liked most about skateboarding, responded, "The money, the money!"[130]

More than a moneymaker, the culture of skateboarding was widely perceived to be the domain of young people, and it operated as a never–never land for some. Skitch Hitchcock, a 24-year-old professional skateboarder, enthused, "I got to be a kid forever, Peter Pan."[131] Indeed, skateboarders were frequently defined as "junior high and high school students"[132] or "teens and pre-teens."[133] *Family Health* defined skateboarders as "generally boys in their teens and pre-teens."[134] Print journalists maintained the barrier between young skateboarders and adults by publishing lists of skateboarding slang, indicating that skateboarders had a language of their own. *Sports Illustrated* listed a variety of slang terms to which promoter "Riordan and his middle-aged colleagues" had to become accustomed.[135] The *Washington Post* claimed, "[S]kateboarding is still something of an outlaw art, its grace and beauty heightened by the ever-present possibility of the board's betrayal. It's an esoteric world as well, its language nearly incomprehensible, its mythology rich with teenaged heroes who have found fame and fortune in a world of nearly perpetual motion."[136]

The *Los Angeles Times* remarked that skateboarding "may be the ultimate sport for today's youth. You don't need a natural landscape (a street, sidewalk or driveway is all that is needed), it's something you do alone, and it appears to be something that older people neither understand nor can ever do as well."[137] The ability to skateboard alone, the story explained, meant that skateboarders were not "dependent on anyone."[138] The independent nature of the practice was tied to its relationship to the self. Pro skater Russ Howell claimed that skateboarding "tells you a lot about yourself" and in recent years "the emphasis has been off teams and on the individual."[139] The editor of *Skate Boarder* magazine told the *Los Angeles Times*, "Skateboarding is an individual freedom"[140]

Boys Only?

Skateboarding in the 1970s was still a male-centric sport; however, women were taken far more seriously in this decade than they were in skateboarding's first moment of popularity. The *Los Angeles Times* asserted that 10 percent of professional skateboarders were female.[141] Part of the reason for this shift may be that Title IX, the law mandating equal opportunities in sports participation for men and women, was passed in 1972.[142] But I would argue that changing definitions of skateboarding also contributed to girls' increased acceptance.

These changing definitions categorized skateboarding as two distinct endeavors. The first, as represented in Peralta's documentary *Dogtown and Z-Boys*, focused on defying gravity and included riding in empty swimming pools and racing down hills. This mode of skateboarding later evolved into "vert," or vertical, skateboarding, which is done on large ramps called half pipes. Vert skating is heavily represented on ESPN's *The X Games*. The second mode of skateboarding was more akin to gymnastics or dance and involved performing a variety of tricks with the skateboard on flat ground, including handstands and lifts. Because of its relationship to the more "artistic" pursuits of dance—or even ice skating—women's role in the practice did not seem contradictory. This mode of skateboarding evolved into today's street and flatland skateboarding, which are not as open to women, in part, I would submit, because of their public nature and their frequent reliance on trespassing.

Women, however, were not only represented as graceful skateboarders. Several achieved the status of professionals; Bill Riordan included Ellen O'Neal and Laura Thornhill on his "team" of skateboarders.[143] The *Los Angeles Times* featured 16-year-old Thornhill in June 1977, and the lead picture portrayed her skateboarding on a ramp with a male skater. The article reported that Thornhill had suffered "two major injuries and scores of scrapes," and when asked why she skateboards she replied, "Because it's fun and because of the money—it's nice making money when you're doing something you like."[144] Ellen O'Neal told the paper that she loved the competition associated with skateboarding and that in her first competition she placed second in a field of 200 boys.[145] The *Times* also ran a photo of Desiree Von Essen waiting for the start of a skateboarding race. She's perched leaning backward on her board, holding on to two poles and wearing a helmet, gloves, and elbow and knee pads. She stares intently in front of her, her body is tense, and she appears to be focused and strong.[146] Von Essen, in short, is a far cry from the young girls posing with their skateboarding dogs. One exception to this trend is a story that appeared in the *Los Angeles Times*, which reported the following about the 1976 California Free Form World Professional Skateboard Championships.

> Ernie Martin from the East Coast broke another record by high-jumping 4 feet 7 inches. Bob Jarvis of Laguna Beach whirled through 15½ consecutive 360-degree turns, and little Ellen Berryman performed a freestyle show complete with gymnastic and ballet maneuvers.[147]

This article claimed, "The girl skaters, using gymnastic and ballet techniques, add a soft touch to skateboarding. But some, like Laura Thornhill, are as aggressive as men."[148]

Clearly, women were not achieving equal recognition or respect within the culture of skateboarding, and the same *Los Angeles Times* article that featured O'Neal and Von Essen claimed that most pro skaters were men and many girls associated with the sport were fans looking for "cute guys."[149] Still, it is clear that the sport's relationship to girls and women was malleable and changing. While important on its own terms, this development was also crucial to masculinity. As masculinity and femininity are mutually constitutive, changing norms regarding female participation surely shift the context of skateboarding so that it may allow for alternative definitions of masculinity.

Moreover, even as skateboarding achieved heightened legitimacy via technology, marketing, and new and daring tricks, it maintained a kinship to more "expressive" and graceful modes. Arguably, this kinship, along with skateboarding's riskiness, has created a sporting space in which young men at one and the same time can conquer space, develop more impressive tricks, and express themselves artistically.

A Fading Fad? Skateboarding, 1979–84

In 1977, some industry insiders were already forecasting the second demise of skateboarding. George Powell of the Powell Corporation worried that companies intent on cashing in on skateboarding's success would begin to sell inferior products, though at the same time he suggested that more adults might begin to participate in the sport, thus maintaining or increasing its popularity.[150] Still, in 1979 the *Washington Post* noted that the Consumer Product Safety Commission was reporting such a dramatic decrease in participation that it no longer felt a ban on skateboarding was necessary. *Money* magazine stated that skateboard sales were down 50 percent in 1977–78, and in those same years skateboarding injuries dropped from 140,070 to 87,800. The commission suggested that those who were still skateboarding tended to do so in the more private and safer realm of skate parks.[151]

By 1979, roller skating had replaced skateboarding as the sport du jour, catching on as a sport open to everyone, unlike skateboarding, which appealed to teenagers generally and boys more specifically.[152] The *Washington Post* reported, "'It's got beautiful demographics, just beautiful,' says Sure-Grip's general manager, John Poe. 'Skateboarding was all male, 10 to 15. This is everybody, 5 to 70 with a big bulge in females 40 to 45—that group has never had an athletic program.'"[153] Poe almost certainly was not celebrating the development of sports accessible to women as a feminist gain; rather, he was pointing to the broad appeal of roller skating as an industry. Indeed, women were represented quite frequently with roller skates. Linda Ronstadt posed in them for the cover of an album, and *Playboy* featured a woman wearing only roller skates. Sharon Borstin published *Keep on Rollin'*, which heralded the benefits of roller skating for women, including burning calories, relieving menstrual pain, and "strengthen[ing] vaginal muscles."[154]

By 1981, several reporters were again calling skateboarding a fad, reducing it to a passing childhood phase with little social relevance. Sebastian DiCasoli, the Sporting Goods Manufacturing Association's marketing director, said of roller skating, "It definitely isn't a fad, at least not like skateboards."[155] The *Los Angeles Times* asked, "Wonder what ever happened to skateboard parks?"[156] The *Washington Post* suggested that video games had overtaken skateboards as the go-to youth activity.[157]

Skateboarding's demise in the late 1970s was indeed contested. In February 1979, a skateboarder told a *Los Angeles Times* reporter, "Skateboards were supposed to be a fad," but many people continued to skate and competitions and skate parks continued to be well attended. The skater proclaimed, "It's here to stay, and I think rollerskating is, too."[158] Continued discussion about the safety of skateboarding and potential bans, as well as coverage of events such as contests, skate parks, and exhibitions, suggests that, although its popularity as a marker of youth culture may have faded, young people continued to engage in skateboarding in both public and private.[159] Furthermore, despite being reduced to a passing fad in most media accounts, skateboarding managed to maintain some of its relevance as a marker of troublesome youth, daredevils, and even teen rebellion. A California congressman, Barry M. Goldwater Jr., reported that his staff persuaded him to give up his skateboard because of concern over his "image,"[160] and several articles invoked skateboarding youths as a sign of trouble.[161]

Michael Brooke suggests that skateboarding's second demise can be attributed to its "old nemesis, safety concerns," because many skate parks closed in response to high insurance premiums.[162] He also argues that skateboarding was a victim of its own success; as companies began to gain monetarily from the practice in the late 1970s, corporate values overtook a formerly untainted pastime. As I have demonstrated, however, skateboarding has always existed in relationship to and within mainstream culture, it has always been a product for sale, and it never enjoyed a precapitalist moment when it existed primarily for a mythically pure subcultural group. Nevertheless, even the mainstream media suggested that skateboarding's demise was due in part to the media's interest in it. In 1985, the *Los Angeles Times* quoted skateboard manufacturer Tom Sims as saying, "The sensationalism of the media hurt [skateboarding] tremendously. Media overemphasized certain elements, the more radical turns and maneuvers."[163]

In these interstitial years, when skateboarding no longer dominated mainstream representations of adolescent males, a niche media industry serving dedicated skaters developed. The once popular *Skate Boarder* magazine was transformed into *Action Now* and began to feature a wide variety of "action sports," including horseback riding, but two new publications devoted entirely to skateboarding were released: *Thrasher* magazine was first published in 1981, and *Transworld Skateboarding* commenced in 1983.

Thrasher and *Transworld Skateboarding*, as the two signposts of the skateboarding world, established a discussion that defines skateboarding's existence in relation to mainstream culture to the present moment. Fausto Vitello, who owns the company Independent, a manufacturer of skateboard trucks (axles), founded *Thrasher* with the following editorial statement: "Skateboarding attracts a unique person. It influences the rest of society. *Thrasher* is not about hypocrisy or selling out to corporate America. We are about skate and destroy."[164] Later Vitello told *Sports Illustrated*, "We just wanted to be outlaws. The mainstream thing hadn't worked, so we just terrorized. That was how we saw we could promote the sport."[165] George Powell also told the magazine, "We knew skateboarding had to become a more underground activity to survive, that mystique was good for the sport."[166] Larry Balma, the founder of *Transworld Skateboarding*, conceived his publication as an alternative to *Thrasher*, which he defined as "sex, drugs and rock 'n' roll." *Thrasher*'s tone, he argued, turned off parents and thus potential customers.[167] Despite their divergent approaches, both magazines were clearly interested in developing discursive constructions of skateboarding that would be marketable. Vitello and Powell's statements, especially, drive home the always already commercial nature of skateboarding, even as it is being defined as rebellious and noncorporate. Toggling back and forth between mainstream and subcultural appeals even in its niche market, skateboarding is constantly in correspondence with the broader culture. These two poles of existence are crucial to understanding skateboarding's next wave, during which it was defined as both the domain of punk rebels and a highly athletic endeavor.

"Skate and Destroy" or the New Little League? Corresponding Anew, 1985–93

Skateboarding's decline in popularity was short lived, and by 1985 it was again the subject of feature articles discussing the state of male adolescents. In April 1985, the *Los Angeles Times* ran a story on Tony Magnusson, who was "Believe it or not, a professional skateboarder." The paper noted that "skateboarders see a fight for acceptance as legitimate and long overdue. They may be men in a boys' world, but they're as serious as a 16-foot fall onto concrete."[168] This movement toward mainstream culture was fraught with contradiction from the beginning. Magnusson described skateboarding "danger . . . freedom . . . a big rush, like walking on the edge of an out-and-out disaster," but the paper said, "it is also brutally competitive and serious stuff to the man-child heroes who don the equipment and risk its indiscretions."[169] Skateboard manufacturer Tom Sims characterized the industry as "more of a grass-roots thing but climbing on a solid basis."[170] The *Los Angeles Times* also ran a story on Russ Howell, "The Pied Piper of Sidewalk Surfing," in which the reporter wrote, "You hope the sport is making a more wholesome comeback, but you know it has a long way to go before society accepts it."[171] A "wholesome" sport with a punk image, the domain of men-children, a multi-million-dollar grassroots industry, and an edgy but serious endeavor, skateboarding in 1985 was loaded with contradictions, and these oppositions and incongruities have followed it to the present moment.

By 1986, skateboarding was again popular enough to be featured in *Sports Illustrated*, this time with Tony Hawk as the central character.[172] His role as skateboarding's spokesperson is deeply contradictory and has been received in various ways by contemporary skateboarders, as I discuss later. *Sports Illustrated*'s 1986 profile helps to establish these contradictions. Of the sport more generally, the magazine reported:

> Today annual skateboard and accessory sales are again approaching $300 million. Models pose in Macy's catalog in skateboarding garb; MGM moguls are talking feature-length movies. But the sport is still struggling, split right down the middle. Anarchists to the left. Little Leaguers to the right. The Defiant Ones—artistic, almost poetic in many cases—live to skate the streets. . . . They're turned on by the breeze blowing in their hair and the nihilistic, satanic sounds of hard-core or speed rock groups like Metallica, Megadeath, and Slayer. . . . Across the fence stands the [National Skateboarding Association]. Its members are no less artistic or inclined to plaster their boards with skulls or skeletons, but the NSA strives for a more clean-cut, competitive and organized image.[173]

Sports Illustrated associated the former with *Thrasher* magazine and the latter with *Transworld Skateboarding* and reported, "Tony Hawk admits he sits 'right between' the two magazines in this culture clash."[174] The magazine's description of Hawk's "punk hunk look" emphasized his space in between: "Blonde hair spills like a waterfall over the left side of Hawk's soft-featured face. He comes across as articulate, sensitive, unswayed by others," but his knees are also "bloodied and scarred by cement."[175]

Sports Illustrated's depiction of Tony Hawk and skateboarding represents not only the practice's existence between what might be traditionally called "subculture" and "mainstream" but also the multiple masculinities encouraged by and represented within skateboarding. Both "hardcore" and "sensitive," "aggressive" and "poetic," skateboarding boys can maintain the power implied by aggressive or dominant masculinities while expanding the realms of masculinity to thoughtful self-expression. The multiple discursive markers that follow skateboarding from this moment into current depictions are surely part of the reason that skateboarders in the new century can proclaim alternative masculinities that are not antipatriarchal without appearing to notice the contradictions in their claims.

Between 1985 and 1993, skateboarding was represented equally as a practice for both punk teens and innocent schoolchildren. In 1985, Tony Hawk's father Frank, president of the NSA and a former Boy Scout leader, convinced the Boy Scouts to take over the Del Mar Skate Ranch in order to alleviate its insurance difficulties. Although the Boy Scouts would remain, for all intents and purposes, an invisible partner, the organization did train the skate park employees "in the goals and principles of Scouting: citizenship, patriotism, character building and such."[176] In 1987, a sporting-goods store owner, Steven Grigorian, told the *New York Times:*

> Some people think it's a radical activity, some kind of rebellion, involving a lot of hippie-types. Actually it's a very healthy sport that has a national sanctioning board. . . . A lot of kids use their boards for transportation, riding them to school, for example. And some use them for their paper routes.[177]

American Health magazine suggested that skateboarding is an activity through which teenagers can channel their energy and aggression;[178] a letter to the *Washington Post* called skateboarding "wholesome and time-consuming fun";[179] and the mother of an 11-year-old boy with HIV defended him as "a regular kid," declaring, "He loves to skateboard."[180]

Between 1987 and 1992, skateboarding fashion became a clear marker of youthful cool,[181] and in 1992 Curad released neon bandages designed to match "kids' fashions, rollerblades and skateboards."[182] Skateboarding fashion was relevant yet hip enough in 1992 for *Vogue* to run a feature article on it. Declaring skateboarding "a lasting subculture with its own patois, rituals, and fashion,"[183] *Vogue* praised both the "grace"[184] and the "outlaw aura"[185] of skateboarding. Featuring a variety of photos of black and white teen males wearing baggy jeans, oversized shirts, and graffiti-style logos, the article concluded, without a hint of irony, "Skateboard culture may already be suffering the fate of punk: it's being institutionalized and marketed for a mass audience."[186]

Indeed, skateboarding had become a marker of youthful cool in the mainstream music, television, and film markets. Skate-punk hip-hop artists the Beastie Boys released their first number-one album, *Licensed to Ill*, in 1986,[187] and the TV network Nickelodeon was launched in 1986 and began airing *SK8TV* in 1990.[188] In 1987, the *Teenage Mutant Ninja Turtles* animated series began, and the turtles loved not only pizza but also skateboards. Perhaps the quintessential radical skater and innocent child, Bart Simpson, came to network television in 1990.

Despite the skateboarding industry's—and *Transworld Skateboarding*'s—efforts to convince the public that skateboarding was simply a new mode of competitive sport, many media outlets continued to portray it as a highly rebellious activity. *People Weekly* introduced "the world of thrashing," a subculture of skateboard "punks—mohawked, skinheaded, tattooed types, proud of their bravado and oblivious to the dangers of hard surfaces."[189] A 1985 *Los Angeles Times* article also included young women in its depiction of rebellious skaters. The article suggested, "Audrey Ritter is strong, if not admirable. The 14-year-old . . . considers herself hell on four wheels. 'I skateboard, but I'm dangerous,' said Ritter. . . . 'I'm suicidal—a suicidal skater.'"[190]

Aside from these two articles, however, the press ignored female skaters, and by the early 1990s, as I will discuss, skateboarders were defined exclusively as male. In the interim, discussions of skaters as rebels continued. *Maclean's* dubbed skateboarders "hell on wheels,"[191] and *Time* ran an article describing them as "bigger, badder, radder and more streetwise than ever." The magazine also quoted one skateboarder as declaring, "I mean, this is not a 'nice' sport like golf," and *Thrasher*'s Kevin Thatcher proclaimed skateboarders to be "the punk-rockers of the sport set."[192] In 1990, the *Washington Post Magazine* depicted skateboarders as

> lighting up smokes and swigging Cokes. . . . [S]tripping down to T-shirts that reveal biceps decorated with some truly baroque tattoos. The boom box blares Metal Church—music that sounds like the midnight shift at the steel plant or a psychopathic dental drill or a garbage disposal eating a beer can.[193]

This article also made it clear that women in this group serve solely as girlfriends and spectators. "Two skate bettys in black leather jackets," it reads, "sit watching [the skateboarding] with no noticeable interest." The article depicts the young women reading books, smoking, drinking, eating, "and gossiping" about clothes and ruining the skateboard ramps so that the skateboarding boys will be forced to stop skating.[194] To channel John

Berger, "Men act and women watch and appear bored."[195] Though here we see women watching men rather than vice versa, the men are still doing/acting/performing—displaying their agency—while the women are sitting on the sidelines.

Placing Boys on Display

Between 1989 and 1992, several articles took pains to define skateboarding as the domain of young men. Reporter Peter Watrous described the "perfectly formed surfer bodies" of the rock group Red Hot Chili Peppers and the Urban Dance Squad's music video for "Deeper Shade of Soul" as "advertisements for the good life in California, where boys can do what boys do, which is play music and skateboard. Clearly this is a closed world that posits a type of joy and community without female interruption."[196] Similarly, a 1989 article in *Seventeen* magazine titled "Why Boys Have More Fun" suggested that while boys "are attempting to perfect the art of bouncing a skateboard from their feet to their hand" girls "are plotting a course that will lead them to become solid, self-sufficient grown-ups."[197] The girls are making a poor choice, for "worrying about things like your future *twenty-four-hours a day* is not going to help."[198] These two reporters invoked a tired stereotype of women as civilizing figures,[199] and they did so at a moment when a backlash against feminism was consolidating in mainstream culture.[200]

Not simply an aggressive subculture, skateboarding had morphed into a never–never land where young men could continue to act like boys, content in their playful immaturity. In 1991, Spike Jonze, then 21, teamed with several others to develop *Dirt*, a spin-off of the popular magazine *Sassy*, as an alternative to teen magazines such as *YM* and *Seventeen*. Its editors had earlier been employed with small BMX and skateboarding magazines. *Dirt* was designed as a general interest magazine for teen boys, but it relied on skateboarding as a cultural marker.[201] By 1995, *Dirt* was defunct.[202] Spike Jonze later went on to produce a variety of niche skateboarding videos and now owns two skateboarding companies, "girl" and "chocolate."

This playful boys' culture, however, was also clearly a space in which boys were being looked at. Surveilled by authoritative adults, skaters also became the object of marketers. Peter Watrous discussed skateboarding as part of a new era of "beefcake" in depictions of men, suggesting that "Feminism, in its attempt to give decision-making powers to the exploited, inadvertently allowed for a whole new type of commerciality" in which women (and apparently men as well) exploit themselves as a mode of power. Images of skateboarders in videos are, for Watrous, both characteristic of a moment in which men must be vigilant of their own bodies and signs of a men-only playground.[203] *Sassy* also discussed skater boys' performances in an article titled "Skater Babes: Asexual or Not?" The article gushes, "Skater boys. Yummmm," and suggests, "Practically every girl knows why all skater boys are babes: They are the perfect combination of attitude and excess fabric." But 16-year-old author Mary-Kate Arnold noting skaters' lack of interest in women, said, "that's probably the very reason we're so attracted to them." Her article makes it clear that skateboarding is a boys' culture, and, despite their apparent disinterest, skateboarders are defined as heterosexual. But, the article claims, "they're just not worthy of our attention. They're too obsessed with their concrete fantasies to ever give a relationship the attention it deserves." Perhaps more important, Arnold points out the discomfort many male skateboarders exhibit when being watched. "Sort of like how girls feel when guys watch them walk down the street, eh?" she teases.[204]

Sassy's short and snappy critique keeps heterosexuality firmly up front, a move particularly necessary for denying homoeroticism in boys-only cultures. Although Watrous suggests that women finally have enough power to exploit themselves, the exclusion of girls from boys' culture only serves to further marginalize them. In the late 1980s and early 1990s, the adolescent girls on the edges of skate culture played one key role: they watched the boys in order to shore up the heterosexuality of skate culture. Not quite the innocent white youths of the Little League, but also not overtly rebellious teens like Dogtown's Z-Boys, the skaters of this moment were positioned as cool, cute, and stylish boys who hovered on the outskirts of mainstream culture.

Teen Demographics and The X Games, 1995–97

In the mid-1990s, the teen youth market began to grow in part because of an increase in the number of teens. In 1994, the Rand Youth Poll reported that American teens were spending 61 billion dollars a year on goods for themselves and were influencing 139 billion dollars' worth of their parents' spending decisions. What's more, the experts at this time predicted that this spending would increase between 12 and 15 percent each year through 1999.[205] Surveys in 1998 showed that teenagers were helping their parents with the shopping, and therefore were highly influential in the choice of household products, but were also spending lots of money on themselves.[206] By 1999, *Advertising Age* reported that "Teen boys pack spending power estimated at $650 billion a year."[207]

In 1995, ESPN introduced *The Extreme Games*, which *TV Guide* described as "the first truly 'gnarly' (translation: cool) made-for-TV sports show."[208] According to ESPN lore, *The Extreme Games* were conceptualized by Ron Semiao, a programmer for ESPN2, after he took note of multiple advertisements utilizing extreme sports. From the beginning, *The Extreme Games* were designed to take advantage of this trend, and the programmers worked to maintain the "extreme" tone of these individualistic sports through extreme production values. "[E]xpect wild camera angles, rock music, and announcers who know each sport's slang phrases," *TV Guide* declared.[209] *TV Guide* further shored up the notion that the sports featured in *The Extreme Games* were different from other sports by pointing out that the prize money, totaling 370,000 dollars for the entire event, was a pittance compared to that of other sports. There was no reason to worry, the magazine noted, because "Most extremists insist that they compete for the love—and thrill—of their sport, and they probably do."[210]

The Extreme Games—renamed the X Games in 1996—cut a skillful path through the counterculture-mainstream athlete dichotomy set up by *Thrasher* and *Transworld Skateboarding* magazines. The event represented "outlandish, on-the-edge sports"[211] but also "true athletes."[212] The network marketed its event skillfully, deeming extreme sports "sheer unadulterated athletic lunacy" in its promotional materials. Marketing executive George Bodenheimer claimed, "These sports come from the streets, not from a TV studio."[213] At the same time, as Robert E. Rinehart notes, *The X Games* worked to incorporate a mainstream sporting ethos into the skateboarding lifestyle, positioning it (and other extreme sports) as a sport tied up with competition, risk, and pain. Despite such incorporation, it must be pointed out, contra Rinehart's view that "In extreme sport, in the mid-1990s, branding was unknown,"[214] that skateboard culture since at least the 1980s had worked to brand itself in multiple ways as both mainstream and subcultural. *The X Games* hadn't *completely* co-opted and changed skate culture; skate

Tony Hawk on a half pipe in ESPN's *Ultimate X: The Movie* (2002), a celebration of *The X Games*. His athleticism is clear, as is the epic nature of the depiction. (Courtesy PhotoFest.)

culture had always had a contradictory stance vis-à-vis mainstream sporting culture. For skateboarding specifically, the mainstream press made it clear that despite its success in the wake of *The X Games* and an Olympic show-case, "skateboarding has not entirely shed its underground image, which might explain its attraction to teenagers. . . . It may be the only sport in which participants can get arrested."[215]

The X Games also showcased the branding power of extreme sports. Marketers for the first games included Taco Bell, Mountain Dew, Chevrolet trucks, Miller Lite Ice beer, and the Pontiac Sunfire.[216] Marketers delighted in the show's alignment with their consumers. Janine Bousquette of PepsiCo claimed that *The X Games* "reinforces [Mountain Dew's] active and cutting-edge image," and Peter Waller of Taco Bell said, "*The X Games* are a distinctive property with an outdoor attitude that delivers a pure audience. *The Games* reflect the free-spirited, energetic attitude of our consumers."[217]

More than an "energetic attitude," *The X Games* represented a shift in interest from team-based to individualized sports. In 1997, the *New Yorker* ran an article discussing the new marketing strategies of the National Football League (NFL), which had hired MTV's copresident, Sara Levinson, to remake its image. Levinson's hiring represented a major shift in the NFL's strategy and not simply because she is a woman. The league wanted Levinson to bring MTV's noncomformist values and rock and roll aesthetic to the traditionally disciplined, team-based sport without, of course, alienating its older and more traditional fans. The article notes that changes in the sport's rules (the introduction of free agency meant that players could go on "the open market" four years after being drafted) encouraged players to see and market themselves as individuals rather than team players. Further, more general cultural shifts from an economy based on physical labor to one based on information and entertainment encouraged us to value creativity and individuality over a willingness to follow rules. Levinson explained that the NFL did not have a "rebellious" image that young people could relate to. Rick Welts, the president of NBA Properties, explained that youths were responding well to the National Basketball Association's (NBA's) personalized marketing of individual players, but "Football players, on the other hand—hulks behind helmets—are faceless performers for the team. Football is about character, not personality."[218]

Such cultural shifts are surely crucial to understanding the rise of the individualistic sports represented in *The X Games*, though participants also invoke a more personalized dissatisfaction with the on-the-ground patriarchy that traditional sports—and their coaches—represent. Shaun Palmer, a snowboarder and mountain biker, told *Time* that "individualistic extreme sports are 'a lot better than going to football practice every day and having your coach yell at you.'"[219]

Co-optation and Rebellion, 1998–2001

By 1998, the mainstream press was beginning to discuss the ways in which extreme had gone mainstream while at the same time maintaining that extreme sports were alternative and edgy. As *Forbes* reported, "Extreme sports are coooool. Edgy, adrenaline-inducing pursuits."[220] In fact, *The X Games* was so cool that NBC launched its own version, *The Gravity Games*, in 1999. Still, *Forbes* claimed, "These guys are no Michael Jordans," for the athletes' involvement in extreme sports was not resulting in huge incomes.[221] *Sport* suggested that, while extreme sports "emphasize freedom and self-expression and are fueled by equal parts talent and adrenaline," their stars, such as Tony Hawk, were "overexposed."[222]

Marketers were indeed wary of attempts to co-opt this subculture. *Forbes* warned of the fate of Nike's 1995 attempt to break into the skate shoe market. Although the company waged an award-winning marketing campaign depicting golfers, runners, and tennis players being chased by police and asking, "What if we treated all athletes the way we treat skateboarders?" a boycott led by the skateboard manufacturer Consolidated Skateboards rendered the shoe unsuccessful. Tony Hawk told *Forbes*, "Nike has a tainted image, because people consider it cashing in on skateboarding's success." Still, *Forbes* reported, many marketers had been successful in their appropriation of skateboarding, and Hawk advised, "You have to make sure that whatever you're doing is hard core."[223] He later told the *New York Times* that he had rejected a proposal to market pasta shaped like him,[224] and his manager and sister, Patricia Hawk, refuses to sell the Tony Hawk clothing line anywhere but in department stores.[225] In a later article, *Forbes* explained the limits some extreme athletes were putting on their endorsements, including refusing sponsorships by alcohol and tobacco companies and "reject[ing] brands that depict their sport as a sideshow."[226] *Business Week* discussed shoe company Vans' strategy for maintaining its authenticity, noting that it focused its efforts on "events, sponsorships, and even a documentary film [*Dogtown and Z-Boys*] to celebrate the outlaw nature of skateboarding culture." Vans' efforts were apparently successful, for in 2001 its sales were up 23 percent from the previous year.[227] As Rinehart explains, ESPN maintained *The X Games*' aura of authenticity by anticipating charges of co-optation and preempting them with clever rationalizations.[228]

Despite their mainstream inclusion, extreme athletes, and skateboarders more particularly, were still defined as edgy or alternative. Reporting on the Gravity Games, *Advertising Age* claimed that the festival's athletes weren't "clean-cut, All-American types" and after a rainout the show's organizers were worried that they might spend so much time partying that they would not be able to resume competition. *Rolling Stone* ran a feature on the professional skateboarder Bob Burnquist, describing him as a "Fearless skater who completes death-defying tricks with ease."[229] Jake Phelps, the editor of *Thrasher*, told *Rolling Stone* that he had discovered Burnquist in Brazil and skateboarding "is about the constant thrill of scaring yourself."[230] Although Burnquist's father is American, and he reads, phenotypically, as white, his Brazilian roots may contribute to the construction of him as fearless. As with much of its discursive history, these rebellious attributes were a source of conflict. Jim Fitzpatrick, executive director of the International Association of Skateboard Companies, told the *New York Times*, "They're not urban gangsters or terrorists who are hell-bent on destroying significant and historic locations,"[231] and a Parks and Recreation director told the paper that in spite of their clothing and chain wallets skateboarders "are the leaders of their high school. . . . Many are honors students or Eagle Scouts."[232] Not "urban gangsters or terrorists" but "Eagle Scouts," skateboarders' construction as rebellious quite easily brought up signifiers of race. Fitzpatrick's claim is notably fraught with racist stereotypes; he all but says skateboarders are white kids, and so one need not worry about them. Clearly, industry folks and authority figures had an interest in determining whether skateboarders were participating in a harmless rebellion expressed sartorially— the domain of white kids who during the week were honors students—or the dangerous, scary, and purposeful destruction of "significant and historic locations," apparently the work of "urban gangsters" (read black kids) or terrorists (read Arab kids). Whiteness, it seems, was good for business.

Whether skateboarders were defined as rebellious troublemakers or all-American good kids, they were certainly utilized as markers of youthful style. *Advertising Age* suggested that "the adrenaline athletes are more accessible role models for the baggy-pants crowd, and they're beginning to show up as endorsers of everything from sneakers, sports drinks and fast-food to telecommunications products and automobiles."[233] Between 1994 and 1999, several publications invoked skateboarding style as trendy and hip. A "cool hunter" for Converse shoes deemed skateboarders, along with transvestites, "the most innovative and experimental of dressers,"[234] and in 1998 the *New York Times* reported that Calvin Klein had appropriated the skateboarders' wide-legged jeans.[235]

Although at times they were still regarded as rebels or troublemakers, extreme athletes were also aligned with "American" values. Several journalists attempted to explain the popularity of extreme sports in terms of the cultural moment, and each suggested that risk taking was part of the American fabric.

> The early explorers—men who were willing to set off in the direction of the edge of the world with no clue where they were headed—were extreme, as were the Western Pacific Islanders who jumped off cliffs with vines knotted around their ankles.[236]

Invoking both the white masculinity of early explorers and the "exoticness" of islanders, the paper manages to suggest that extreme sports are a part of a long history of daring, adventure, and achievement. *Time* magazine also made such claims.

> America has always been defined by risk; it may be our predominant national characteristic. It's a country founded by risk takers fed up with the English Crown and expanded by pioneers—a word that seems utterly American. Our heritage throws up heroes—Lewis and Clark, Thomas Edison, Frederick Douglass, Teddy Roosevelt, Henry Ford, Amelia Earhart—who bucked the odds, taking perilous chances.[237]

The magazine also suggests that Americans would be more interested in creating opportunities for such chances during a time of relative peace: "[A]t the end of a decade of American triumphalism abroad and prosperity at home, we could be seeking to upsize our personalities, our sense of ourselves."[238] Such risk taking could be the path to greatness, the magazine suggests, but it also helps to explain why Americans were so "forgiving" of Bill Clinton during "Monicagate." *Men's Journal* editor Mark Bryant told the *New York Times* that extreme sports helped Generation Y "reject the apparent dullness of modern life" in a successful economy.[239]

Tony Hawk provided perhaps the most direct image of skateboarding as all-American. Portrayed frequently in his roles as husband, father, and entrepreneur,[240] Hawk also often espoused the value of hard work. He told *Sport*, "[T]he kids who see us really understand the level of athleticism and dedication required to succeed—that it's not just a 'go for it' sport that takes guts to try,"[241] and he told *Sports Illustrated for Kids*, "When I skate, I never go half way. If I don't do my best, it eats at me. It kills me inside."[242] Hawk also continued to lobby for skateboarding's acceptance: "[W]e are finally getting the legitimate coverage about the talent and athletics instead of the lifestyles, the tattoos and the hairdos. Maybe that's part of our culture, but that's not what the emphasis should be," he told the *Providence Journal-Bulletin*.[243]

Women's Sports and Fitness also suggested that extreme sports are "a mode of self-expression . . . a reaction against everything considered to be mainstream" that was "co-opted as a way to sell stuff."[244] The *New York Times* was even more direct: "While high-risk, attitude-laden extreme sports . . . might have once been about having fun and busting free of the confining rules of traditional sports, they are now increasingly about money."[245] And in October the paper claimed, "Mere skateboarders have become nearly as dull as the once-amazing triathletes and endurance athletes."[246] An ad for Wild Turkey Kentucky Bourbon made fun of extreme sports' trendiness,[247] and *Sport* deemed "the skateboarder-as-tattooed-troublemaking-outcast-teen . . . a tired cliché."[248]

The *New York Times* also quoted Kevin Thatcher of *Thrasher*, who declined ESPN's invitation to work with the network on *The X Games* skateboarding contests because "TV flattens skateboarding into one big ad." Kevin Semiao, the creator of *The X Games*, retorted that the event encouraged more kids to skateboard and so was highly supportive of the industry.[249] In many ways, the debate between Thatcher and Semiao skillfully manages and reinforces the false dichotomy between subculture and mainstream by suggesting that skateboarding should be—and was at one time—one or the other. As I have noted, *Thrasher*'s long-running campaign to define skateboarding as subcultural was in and of itself an effort to market the sport. Although *Thrasher* promotes itself as an "authentic" part of a "pure" skateboarding culture, the culture to which it refers never existed. On the other hand, as my interviews with skateboarders reveal, *The X Games*' focus on competition does feel, in part, like a corruption of the practice's values, for many skateboarders are in fact attempting to escape the competitive world of traditional sports.

Mythmaking, Brand Making, and Authenticity, 2001–6

In 2001, former professional skateboarder Stacey Peralta released *Dogtown and Z-Boys*, a documentary depicting the lives of the Zephyr Skateboarding Team based in South Santa Monica and Venice, California (Dogtown). As I have noted, this award-winning documentary positions the 1970s skateboarding era as a moment of working-class teen rebellion.[250] More than telling a partial history of skateboarding, this documentary produces a myth central to skateboarding's current definition as a mainstream but edgy culture. Released just as the mainstream media were beginning to worry about marketers' co-optation of skateboarding, the film serves as a cultural reminder that the practice is supposedly rooted in rebellion and thereby, I argue, mitigates the dampening effect that marketing may have on skateboarding's image.[251]

Although the mainstream press noted the self-mythologizing that was operating in the documentary—it does, after all, feature Peralta and his friends prominently—critics were generally enamored by what Roger Ebert called its "infectious enthusiasm."[252] More important, the press used the film as an opportunity to discuss skateboarding's "roots." The *New York Times* reported in one article:

> The golden days are resurrected in explosive, freewheeling montages that synchronize old home movies and [skateboarding photographer Craig] Stecyk's photographs with a rock soundtrack . . . into a synergistic rush that captures the sport's exuberant bad-boy aesthetic and lends it a mystical glamour. Beyond being an exhibition of physical prowess and daring, the essence of skateboarding excellence is that elusive personal quality known as style. That's why the movie's suggestion that skateboarding is an art form—with its emphasis on grace, inventiveness, and self-expression—doesn't seem so far-fetched.[253]

Dogtown and Z-Boys reinserted notions of style and expression into discussions of skateboarding that had come to be dominated by a focus on *The X Games* and competition. Of course, *Dogtown*'s styles were quickly appropriated by the fashion world. Vintage skateboarding T-shirts and Vans became popular, and high fashion picked up on this trend. One fashion industry insider said of the *Dogtown* style, "So much of youth culture has been overexposed and this feels so fresh. They had so much attitude and style, and it was so natural—the bright, colorful, sporty, fun feeling." Another said, "That whole Dogtown look is really so much about lifestyle and belonging, and the mix of sunshine and rebellion is really intoxicating."[254] The appropriation of this image did not seem to negate its power, for even 2005's fictionalized version of *Dogtown*, titled *Lords of Dogtown* and written by Stacey Peralta, was well received. The *New York Times* credited director Catherine Hardwicke (who also made *Thirteen*) for its "appropriately scruffy, unpolished look consistent with the resourceful, do-it-yourself aesthetic of the place and time it depicts. . . . [The] scenes have both the loose, stop-and-start rhythms of a long summer day and the restless, competitive energy of young men in the heat of adolescence." The reviewer continued, "[T]here is something about it that feels right—the looseness of its construction, the eclectic welter of its soundtrack, the faces of its cast."[255] *Entertainment Weekly* deemed the film "rare in its grit and authenticity" and praised its use of "a God-on-the-street's-eye view of skateboard heaven."[256] Although these point-of-view shots evoke reality in their tone, they are also a convention of the niche skateboarding videos, which I discuss later.

Kyle Kusz offers a scathing critique of the racial politics of both *Dogtown and Z-Boys* and *Lords of Dogtown*. The documentary version of the Z-boys' story, he argues, enacts "a new cultural racism" that reinscribes the dominance of whiteness by depicting young white men as socially marginalized heroes who can do no wrong (despite their criminal behavior).[257] The film particularizes the boys' whiteness by referencing their working-class status and superficial relationship to racial "difference" (via skate shop owner Jeff Ho, Z-"boy" Peggy Oki, and Z-boy Tony Alva's nonspecified race). By making these claims to difference while maintaining the centrality of the boys' whiteness, Kusz argues, the film recenters whiteness. *Lords of Dogtown*, while still noting the boys' economic marginality, positions the skaters as lords, as masters of their domain. In the post-9/11 world in which that film was made, Kusz argues, cultural texts worked to present men as imperi-

Rebellious boys skating in an empty swimming pool in *Dogtown and Z-Boys*. Simultaneously gritty and utopic, the image captures the contradictions of skate culture. (Courtesy PhotoFest.)

alistic dominators rather than a group besieged by the powers of women, people of color, and the LGBT (lesbian, gay, bisexual, transgendered) community. Both of these texts, then, walk the line between images of white male dominance and youthful rebellion. The *New York Times* summed up skateboarding's image as such.

> Much of its current appeal comes from the image of skaters as loners whose very status as outsiders makes them all members of a tribe of sorts. This quality of being an individual and yet still belonging is classic Americana— and it's what corporations and magazines try to sell with T-shirts that say

'Skate or Die.' Perhaps this makes skateboarding not an extreme sport, but a trick of balancing extremes.[258]

Skateboarding certainly did begin to balance extremes, as I have been arguing, and *The X Games* also worked to maintain the edginess of extreme sports even as it proclaimed their centrality to modern athletics. "While business has gotten bigger," *TV Guide* reported, "the sports themselves are still conducted in a heady cloud of street-style, indie machismo. Competitors perform against a pumping wall of music."[259] The industry continually worked to maintain this image. *New York Times* reported:

> An insider's understanding has kept the lucrative board-sports industrial complex—skateboarding, snowboarding and surfing—mostly in the hands of hard-core practitioners, even as these sports have grown more popular. Mainstream companies like Nike that have easily penetrated other sports often find themselves on the outside looking in, struggling to gain traction with action-sports athletes and fans who define their world by its anti-establishment bent.[260]

The article further explained the meaning of *authenticity*, which in large part relied on distribution decisions rather than a perceived level of sales. Lora Bordmer of Action Sports Retailer, a board sports industry trade show, explained that exclusive distribution to smaller board shops—rather than large retailers—is a key component of authenticity. In 2006, Nike was more successfully breaking into the skateboarding market by distributing its shoes in board shops and sponsoring small contests; Pacific Sunwear, a mall chain that sells extreme sports apparel, made a major mistake when it ran an ad in skateboarding magazines with a skateboard's trucks (axles) on backward.[261]

By the time *Dogtown* was released, Tony Hawk had become both a myth and a brand. Stacey Peralta called him "a part of American culture," and *Sports Illustrated* deemed him "a one-man marketing phenomenon" and "a legend in the world of skateboarding." The youth marketing company Alloy found him to be the "coolest big-time athlete" in a survey, and fellow professional skateboarder Bucky Lasek claimed, "He could put his name on toilet paper and sell it to the world."[262] Although, as I have noted, Tony Hawk claims that he has made careful choices in order to preserve his authenticity, his history in the sport, as well as his sheer talent, has also served this purpose. Still his image is constantly in question.

Marketer John Griffin called Tony Hawk "a guy who, for corporate America, can reach parents. You get a family guy, a squeaky-clean guy." But Hawk's image is not all goody-goody, for he appeared on MTV's *Jackass* and *Viva La Bam*, and *Jackass*'s executive producer, Jeff Tremaine, reported, "His concern about damage to his image doesn't override his sense of humor."[263] Crucial to Tremaine's claim is the notion that Hawk appeared in the MTV shows because he found them amusing, not because they would balance his family-guy image well and remind viewers of his roots in the skateboarding community. These roots have been used by corporations to project the legitimacy of various mainstream products. *The X Games* owes its success in part to Hawk's early involvement, as "He signed on and enlisted cool skateboarders who might otherwise have rejected the event as crass commercialism."[264] Hawk also brought such authenticity to Activision's line of Tony Hawk video games. "An avid gamer, Hawk insisted on creative input," advising the developers on the game's combinations of skateboarding tricks as well as nixing over-the-top moves and cheesy settings.[265] In 2006, Hawk participated in a major cross-promotional endeavor with Jeep, *Rolling Stone*, and Activision, which included an "advertorial" in *Rolling Stone;* a Jeep Wrangler outfitted with a skateboard, snowboard, and surfboard; an appearance by Jeep and its Toledo, Ohio, factory in the latest Tony Hawk video game; and several other initiatives. Pat Hawk again made clear Tony's commitment to authenticity, noting that he was once a teenager intent on spotting sellouts. She told the *New York Times*, "That's why Tony doesn't have a deal with Nike" or Gap—because skateboarders do not buy Nike or Gap products. Conversely, Tony Hawk has explained that he endorses McDonald's because "I take my kids to McDonald's. I always order a No. 2."[266]

Hawk's image, carefully maintained, is also carefully naturalized. His company, Birdhouse, sponsors a team of street skateboarders (whose legitimacy has been less frequently challenged than that of the vert [vertical] skateboarders who are featured on *The X Games*), and he makes surprise appearances on their tours in such mundane places as Fargo and Wichita. Hawk also maintains a foundation that sponsors public skate parks, and his demo fees support the foundation. He defends himself against claims of selling out by arguing that he skateboards for the love of it rather than for the money or fame.[267] He told *Time:*

> I always keep the focus of what I do on the skating itself. I've turned away plenty of endorsements and promotional opportunities when the basis was not around skating. Quality skating will always be at the fore-front of the image I project, and if I start sucking, then I don't deserve any of this stuff, and I won't be out there promoting it.[268]

This argument is supported in part by Hawk's history in a sport that has not always been popular. His autobiography, distributed by Disney, takes care to detail Hawk's struggles when street skating became more popular than vert, and he is routinely characterized as a skateboarder who did not take his success to heart at earlier times when skateboarding was popular.[269]

In fact, Hawk is positioned as a success story in the face of other skateboarders who allowed fandom to go their heads during skateboarding's earlier heyday in the 1970s. Several cautionary tales enforce this notion while at the same time reminding audiences of skateboarding's rebellious undertones. *Stoked: The Rise and Fall of Gator,* a 2003 documentary by Helen Stickler, tells the story of former professional skateboarder, Mark "Gator" Rogowski, who is in jail for murder and rape. The film positions Gator as a legend of the 1980s skateboarding scene, an early professional who was making 100,000 dollars annually in 1984 at the age of 17. The *New York Times* reported that "the fame would prove destructive. Mr. Rogowski grew arrogant, alienating himself from his skateboard buddies, falling into trouble with the law." In one scene in the movie, Gator says, "I love getting arrested. I'm one of the most illegal skaters in the circuit."[270] Filmmaker Helen Stickler, a former stripper, pushes this cautionary tale even farther, suggesting that she could identify with Gator in that both skateboarding and stripping are "alternative communities, industries where 'youth and vitality are sold.'" Youth, she said, is fleeting and easily lost, and without it Gator had nothing.[271] Although a review of the film notes that Rogowski showed symptoms of manic depression, much of the film focuses on his poor response to fame.[272] These discussions, of course, ignore the way in which patriarchal structures encourage the gender inequality that contributes to the existence of rape.

In yet another cautionary tale, *Sports Illustrated* ran a feature story on former professional skateboarder Christian Hosoi, who was a champion vertical skateboarder in the 1980s and 1990s with Tony Hawk and was invited to be a central contestant in the first Extreme Games. Hosoi did not attend the games, however, because in the zeal of his early fame and fortune he had descended into drug addiction and was on the run from the authorities. *Sports Illustrated*'s overview pits Hosoi and Hawk against one another, pointing out that Hawk's father instructed him to do calisthenics before contests while Hosoi's father "would alternate sucking pure air from an oxygen tank and taking bong hits."[273] Furthermore, Hosoi was highly successful in the mid-1980s, sponsored by Oakley and Swatch and appearing in a Beastie Boys video as well as Coke and Pepsi ads. In response to that success, he "bought a Mustang, a Harley-Davidson, a tricked-out Jeep and a McLaren sports car, all before he had a driver's license. He hung out with the Red Hot Chili Peppers, the Beastie Boys, Ice-T and the actors River Phoenix and David Arquette," unlike Tony Hawk, whose father urged him to invest his money in a house.[274] Hawk reported, "I didn't fall into the trap of celebrity and partying and burning out, so when things turned back around, I was one of the only guys from that generation still skating hard."[275] By 2005, Hosoi had been released from jail and was serving as an announcer on *The X Games*, solidifying the notion that Hawk had taken the correct path.[276]

Hosoi and Rogowski's stories serve several purposes. They operate as mythic cautionary tales, reminding audiences of a moment when skateboarding was supposedly rebellious, underground, and "subcultural." They suggest that skateboarding has a long history that should be remembered reverentially and that its rebellious roots are somehow innate to the practice, not a construction of the niche industry. At the same time, these stories remind us that Tony Hawk was a part of an industry that crashed and that, through both business acumen and dedication to the practice, he managed to survive. Hawk, then, cannot be a sellout, for he clearly loves skateboarding so much that he stuck with it even when times were tough for other skateboarders. Finally, these tales remind us that fame can have consequences and current skateboarding stars should not get caught up in money, attention, or celebrity. Rather, they should, like Hawk, keep their focus on skateboarding.

Alongside these reminders of rebellion, however, the mainstream press between 2003 and 2006 began to suggest that attitudes about skateboarders were changing. By 2002, the press was certain that skateboarding and extreme sports had become firmly entrenched in youth culture. One 26-year-old man told *American Demographics*, "Extreme sorts are my Monday Night Football,"[277] and the president of American Sports Data, Inc., said "These new sports are an authentic slice of the wider youth culture and not just a fad."[278] In 2002, *Better Homes and Gardens*, which had long decried the dangers of skateboarding, noted, "The label 'extreme sport' is outdated for skateboarding, as is the stereotype of skateboard kids—radical daredevils with multicolored hair who hang out on street corners." The magazine deemed the practice "a mega sport that attracts the whole family," pointed out its cooperative nature, and noted that professional skater Bob Burnquist likened it to a new form of playing catch.[279]

Hartford, Connecticut, was dubbed a skateboarding hot spot, and, rather than fighting this designation, town leaders embraced its potential for increased tourism. While the owner of a local skate shop there worked to promote Hartford's skateboarding potential, convincing national skateboarding companies to tape parts of their videos in the town, local officials tacitly and explicitly supported the effort. The Hartford mayor, rather than denouncing the skaters' increased presence, said, "I hope they're spending money in our city," and local businesspeople, while they worried about liability and asked skateboarders not to use private property, characterized the practice as "exciting" and the skateboarders as "friendly." Local fast food restaurants enjoyed increased revenues, and an employee of Hartford Proud and Beautiful stated vigorously, "Don't you write anything bad about those kids. Skateboarding is just youth and exuberance."[280] In November 2003, the *New York Times* reported, "Demographers who made a fetish of soccer moms in the 90s may well be swooning over skateboard moms by this decade's end," as many suburban parents were supporting their children's skateboarding by allowing them to build ramps in their backyards. The newspaper also reported that liability was not a major issue at public skate parks, for the Consumer Product Safety Commission had found that skateboarding yielded a smaller percentage of injuries than basketball and football. Doug Wyseman, who served local governments as a risk management consultant, noted that skateboard injuries did not often result in lawsuits, for skateboarders saw them as "a badge of courage."[281] In 2005, the Manhattan Parks Department in New York City decided to redesign the

Brooklyn Banks near the Brooklyn Bridge as a "skateboard-friendly park' that would include benches, ramps, and planters on which skaters could practice, as well as areas to be used in other capacities.[282] More than a brand and more than a myth, skateboarding has again been legitimized as a relatively harmless—but still cool—practice.

It remains to be seen whether skateboarding's continued acceptance in mainstream culture will cause its eventual downfall. Although I have argued throughout that the practice's subcultural roots are mostly a discursive production of the media, skateboarding is, nonetheless, an activity that has generated its own niche industry and culture and is supported by enthusiasts who regard it as a location of difference, as I note in the next chapter. Skateboarders are in constant correspondence with these depictions of their culture, and in their own spaces—particularly the skate shop—they teach one another how to manage skateboarding's appropriation. Through their discussions about and with niche skate media and their explications of skateboarding's appeal, skateboarders construct a seemingly "authentic" definition of their practice.

Talked about how skateboarding was
up & down in popularity

"Freedom on four wheels"

Individuality, Self-Expression, and Authentic Masculinity in a Skateboarding Community

Skateboarding is freedom on four wheels.
—Brian, age 29, Ann Arbor

During the summers of 2002, 2004, and 2006, I spent much of my time in a small skateboard shop tucked below the street in Ann Arbor, Michigan. There, amid a jumble of gear, boys gather regularly to meet before skateboarding sessions, to take a break from skating, to watch skateboarding videos, or simply to hang out. More a clubhouse than a place of business, the skate shop is home to a few worn-out lounge chairs, a 13-inch television/VCR, and a metal rail approximately 8 inches off the ground on which skateboarders can practice their tricks. Jammed in the shop's exposed metal rafters are a multitude of worn-out or broken skateboard decks (the board without the wheels and trucks—the axles—attached). Each of the four walls is covered with handmade pictures, professional posters, and racks of skateboarding shoes and new skate decks, and the shop's glass counter, which houses wheels, trucks, and ball bearings, is peppered with stickers issued by various skateboard companies. The area behind the counter is littered with shoe boxes, CDs, skateboards, magazines, and videos, and crowded racks of skateboarding apparel are gathered in the center of the room.

It is in this comfortable and stimulating space that the Ann Arbor skateboarding community is consolidated. Although to some degree skateboarding is still imagined to be centered in the sunny climes of California, skateboarders find both the time and the space to skate in locations across the country. Michigan skateboarders frequently battle cold weather, but as long as sidewalks, streets, or parking lots are clear of snow they are able to practice their sport. Still, sometimes weeks go by between sessions, and it is during those weeks that the skate shop becomes particularly important; if nothing else, the skaters can practice on the low bar in the middle of the shop on which they are meant to practice their tricks, grinding and sliding their boards.

Neither singular nor self-enclosed, the skateboarding community is characterized by movement: individuals move in and out from season to season, members enjoy differing levels of intimacy with one another, and individuals gather at varying levels of regularity. That is, within the large community of skateboarders who come to the shop regularly, there exists a variety of peer groups, cliques, and relationships. The shop operates as a space in which individuals who might not otherwise know one another meet and relate as skateboarders first and foremost. It is here that the community, as a corresponding culture, develops and articulates the norms of the culture, its primary values, and so on. Corresponding with one another and the media of skate life—particularly videos and skateboarding magazines—and exploring the variety of ways in which their sensibilities correspond with mediated images, the boys instruct one another and themselves about their culture's norms of masculinity and the values of skateboarding.[1]

The skateboarders who populate this shop love skateboarding, imagine it as central to their lives and identities, and consider it an everyday part of their lives. As 24-year-old Kiran told me, "It's like addictive, too, you know. If I don't skateboard for three or four days, I start going crazy. I'm just like, 'Oh man, I need to skate!'" Through their discussions of the skateboarding community and the practice of skateboarding, it is possible to glean those values central to the skateboarders' lives and in turn to examine the ways in which these values align with those produced in the media of skate culture. This chapter serves as an analysis of those values, and in subsequent chapters I discuss the media associated with the subculture.

This wide-ranging analysis of skateboarders as first and foremost a community—and only secondarily an audience—distinguishes my work from most audience research, which often defines its audience by either demographic variables[2] or fandom of a particular media text.[3] Although such work offers a great deal of insight in its own right, mine approaches audience studies more holistically, placing skateboarders' media use in the context of their everyday lives, their multiply produced ideologies and values, and their interactions with one another. Examining how media and skateboarders' lives correspond in the production of their identities, my research is not primarily a consideration of how skaters talk back to media but instead constitutes a discussion of the construction of male youths' identity and the media's contribution to that construction. What follows is an elaboration of the values and ideas central to skateboarders' identity.

Without fail, skateboarders speak passionately and lovingly of their practice; they make it clear that skateboarding is deeply important to their lives—some even suggest that it has changed their lives—and their descriptions of the community and its practices are delivered with a sense of reverence that contrasts deeply with the irreverent images of young men we see in most media. Although mainstream culture has managed to paint skateboarders as an aggressive, highly competitive group of adrenaline junkies or as slackers and stoners, skaters are far more passionate about the value their culture places on freedom, individuality, and self-expression. That is to say, skateboarders imagine skate culture as a location of difference, an alternative to dominant demands that adolescent boys, as exemplified by "jocks," should overvalue competition, physical dominance, and emotional repression. For skaters, the culture's esteem for freedom and individuality seems to be an alternative to mainstream adolescent culture and an opportunity for various expressions of masculinity. Interestingly, however, it is this very reverence for freedom and individuality that places skateboarding culture firmly within mainstream America. What could be more American than a freedom-loving, individualistic group of young men?

Still, for skaters the unquestionable dominance of individualism and freedom means that skateboarding culture can also allow for an emotional, cooperative, and artistic expression of identity that is clearly tied to their dissatisfaction with dominant notions of masculinity. Although this mostly white, mostly middle-class, mostly heterosexual group of young boys occupies a clear position of social dominance, skaters nonetheless feel limited by social expectations about their identity. It is in this difference within dominance that skateboarders enact a critique of patriarchy that is not necessarily antipatriarchal and offer an alternative to masculinity that does not necessarily strip masculinity of its social power.

The complexity of skateboarders' social position and their expressions of a personal mode of politics reveal the inadequacies of current theories of identity, power, and politics. Although conventional academic knowledge suggests that identities are constructed via binaries—male or female, homosexual or heterosexual, black or white, and so on—the skaters' struggles with masculine identity make it clear that these binaries are multiple and complex. Although Kimberle Crenshaw and Valerie Smith have offered "intersectionality" as a theoretical and methodological approach complicating our knowledge of identity, it is not enough to consider gender along with race along with sexuality along with class along with nationality.[4] In fact, we must consider the multiplicity of masculinities in relation to the multiplicity of whiteness and so on. That is to say, it is only through evaluation of the ways in which various masculinities are articulated with national ideologies and tracing the ways in which particular expressions of masculinity (e.g., the sensitive new age guy, the urban cowboy, the male cheerleader) traverse expressions, locations, and identities vis-à-vis power relations that we can understand the political implications of these identities and their mediated depictions.

In her analysis of gender relations among children in elementary schools, Barrie Thorne offers a useful model for understanding skateboarders' expressions of masculinity. Thorne notes that the boys who were able to cross gender divides during playtime without repercussions (in the form of being socially ostracized) were those who otherwise displayed a high level of athletic skills and were popular. Describing one boy who volunteered to play on the girls' teams and willingly participated in a dance performed by a school visitor, Thorne says, "His unquestioned masculinity as one of the best athletes and most popular boys in the school was like money in the bank."[5] In other words, by displaying dominant modes of masculinity (athleticism and leadership) in most aspects of his life, this student was able to "play" with gender norms without being mocked. In a similar manner, skateboarders disrupt some gender norms (by devalorizing competition, for example) without disrupting the dominance of masculinity. Skateboarders are neither radically different nor conservatively alike; they are neither challenging male power nor violently maintaining it. Rather, they are moving through

challenge norms

youthscapes that operate as alternatives in a manner appealing to these boys while shying away from an explicit engagement with gender politics.[6]

There's something simultaneously progressive and regressive going on here.[7] The skateboarders' individualistic standpoint belies a lack of concern with issues of social equality and structures of power, but their passionate explanations of skateboarding's appeal—its acceptance of difference (within particular parameters of gender especially), its space for self-expression, its cooperative nature—suggest that skateboarders harbor a dissatisfaction with traditional masculinity that should complicate scholarly notions of male identity.

The point to be made here is not that skateboarding operates as the only available culture in which adolescent males can challenge dominant notions of masculinity. Perhaps interviews with skateboarders' proclaimed opposite—the jock as imagined through football players—would reveal similar dissatisfaction with competition and emotional reticence. The point is that in both their conversations and their media, skateboarders offer up a version of masculine interaction that contrasts with images of athletes competing for physical dominance or even rock musicians dominating stages.

Of course, a key caveat is that dominant identities—masculinity, whiteness, heterosexuality—rely on their multiplicity for their power. That is, it is precisely because dominant identities can shift and take on various expressions while keeping their institutional and social power that they are so easy to live in. However, I would suggest that in explicating skateboarders' negotiation of the multiplicity of adolescent masculinity—in addition to the mainstream and niche media's depiction of the multiplicity of this identity—we can elaborate on the routes through which adolescent boys both maintain and challenge power relations.

Power is not simply something that white men continually exert over everyone else (though one can quickly conjure up numerous instances of such exertion). Following Michel Foucault, power is part and parcel of the production of knowledges; it moves through every relation and exerts itself on all expressions of identity.[8] Skateboarders' enactment and negotiation of masculinity serves as both challenge to and protection of power, as both critique of and subscription to dominance. Skateboarders are clearly dissatisfied with the status quo but only with the limitations placed on their own lives. Their dissatisfaction does not extend to the limitations that women, homosexuals, or people of color may face on an everyday basis. Still, I believe that the development of masculine emotional capacities, self-expression, and cooperation are part and parcel of the progression of power relations, that is, they serve as a modest beginning, a location of some promise, a glimpse into the possibility that young men can operate for social progression.

Skateboarding's Appeal and the Construction of Adolescent Masculinities

As Fred Pfeil noted in 1995, feminist scholars frequently think of masculinity as monolithic without taking into account the variations in power afforded by class, race, sexuality, and so on.[9] Critical race and queer theory have begun to explicate masculinity via its intersections with other axes of identity, and a mere glance at the title of R.W. Connell's oft-cited *Masculinities*, published in the same year as Pfeil's *White Guys*, reveals that at least some scholarly work on male identity has taken into account its multiplicity.[10] In his extension and critique of scholarly discussions of the 1990s white male backlash, Sean Brayton argues, rightly, that "rather than conceiv[ing] of masculinity as some homogenous category of manliness, it is more useful to recognize a series of masculinities."[11] Still, scholars continue to struggle with analyzing male identity. What to do with such multiplicity? How to pin it down? How does one make a claim about male identity when it seems to be constantly shifting? One strategy is to examine how masculinity is negotiated by men—how they justify and respond to their particular expressions of masculinity—and then align these expressions with men's particular expressions of or encounters with power. That is, rather than assuming that masculinity equals power—or even that straight, white, American, middle-class masculinity equals power—we should first explicate how that masculinity is expressed and how, in turn, it does or does not manifest itself as various demonstrations of power.

In discussions of their identity as skateboarders and their devotion to skateboarding culture, skaters reveal that masculinity poses a problem for them. In reverent descriptions of the experience of skateboarding, the adolescent boys I interviewed disclosed a yearning for the opportunity to express themselves and a space in which to feel a sense of freedom or transcendence. Although at first glance it may seem as though white middle-class boyhood is entirely focused on freedom and self-expression, in the minds of the skateboarders male adolescence and even adulthood are characterized by institutions that serve to stifle such individualized joy. Work, school, family, and, most important, organized team sports all operate as personifications or institutions of patriarchy that place limitations on the type of transcendent, inspirational, and boundless sensation imparted by skateboarding.

The expression of such desires—and the suggestion that they are limited by work, family, school, and home—hovers dangerously close to legitimizing an evasion of responsibility that frequently leaves women, in particular, alone to contend with financial constraints and familial demands. However, when read with the demands of patriarchy firmly in mind, the skateboarders' desires reveal a nascent critique of dominant modes of masculinity; a movement toward expanding the possibilities for male emotional, spiritual, and bodily expression; and a sense that things are not as they should be. In other words, the skateboarders' descriptions of transcendent pleasure and self-expression, individualistic though they may be, stand just outside the norm and give the lie to the caricatured angry or emotionally reticent male teenager who can express himself only through violence, competition, or sex. More than "sensitive new age guys"—and certainly not simply adrenaline junkies or slackers—skateboarders seek sustenance in the transcendent experience afforded by their boards.

This ever so small step outside of dominant norms suggests that the possession of societal dominance, as afforded by masculinity, whiteness, middle classness, heterosexuality, and American citizenship, does not necessarily bring about an absolute adherence to hegemonic standards. It is nothing new to define hegemony as an ever shifting process by which new or alternative ideas are subsumed by the mainstream; however, the boys' negotiation of masculinity suggests that even while a community may challenge one ideological entity it may do so while holding fast to another swathe of dominant ideas. Although skaters may challenge masculine norms ever so subtly, they are doing so in a community that places great value on larger American norms such as individuality and independence. As such, their experiences do little to challenge the status quo.

Skateboarders' dominant identities do not entirely safeguard them from being restricted and policed, and so they are aware of the experience of being targeted as troublemakers by the authorities. However, their own encounters with the limiting effects of institutions have not been translated into a sense of empathy for groups outside their community. In fact, as they seek freedom in the skateboarding community skaters actively (though not always consciously) exclude women, gay men, and people of color. Their exclusionary practices stem in part from a desire for dominance and in part from contemporary understandings of diversity, as I will discuss at length.

Finally, as self-proclaimed and sometimes willful outsiders and as a group seemingly committed to insulating itself from mainstream demands, skate culture's correspondence with mainstream culture—particularly the mainstream media—remains of paramount importance. In fact, discussions with skateboarders make it clear that their simple presence within mainstream culture is not entirely troubling; rather, it is the mainstream's presentation of their masculinity that skateboarders find troubling. The skaters exhibit a type of relativistic tolerance for media portrayals; they suggest that, while mainstream media may make mistakes in their portrayal, it is only the continued existence of "true skaters" that is of importance. That is to say, as long as skaters can rely on their fellow skateboarders to stay true to the key values of the culture, they are ensured that a community exists in which they can experience transcendence, freedom, and individual expression. As such, a key element of skate life is constant correspondence with each other and various media in an effort to communicate the culture's core values.

"A desire to be different": Subcultural Aspirations, Mainstream Actualities

Skateboarders imagine their practice and their community to lie outside of mainstream happenings; they proclaim themselves to be "outsiders," a "minority." As 21-year-old Jeremiah, an employee of a chain skate shop, explained, "I wasn't really attracted to skateboarding by the actual sport. I was more attracted to the fact that nobody did it and I was like wow, this is cool, I'm going to try this. And that's pretty much how I got into it. A desire to be different, I guess, at a young age." A former hockey player, Jeremiah explained that as a middle-school student he began to feel dissatisfied with his then current group of friends and turned to "underground" music—punk and indie rock—along with skateboarding in an attempt to differentiate himself.

Although, as I have noted, skateboarding's relationship to mainstream culture has certainly shifted in the time since Jeremiah was a middle schooler, skateboarding continues to be presented as an oppositional activity. Despite its expansive presence in advertising appeals and preteen and teen media and its general importance to such mainstream behemoths as the Walt Disney Company and its networks, ABC, ESPN, and Disney, skateboarding has been used primarily for its rebellious, subcultural image. Although many skateboarders object to the culture of extreme exemplified by *The X Games* and Mountain Dew's advertising campaign, they also frequently remind one another and themselves of the numerous run-ins they have had with police, business owners, parents, and teachers who disapprove of their activity of choice. As such, although the mainstream amplification of skateboarding's extreme, risk-taking nature mischaracterizes their culture in most skaters' judgment, skateboarding's illegality and general aura of rebellion is appealing. In this way, the skaters correspond with the interstices of media representations of skate life, critiquing and accepting their portrayals in a fluid way.

Skateboarders' attachment to their practice's association with rebellion, however, pales in comparison with their firm insistence that it offers an alternative to other teen boy activities, most notably mainstream sports. Timmy, a 20-year-old skateboarder who worked at a local diner, explained, "It's not like a sport. It's not organized, there's no teams. . . . It's completely up to you, how much better you get and what you want to work at, and it's like self-propelled." Matthew, a 21-year-old college graduate, claimed:

It's just like disassociated from the rest of the normal world almost. . . . With the snowboarding . . . you're in the mountains, in a place where they allow you to be, where you pay to go there, and you ride a chairlift and go down the mountain and everything, they have little slopes built for you, but skateboarding is not like that, you know. You are in places that you are not meant to be for skateboarding, and . . . you have to look at things like, "How can I use this for skateboarding, even though it's not meant for it," you know. And, I don't know, it makes you think a little different, right?

Sixteen-year-old Jack, a student simultaneously earning his high school diploma and an associate's degree at a local community college, made this point most adamantly.

no one is depending on U

> And that's not what skating's all about, you know. The whole competitive thing. I'm just really not into it at all. It's like, "He made *The X Games* and got a gold medal!" It's just like, that doesn't mean anything! This isn't the Stanley Cup! . . . The other thing is that skateboarding is NOT a sport. . . . It's just that you don't skate to be better than anyone; there's not a coach who's saying, "I want you to do a 360 first, and then a kickflip, by the end of the week!" you know? You don't have to wake up at 5:30 in the morning to go skate. That's what sports are all about. It's like tournaments. They're not worth it! You better be good, and that's not how I see skating.

all about you

Jack also explained, "The possibilities are endless in skating, and there's no restrictions, there's no, like, codes, there's no rules; it's just like, open, you know. Just get on your board and ride." Thirteen-year-old Eric explained:

> Like a team sport, you have like, coaches yelling at you, and people depending on you. You have a time limit. But, um, with skateboarding you're on your own, you're like on your own team, you just push each other. It's not, it's not, you don't compete against each other. Like, you see *The X Games*, it's not skateboarding, like it's not about competing. It's just skating together.

Jim, age 15, said, "It's just awesome, to ride and do it wherever you can do it. There's not a court, it's not like basketball or something that, where you have certain limitations. There's like no limitations at all. And you can do it wherever you want, and do whatever you want or anything." For each of these skateboarders, the trappings of team sports, including sanctioned spaces for participation, established rules, and coaches, all signify patriarchal control, and for skateboarders their practice offers an escape from such control. The Ann Arbor skaters' claims mirrored closely those made by Becky Beal and Charlene Wilson's participants, who "contrasted their style with 'jocks,' who were usually identified as football players, claiming that they were more intellectual, creative, and independent."[12] And the attention the skaters paid to attitude aligns with researchers' findings in studies of other "extreme sports." Belinda Wheaton points out that participants in activities such as skateboarding, snowboarding, surfing, and other action sports frequently argue that it is the "style of life" attendant on the practice that is important, not the practice's existence as a physically demanding or competitive sport.[13]

Still, not all of the skateboarders felt quite as adamant about defining skateboarding in opposition to sports. Eleven-year-old Adam, for example, explained, "It's not a sport to a lot of people—it's more like how they live their lives, what they do and stuff. Skateboarding for me, it's a sport, but it's also a lifestyle, and how like, knowing that other people can help you if you're having trouble skateboarding or something, like knowing that you have friends." Despite considering skateboarding a sport, Adam still found the cooperative nature of the practice to be key. His focus on other people's help was not surprising given that many of the older boys in the skate shop were willing to give the younger skateboarders advice not only about how to skate more successfully but also about the values of the culture. That is, skateboarders frequently communicate to instruct one another in skateboarding's core principles and values. However, such instruction is contingent in form, for were it too direct or formal it might begin to resemble the restrictions skaters see in traditional sports. As 29-year-old Brian suggested:

> If you want to treat it like a sport, it could be a sport. . . . Where I can see a lot of people saying it isn't a sport is because they don't look at it from a competitive point of view, okay. Um, just 'cause that's so, it is a sport. Just like waterskiing, or surfing, it's a sport. The only thing that makes it different as a sport is it doesn't have to be for trophies and stuff like that. . . . You just choose not to treat it like a sport, 'cause you get this crazy idea, that set notion that a sport has to be win, lose, competition, competition, competition, but not necessarily.

Brian's directive—"If you want to treat it like a sport"—demonstrates the contingency I have discussed. The boys avoid controlling one another while at the same time maintaining the boundaries of skateboarding's values. John, a 21-year-old university student and skate shop employee, explained that as a teenager he skateboarded while continuing to participate in football and basketball. Jeremiah pointed out that while skateboarding "doesn't have the limitations that other sports do have," such as rules, the practice still requires physical prowess. He said, "You see something, you try to do it, the only limitation you have is your own natural ability. It's cool in that sense. Other sports aren't like that."

Although, clearly not all skaters feel strongly about distancing their practice from traditional sports, the relative lack of organization, rules, routines, coaches, playing fields, game times, and so on in most types of skateboarding is appealing to many skateboarders. These skaters and others also approach their characterization of the practice by discussing its artistic and individualistic nature, as I will discuss. Whether or not skateboarding is wholly distinct from other sports—one could claim, for example, that runners frequently operate independent of the organized sporting world—skateboarders' imagined outsider status is important to their identity and is arguably encouraged by both mainstream and niche skateboarding media. Furthermore, their often adamant assertion of difference suggests that they find traditional sporting culture—still a central domain of adolescent boys—dissatisfying or even stifling. When I asked 19-year-old Joe, "Do you think there's a difference between kids who are skateboarding and the kinds of kids who join the football team or something like that?" he replied, "Yeah, there's definitely a difference. They're told their whole life that that's what they should do 'cause their dad probably was a football player for [the university] or something, and sometimes their dads won't even let 'em skateboard. I've seen it happen." For Joe and the other skateboarders, participation in football represents submission to patriarchal demands.

Skateboarders' descriptions of the traditional sporting world, with the demands of coaches, set practice times, and fellow players, also allude to the highly disciplined male subject that David Savran describes in *Taking It Like a Man*.[14] Although the skaters' complaints hinge on the idea that someone or something else will be regulating their activities in the sporting world, Savran's self-disciplined, overly policed, pleasureless male subject is still applicable, for the sporting world absolutely esteems self-discipline. Savran's argument suggests that a self-flagellating ideal male subject has given rise to a culture in which male self-violence is a foundational aspect of white masculine identity, and, in her analysis of the movie *Fight Club*, Lynn Ta reveals that even texts that seem to be critical of such norms end up resorting to self-violence.[15] I would suggest that skateboarders' rejection of the perceived norms of sport culture—as well as their discussion and performance of the norms of skateboarding culture—enacts a different mode of adolescent masculinity that does not rely on male self-violence and in fact operates as a promising alternative.

Skateboarders place a tremendous amount of importance on their ability to act as individuals and the feeling of freedom facilitated by skateboarding. Their breathless descriptions of opportunities to both express one's individual style and practice self-guidance bring to light the highly American nature of skateboarding. The related desire for a sense of freedom is also highly American, but the ways in which skateboarders describe a feeling of bodily transcendence reveal a particular experience of freedom that lies outside traditional white male rationality. The skaters' correspondence with mainstream American culture is complex in its various assessments of mainstream codes. The values and ideologies central to skateboarding culture blur the boundaries between subculture and mainstream and reveal that, while masculinity may operate as what I call a "location of difference" for skateboarding culture, other ideologies—such as freedom and individuality—lie firmly within mainstream America.

"It's just you and your board": Individuality and Self-Expression

In sharp contrast to their sometimes adamant rejection of the norms of traditional sports, many skateboarders wax poetic about the expressive and individualistic nature of skateboarding. Responding to the question, "Why do you skate?" with descriptions of their love of the practice, skateboarders usually shifted tone and stared into space, grappling for words that would describe the joy of the experience. Far from the overly aggressive, in-your-face skateboarders on mainstream television, these boys spoke quietly and passionately of their devotion to skating.

> It's just you and your board. . . . It's like an art form in a sense. The only limitations you have in skateboarding [are] your own. And the idea that you can just take a thought, a pure idea, a thought in your head and go attempt to do it, it's kind of like art. (Jeremiah, age 22)

There's not too many, you know, like there's teams, or whatever, but they're not teams; it's not like they huddle. There's not a game plan. And it's not a choreographed thing, so it's not like you go out and have a play, you know. It's like, the play is in your head, you make it up. Um, that's part of the art of it, too, it all just comes from your soul and your heart. . . . And I think that's part of the joy that builds up in style. (Mike, age 29)

It's pretty much about expressing yourself! (Eric, age 13)

It's an art. That's the only way you can define it. Just like, the way I see it, there's so many different styles of painting and stuff, and music, too. . . . That person, like, I'm just saying, if you can know what their personality is, you know their art. . . . So with skating, like I take who I am as an individual and bring it to my skating. . . . Watching a skateboard video, you'll see people with . . . dreads and stuff, they'll have the whole rude style, and the hesh rats, and like, I don't know, it just seems that you take the exact individual that you are and put it in your skateboarding. (Jack, age 16)

The skateboarders' claims move easily from imagining skateboarding as a concrete representation of an abstract sense of self or, in Jeremiah's words, "a pure idea," and imagining skateboarding as an extension of style. While the former suggests that skateboarding is expression for expression's sake, for the joy of baring, as Mike claimed, "your soul and your heart," the latter connotes a more superficial, outwardly motivated desire to demonstrate to the world "who I am as an individual." Jack's quote not only exemplifies the notion that skateboarding is a space of self-expression but also that such self-expression is imagined via lifestyle or style and is manifested via such stylistic markers as dreadlocks. Their self-expression, that is, could still be based in the consumption needed to mark particular personalities and styles. Fifteen-year-old Braden, a close friend of Jack's, echoed the discussion of expression via style in his explanation of the "roots" of skateboarding as represented in the film *Dogtown and Z-Boys*.

Everyone had their own style. They were all progressing. So, it's all about progression and individual style. Um, basically, like. Like, having, um, define style. I'd say just skating and doing what you want. . . . And that's the big thing of skating, like it's for you. Like, just individual art. Art not sport! And, uh, it's all about doing things for yourself.

Twenty-nine-year-old Mike, a bartender, explained how one expresses style via skating.

> Once you learn a trick, you start to appropriate your own style, like squeak out a trick, like slide it out, the way you use your foot. . . . You just teach yourself, like different ways, like you would do it the way you're more comfortable. And when you teach yourself that, you know, you completely make it your own at that point because not only have you learned to do the trick, and maybe do it quite well, but you're able to put your piece on something that's already been done many times, and you do it in a way that no one does it. . . . You're not just doing any old trick all the time, that's just gonna get boring, so you kind of make it creative.

Self-expression for the skaters is, in part, about asserting one's individuality—"you do it in a way that no one does it"—and the individuality of skateboarding also permeates skateboarders' pride in being self-taught. Mike explained that skateboarding "feels good. It's part of me. I've done it so much. It's one of the 3, 4, 5 things that I'm really good at. I taught myself everything. That kind of meant a lot. So I just did a trick or whatever and just want to keep learning. You teach yourself. I didn't really have anyone to help me out." Matthew, age 21, echoed Mike's claims.

> It's very individual, you know. It's, uh, it's like you don't have to rely on anyone else, you can do your own thing, you know. Just have fun, skate the way you want. . . . I didn't have to stay after school and go to practice for anything. I didn't have to like rely on other people. I could go out by myself and just practice. . . . It's like an individual activity. It's for yourself, you know. And, uh, what you can make yourself do, what you can, like, push yourself to do, right?

Although such individual effort echoes, in some ways, Savran's self-surveilled man who must embrace pain in order to become a fully realized individual—to be a good skateboarder, you must "push yourself," presumably through some pain—the skaters' frequent claims that when skateboarding one should "Just have fun, skate the way you want" and that it "feels good," suggest that the general experience of skateboarding is one of pleasure not pain.[16] Such pleasure also rejects the constraints associated with masculinity by allowing young men to experience a range of emotions and revel in mental pleasure.

In fact, even though, as I discuss later, many representations of skateboarding foreground pain, skateboarders themselves rarely discussed it outside of notions of hard work. Representations of self-inflicted pain such as those depicted on *Jackass* are, as I argue in the next chapter, largely ironic and so do not seem to register with the boys. In short, though it seems as if pain is central to skateboarding, for the boys pain is not central to the experience.

"It's like spiritual fulfillment": Skateboarding as Escape or Transcendence

Contra Savran's self-flagellating male, the boys consider skateboarding a way to escape pain rather than a demonstration of their ability to feel it. Although (and in part because) skateboarding requires a high level of concentration, it offers a sense of transcendence, escape, meditation, or fulfillment seemingly unavailable in the boys' other domains. School, work, families, and relationships all produce stress in the skaters' lives; the practice of skating mitigates that stress.

> There's so much enjoyment and community in just riding around a parking lot, just cruising around the streets downtown. . . . But the reason I skate is just the pure enjoyment I get. (Jack, age 16)

> But it's freedom! I feel free when I'm skateboarding, and I can forget about everything that's bothering me for that hour or two of the day. It's like liberating, so it's kind of like therapy as well. . . . Some people do meditation, some people do yoga, I skateboard. That's my meditation, I guess. It's the one thing I can focus on and not think about anything else. (Brian, age 29)

> There's this certain feeling that I get. Like personally, when I bomb a parking

structure [skate down its ramps rapidly], which I usually do two times a day, there's just a feeling that you get when you're on the edge of control, like cruisin' around the corner on a big skateboard. . . . You get an adrenaline rush, and it, it keeps me young, too. (Jason, age 32)

It's just so fun, it's like, you're just in your own world when you skate. Like it's really fun. . . . You're focused just on skateboarding, and . . . you can like get away and stuff, you know. (Marc, age 15)

You get stressed out with school or work or just like relationships and stuff, and when you start skating, it's like the only thing in your head is just cruising down the street, it's super relaxing. And you can't beat it, no one can take it away from you. (John, age 21)

When you're skating, there is sort of an escape involved. Like, when you're really concentrating on just skating, I mean, it's that sense of focus that you don't really, I don't get it from anything else. I've got all sorts of other hobbies, like music, but, I don't know, skateboarding is the true, like, it's almost like meditation in a way. . . . It even helps me think about things. . . . It just makes me feel good about myself . . . and, I don't know, it's just cool, too! (Timmy, age 20)

When I'm skateboarding, there's nothing else on my mind but skateboarding. So, in that aspect, it's freeing. If I have exams or stress from anything else . . . like, I could have a midterm tomorrow and I go skateboarding, I, for that time . . . I'm thinking about nothing but skateboarding. And just, like, totally immersed in how much fun I'm having, you know. (Matthew, age 21)

It's just like, orgasmic. . . . I'll fall in love with skating when I'm just alone in the middle of an abandoned street. . . . You get a lot of thinking done. (Braden, age 15)

And like . . . this is gonna sound cheesy, but it's like spiritual fulfillment. In a way, where it's just, if there's any problems any time, you go skating and you don't really think about it and it feels good. (Kiran, age 24)

In these descriptions, the skateboarders elaborate on the emotional, spiritual, physical, and mental pleasures that accompany skateboarding. Of course, as skateboarder Jason suggests, much of the pleasure they describe is probably a result of the adrenaline that accompanies the type of risk taking that is typical of sporting culture generally and mediated depictions of skateboarding more particularly; clearly, these skateboarders are not fully rejecting physicality, risk taking, and bodily harm, all clear markers of dominant masculinity. As Alana Young and Christine Dallaire note, by taking pleasure in the type of risk taking associated with skateboarding (what Stephen Lyng calls "edgework"),[17] female skateboarders, for their part, "challenge hegemonic femininity."[18]

Despite the fact that skateboarding is inherently risky to some degree (and thus conventionally masculine), skateboarders' reflective and passionate tones contradict dominant images of surly white male teens as well as notions that men are not and cannot be expressive, emotive, or introspective. Furthermore, their discussions of stress and problems belie suggestions that young men are unable to reflect on or talk about what's troubling them. Both the practice of skateboarding and skateboarders' discussions of it provide skaters an opportunity to engage in a manner contradictory to dominant norms of masculinity, and, as their passionately stated descriptions reveal, they place a high value on this opportunity.

Nonetheless, although skaters are highly devoted to the notion that skateboarding is pure fun, the emphasis that they place on independence and the progression of skills reveals a continued loyalty to the value of hard work. In fact, the skaters seem to be expressing the American dream via skateboarding: they are self-taught, successful, skilled, and dedicated. Although skateboarding usually earns them no monetary rewards, the development of their skills seems to be enough to merit such devotion.

Tied closely to the skateboarders' ideas about self-expression is a clear sense that it evokes a type of passion or love not produced by other activities or hobbies. Their expressions of passion also seem to belie the hyperrationality of masculinity and whiteness, but the attendant importance of devotion and dedication to the advancement of skateboarding culture and the progression of individuals' skateboarding skills suggests that the passion is easily translated into traditionally American modes of masculine engagement. As Jack elaborated, "I eat, drink, sleep skate, you know.

. . . When you're a skateboarder, you have that love, that strong love for it."
Brian suggested that, despite having taken up skateboarding because of its
subcultural or outsider status, he continues to skate because of "passion."

The subtle shift in skaters' descriptions of skateboarding—from expressive art form to the product of individual hard work—demonstrates the
ways in which traits associated with masculinity and American identity
are dynamic in their relationship to normative identities and expressions
of dominance. Skaters' breathy descriptions of the art of skateboarding
certainly challenge masculine norms of rationality and emotional reticence,
but the underlying commitment to such masculine American values as independence, progression, and physical work reveals the enduring nature of
these values, their flexibility in relationship to other expressions of identity,
and the inextricable relationship between dominant norms and subcultural
alternatives.

Claiming the Outside/Maintaining the Inside: The Preservation of Power in Skateboarding Culture

"Wanna talk about a real minority": Demonstrating Individuality via Outsider Status

Skateboarders construct their identity, in part, by claiming outsider or even
minority status. Although some of these claims clearly imply a sense that
minority groups are asserting, unfairly, that their own experiences with
oppression are unique (see especially Brian's subsequent discussion), others suggest simply that skateboarders do imagine themselves as standing
outside of mainstream culture generally. Many skateboarders take pride in
this outsider status, arguing that it has provided them with a unique out-
look on life. Again, individuality becomes paramount to skater identity; not
only have they independently trained themselves to participate in a creative
activity, but they've also developed distinctive identities that supposedly
help them stand out from the crowd.

And we gotta band together. It's the only way we're gonna be able to fight
oppression. We're still being oppressed. Wanna talk about a real minority.
Skateboarders, is a true minority. 'Cause you know, cops hate us, uh, every-

body hates us. Middle-class people, oh we're so dangerous, yet somebody can barrel down the street on a mountain bike, they never say nothing about that. You know what I mean? . . . They profile us, big time, skaters. Just have a skateboard, even if you're walking with one, the cops'll watch ya. It's terrible. . . . I've never been ticketed for skateboarding. I'm proud to say that. Never been ticketed for skateboarding. (Brian, age 29)

Brian's claim that he is continually surveilled but has never received a ticket is curious and at first glance suggests a feeble attempt to claim special status via an unrealized oppression. Studies of whiteness and masculinity have described such behavior, and surely a proclamation of oppression is one manifestation of "the possessive investment in whiteness."[19] After all, it takes only a small step to move from claiming to be "a real minority" to suggesting that other minorities are inflating claims of oppression or asking for "special treatment" when it is not needed. At a moment when affirmative action is continually under fire, such insinuations should not be taken lightly. Notably, Brian had recently arrived in Michigan from California, both states where affirmative action cases have been major news. Nevertheless, after reading this passage, Kiran implored me to communicate that many skateboarders had received numerous 100-dollar tickets "for rolling on the sidewalk/street in Ann Arbor."

Other skateboarders' discussions of difference, however, were aimed toward explaining why skateboarders might think differently from the norm. While in some respects these claims align with the skateboarders' argument that skateboarding is not a sport in that they situate the practice and culture outside of more normative practices, they also gesture toward the origins of skateboarders' sense of dissatisfaction. As I have noted, skateboarders are policed and surveilled, and these experiences, along with their fraught relationship to their nonskateboarding peers, result in the sense that they are outsiders.

And it's a subculture . . . because we get sort of a raw taste of life. We have to argue with people on a regular basis about getting out of the area. (Jeremiah, age 18)

We don't care what other people think about us. (Eric, age 13)

Fifteen-year-old Brandon and Jim, interviewed together, explained.

> *Jim:* I think, like, like, skaters are like, they're more like open, not as uptight. Like we're stupid little kids that got made fun of, like some jock or something would be like, "Dude, that's stupid!"
>
> *Brandon:* Yeah, 'cause basically you get made fun of. 'Cause skateboarding to other people it was like a, a phase that everyone went through, and now it's over or something. So, when you stick to it, you know, you know, like, it's a skateboarder, so they make fun of you, so basically you get used to that, so everything just doesn't really matter anymore. You know, what people say.

> Like, you'll always be accepted into skateboarding, and unlike football or something, kids'll make fun of you if you're small or something like that. Look at me, man, I'm scrawny. I skateboard. Kids, I have a bunch of friends. Kids love me, you know? It's awesome. (Joe, age 19)

The skateboarders' descriptions of being teased about skateboarding or body type and their references to arguments with the authorities about the practice of skateboarding make it clear that they feel as if they have been somewhat forcibly excluded from dominant groups such as the jocks in high school. Skate media and culture do tend to suggest a lanky body type as an ideal—one need only look at Tony Hawk to see this—and I suspect that bulkier men who would be valorized as football players or wrestlers may feel excluded from skateboarding culture. It is important to note, however, that the dominance of this body type in skate culture may play a role in skaters' attraction to it. The boys' assertions of difference serve as a strategy by means of which they establish a sense of agency; if one chooses not to participate in a particular group, he cannot be excluded from it by others. More germane to my argument, however, is that the skateboarders' solution to exclusion is highly individualized and lacks an articulation of larger structural issues such as the idea that a "real man" would be big—and physically dominant—not "scrawny" like Joe. Skateboarding in this sense becomes a type of enclave, a location in which skateboarders can feel comfortable with themselves and escape from the demands of dominant norms.[20] Skaters' inability or unwillingness to live up to established markers of masculinity does not necessarily effect an articulate critique of those norms, nor does it inspire a conscious effort to change them. Instead, it forces withdrawal into a more accepting community.[21]

From Punk to Hip-hop: Style as Cultural Difference

Skateboarders frequently translate their outsider status into assertions of cultural acceptance. Referencing such stylistic markers as music and clothing, skateboarders deemed their community "multicultural" or "diverse" and indicated that their acceptance of multiple peoples stemmed from their own experiences of exclusion or oppression. Using code words such as *Rasta*, *punk*, and *hip-hop*, skaters implied that their culture is racially diverse, but these words seemed to weigh equally with generic terms associated with high school cliques: *geeks*, *nerds*, and so on. The skateboarders' explanations of difference served to elide race, making it seem as though any and all racial differences were easily subsumed by a common devotion to skateboarding. Even when they were explicitly discussing race, as Kiran does below, skateboarders slid easily into references to lifestyle or music.

Such elision is not surprising in a community of youths who have come of age in a culture that celebrates tolerance, diversity, and multiculturalism while rarely explicitly discussing the continued effects of racism and racial difference. In youth culture, race is frequently associated with particular music forms, and contemporary youth culture suggests that "crossing over" via music is acceptable but still problematic. Skaters seem to suggest that anyone can cross over into skateboarding as long as his primary concern is with skateboarding.

> Skateboarders are, they're pretty, um, unbiased culturally, so, 'cause they're outsiders, especially back in the day they were outsiders, even now, still. So, you kind of come up with your own music and you start liking different things, you know? Kids that skate aren't just listening to punk, they're not just listening to pop anymore, they listen to everything. They listen to jazz, all kinds of stuff. (Mike, age 29)

> It's just stupid to define a skateboarder in one way, it's like defining what a person is in any other sport in a certain category. I guarantee you there are

all different kinds of personalities and all different kinds of people. (Jeremiah, age 21)

Brian (age 29): I think the type of people it attracts . . . very multicultural, multidiversity crowd.

Yochim: Okay, do you think it's a diverse crowd?

Brian: Oh, very much so.

Yochim: Do you think in Ann Arbor it's diverse?

Brian: Ummm, that I really can't say for sure. . . . Um, from what I've experienced, yeah. I've seen a whole bunch of different types of people coming from different backgrounds. 'Cause when you're skating it doesn't matter if you're a geek, a moron, a nerd, any of that stuff. It kind of transcends all that kind of behavior.

Joe (age 19): Skateboarding's for everybody. Like everyone can skateboard, and like, skateboarding's full of so many—it's so diverse, like there's so many different kinds of pros. . . . [T]here's like Rasta dudes, there's like hip-hop soldier whatever, there's little like punk rock kids. . . . If people on the outside just see a skateboarder as some kid that grows in a rat 'stache, and those are the kids we hate, that annoys the hell out of us. We hate kids like that.

Yochim: What's a rat 'stache?

Joe: You know, when kids grow a mustache and they don't shave it so it's just like peach fuzz that's growing out of control?. . . . [Y]ou always see ratty white trash kids with 'em. And I hate white trash. 'Cause I'm from Lansing.

[Skateboarding is] a mesh of cultures. . . . You know, people who listen to punk rock music or, and then there's your rocker, there's your hip-hop heads, and then there's everything in between. . . . [L]ike style of clothing, right, you know, like there's people who look like rockers, people who look like hip-hop heads. . . . There's people who dress real nice like [pro skater] Andrew Reynolds, you know, he wears a sports coat. (Matthew, age 21)

Jim: "There's like preppy skaters, there's dirt skaters, there's all different kinds of skateboarders."

Brandon: I mean you could have a football player that skateboards.

One of the things I've always liked about skateboarding is that it's diverse. . . . Like culturally diverse, it's socioeconomically diverse. It's not about rich people that skateboard, poor people that skateboard, middle-class people, there's like, all sorts of different races. It's awesome. There's pro skaters that are half Indian like me. . . . In India there's not really a skateboarding scene, but in most other countries, like in Africa and stuff like that, there's skateboarders, South America. It's so cool. That's one of the things that makes skateboarding, in my opinion, a superior culture to any other kind of youth culture, or like, [any]thing that other people would consider cool. That's one of the reasons that it's cooler than snowboarding. Like who snowboards? Rich white kids. For the most part. . . . I think that's what keeps the majority of people out of it . . . they can't afford to buy a five-hundred-dollar board and lift ticket. . . . Skateboarding's low cost keeps it diverse, and that rules. There's so many different things you can be into and still be a skateboarder. Punk rocker kids, hip-hop kids, metal, whatever. There's dudes that listen to Britney Spears, and they all skateboard. 'Cause that's their common bond. There's diversity. (Kiran, age 24)

As I have mentioned, skateboarders believe their level of cultural acceptance or tolerance to be an outcome of their experiences as outsiders. For skaters, superficial discrimination is inexplicable, and skateboarding's tolerance is another measure of its superiority to other youth cultures. Notably, however, in describing skating's diversity Joe established a clear boundary excluding "white trash kids." Furthermore, the invocation of *white trash* allows Joe, especially, to displace intolerant attitudes onto a group of folks deemed less educated and less accepting of diversity than most skateboarders, who present themselves as middle class.[22] *White trash* signals not simply economic difference but a difference in taste. I would suggest that boundaries of taste permeate skate culture despite skaters' claims that one can wear any style and listen to any type of music and still be accepted into it. Certainly, skaters display a particular sense of "cool" that operates as a requirement for entry into the culture. The clothing skateboarders wear falls into a limited spectrum, and the adoption of tight clothing or business attire, for example, must be suitably ironic. Matthew, for example, described another skater with admiration: "You see a lot of skateboarders that are really, really fashionable. . . . Like, they stand out. Look at [Joe]. He's got like, wears girls' jeans and like a striped sweater. Sometimes I see him rockin' the headband! . . . Yeah, [Joe's] hilarious!"

Although many of the skaters' comments on diversity are centered on issues of style, it is important to take note of Kiran's succinct and smart analysis of the opportunities afforded by skate as opposed to snowboarding culture. Although skateboards usually cost approximately 100 dollars, depending on the level of use they can last a relatively long time. And without the cost of lift tickets and transportation to ski resorts—or even the costs of participating in club sports—skateboarding is a relatively cheap and accessible practice. Of course, Kiran's life experiences—he is half Indian and half Belgian and was born and raised in Belgium until 1990—have probably enabled him to be more attendant to such issues than his white counterparts.

Even after reading this book, Kiran objected to my analysis of race in skate culture. He took issue with my (and other scholars') characterization of it as a white culture, naming a host of professional skateboarders who are not white, including, in Kiran's words, "We got Tony Alva—Hispanic dude, Steve and Mickey Alba—Latinos, Peggy Oki—Asian, Steve Caballero— Mexican, Christian Hosoi—Hawaiian, Ray Barbee, Tommy Guerrerro, etc., etc." At this time, Kiran had moved from Ann Arbor to Austin, Texas, and he told me, "When I go to the skate park by my house there's more minorities than white kids there. I just think the Midwest is pretty segregated and maybe a lot whiter in parts than people realize. But just think about the kids in Ann Arbor, too." He named five skateboarders, only one of whom I had interviewed, and concluded, "all brown or some shade of it." Kiran's point is well taken, and I think it is important to note the diversity evident in skate videos. Still, mainstream depictions of skateboarding continue to be mainly white, and images of diversity in niche videos can also be read as the type of tokenism that maintains the centrality of whiteness.

Skate boarding looks white from the outside

"We just want to skate, you know?" Skateboarding as Transcending Race

Skateboarders' claims to tolerance, even when explicitly referencing race, serve to support their claims that it is the practice of skateboarding itself that is crucial to the culture, not the performance of different lifestyles. In other words, their discussions of tolerance, which in a nutshell say "Race doesn't matter—skateboarding does," assert the authenticity of this culture by suggesting that it is only about the practice of skateboarding and not about appearing to be cool, maintaining power, or developing an exclusionary group, each of which would be aimed toward stylistic ends rather than the experience of pleasure, joy, or transcendence, as I discuss later. The Ann Arbor skaters' discussions of race worked hard to elide race, much like Wheaton and Beal's skateboarders and windsurfers. At the same time, like Wheaton and Beal's respondents, their conversations about race still drew on the normativity of whiteness.[23]

> Skateboarding's open to all different cultures, like African Americans, Asians, all kinds of people. And they wear baggy clothes, whatever you want to wear. It's pretty much accepted in skateboarding. (Adam, age 11)

> Skateboarding is really multicultural. Like if you skateboard it doesn't matter, like, what background you are, what race you are. And usually in society it really matters, like what color your skin is or what your background is, you know. . . . I would say skateboarding is more like a mix of people from all different backgrounds. They're just kind of there to skate. (Alex, age 19)

> *Yochim:* Do you think it's diverse racewise?
> *Matthew* (age 21): Yeah, absolutely.
> *Yochim:* In Ann Arbor, do you think it is?
> *Matthew:* In Ann Arbor, you know what, there's more, um, I seen more, like, uh, white skateboarders then, but you know, like I skate with like, um, some of my friends are black and they skate, you know. Um, but yeah, it's really diverse. I mean, what I see around here, yeah, maybe more white kids skate, but like, that's not true everywhere else.

Yochim: What about race? Is there, from what I've seen it's mainly a white sport.

Braden (age 15): Yeah. Um, I don't have any opinions on anybody doing anything that they want to do, but.

Yochim: I just want to know, like in your experience has there . . .

Braden: Yeah, it's mainly a Caucasian activity, but there's definitely, um, not any discrimination that I have run into between skaters and like minority skaters. So, yeah, it's really no big deal. We just want to skate, you know?

Not as much a race issue these days in skateboarding. Skateboarders are kind of hated, looked at as thumbs down by the rest of society. It doesn't make sense for white skaters and black skaters to not skate together. I evaluate if things are racist, and generally, it's more positive—like, "Wow, black guys have good style when they—or Asian guys." . . . Race is not a problem in skating. (Jeff, age 21)

Despite the skaters' indications otherwise, my own experiences with the southeastern Michigan community suggest that it is mainly white. I interviewed two Latino and one Indian skateboarder; the rest of my interviewees were white. Of the white skateboarders, one indicated, without being asked, that he was Jewish. I encountered one Asian skateboarder, who declined to be interviewed, and no black skateboarders during my time with the community.

The skateboarders' responses to my prompts about race also reveal a sense of discomfort in talking about race. Although the skaters frequently tended to use highly informal language punctuated by linguistic qualifiers and false starts, their unease when explaining race relations in their community was palpable in the extent to which they lapsed into such qualifiers during these discussions. Although Matthew could not vouch for diversity in his own experience, he relied on a sense of diversity in the "imagined community" of skateboarders, and skate media—particularly skateboarding videos—support this assertion in their representation of diverse "teams" of professional skateboarders.[24] Also notable is Jeff's attempt to make clear that he does think about racism and guards against it. For him, positively valenced but still monolithic descriptions of various racial or ethnic groups ("Black guys have good style") are not racist. The boys' uncomfortable and problematic discussions of diversity and race should be understood in the context of their own culture as well as broader American cultural constructions of race.

The disparity between claimed diversity and the reality of the community is not surprising given the skateboarders' general sense that they operate differently from other adolescent groups, their existence in a culture that supposedly values diversity while doing little to promote it, the community's specific location in a liberal university town, and my presence. As a researcher and an educated woman, I surely signified a liberal white who would have no truck with overt racism, and the skateboarders were undoubtedly guarded in my presence even after knowing me for five years. My status as a researcher was always known, and even to those skateboarders who regarded me as a friend I was generally an older, more established— and thus relatively authoritative—figure. As such, the skaters' struggled to acknowledge racial differences and even racism while at the same time denying its presence in their own culture. As one skateboarder told me, "I mean, it could be different in the South and stuff." Like most white Americans, these skaters shunned the notion that their own community might be exclusionary.

Taken together, however, the skateboarders' elision of race and their continued reliance on individualized notions of identity and community served to maintain the power of white, middle-class skateboarders. Because their main claim to difference and their solution to dissatisfaction with other more mainstream groups (as encountered in high school, for example) amount to the repeated refrain that "skateboarders can do whatever they want," the group saw no need to make a conscious effort to include frequently excluded groups. Whiteness and masculinity remained the unstated norms, a status that cultural theorists have demonstrated to be a position of power.[25] As such, the dominance of individuality operates to maintain white dominance in this group.

"You do it for the love of it": Authenticity, Love, and Individuality

The skateboarders' notion of authenticity is firmly grounded in their general ethos of individuality. As such, to be an authentic skateboarder one must be all about

doing so for his own reasons rather than to impress others. Consequently, mainstream images of skateboarders as "extreme," or even competitive (as in *The X Games*), are labeled inauthentic or, in Jack's words, "very wack." Jack elaborated that skateboarders in the media "are portrayed as getting air. Being extreme. It's not about . . . doing tricks! It's all about having fun. And if doing tricks is having fun then that's what it is. If it's riding around a ramp, it's having fun, you know." Jack's somewhat roundabout claim reveals the contradictions that the skaters' primary concern with individuality evokes. That is, if the bottom line for skaters is that each skateboarder takes part in the culture for his own, individual reason, then judgments about what does or does not constitute authenticity become highly contingent: skateboarding is not about doing tricks unless that's what's fun for you; if riding ramps is fun for you, then it's authentic; and so on. Such individualistic evaluations also translated into skateboarders' correspondence with the media. For example, many skaters excused Tony Hawk's excessive monetary success and corporate involvement as a personal choice; as long as he still loved skateboarding and displayed his skills, they suggested, he had every right to participate in its mainstreaming. Skateboarders' assessments of Tony Hawk align with those of Wheaton and Beal's skateboarding respondents, who deemed a skateboard brand authentic if it exhibited "a long-term commitment to the sport [or] demonstrated a working knowledge of" it. What's more, if the brand was perceived to be appealing to "core," committed skateboarders it was more highly regarded than brands perceived to appeal to newcomers.[26]

As much as individuality pervades skateboarders' descriptions of their practice, a sense of true love, fun, joy, or devotion must motivate their participation in it in order for skaters to deem it authentic. Such an emotional commitment to skateboarding—and the attendant devotion to feelings of pleasure—can be read as a negotiation of masculine norms deeming pain to be paramount, as I have discussed with reference to David Savran's work. Still, when developed through the lens of individuality, the skaters' expressions of pleasure lose some of their political steam. That is to say, skateboarders' experiences and descriptions of the pleasure of skateboarding, and pleasure's overriding importance to their sense of authenticity, act as a nascent critique of norms of masculinity. However, that critique remains nascent inasmuch as it relies on individuality for its expression. Individuality, in part, disallows skateboarders from developing a broad-based, institutional critique.

It is important to note, however, that the skaters' regard for individual satisfaction with skateboarding is often couched as the antithesis of commercial interest in the practice. That is, one marker of disingenuity in this culture is the notion that an individual is skateboarding for profit rather than pleasure. To skateboard for profit, one must focus on competition, physical prowess, and constant progress—values antithetical to skaters' ideas about self-expression and cooperation. Skateboarders, then, sometimes communicate a critique of commercial culture; however, the critique is that commercialism disallows individual expression, not that capitalism causes structural inequalities, exploitation of various peoples, overuse of natural resources, and so on. The critique is always located in their valorization of individuality.

> You do it for the love of it, not to be cool, or not to be good at it, it's all the same thing, you know. Its like, the whole jock stereotype, usually you see it in sports, like the football jock, you know, like some guy with slick[ed] back hair, you know, ladies man or whatever, plays all these sports. . . . A lot of them get caught up with skating for whatever reason; they see it and think this'll be kind of fun. And they just skate to be, like, skate to be good. They don't skate; they'll only do something really big and crazy if it's on film or if someone's taking a picture of it. Or if, you know, they just do it to be better than other people and not to have fun. That's not the way all of it is. (Jack, age 16)

> *Jack* (age 16): That's a true shop, you know?
> *Yochim:* What do you mean when you say that?
> *Jack:* True shop? Uh, you know, there's like the main reason, you know, to get money. It's people's career. But they support skateboarding in a really true way, not branching out into some sport shop, like MC [sports], whatever! Because you can be in those true shops, and . . . they know what true skateboarding's all about. They're just there to support the scene.

> I don't think like anything could change skateboarding because [of] kids that actually love it so much that that wouldn't happen. (Joe, age 19)

actual sb

vs

money

all about

When I first started . . . I didn't know people got paid. I just thought it was
something that people were doing, you know, when they weren't working
and it was just having fun. Kids now look at it like, my little brother skateboards and he looks at it like, "Oh, I need to get a sponsor now," stuff like
that. And it's just like, you don't really need to, you know? I mean, I'd be skating if I didn't have any sponsors. . . . Right now, skateboarding, it just seems
like, everybody's trying to start their own company and tryin' to make a lot
of money and just trying to make their own impact on skateboarding, and I
think that the companies who are really down for skateboarding since, like,
they've started, and companies that are all about skateboarding, sound fun,
will survive. And skateboarding companies that are just all about the money
will just die. So it kind of just separates out. Survival of the fittest I guess.
Survival of the funnest, I would say. (Alex, age 19)[27]

Some of these kids just get too, like, "When am I gonna get sponsored? How
am I gonna get sponsored?" This, that, and the next thing. I don't remember
ever having that mentality. I just went out and did it and had fun. (Matthew,
age 21)

If you're not having fun when you're skating, you're skating for the wrong
reasons. . . . Tony Hawk and the 900 makes young skaters think, I need to be
able to do a 900 or a 720 or something, I need to be able to these big tricks.
And they're not satisfied with how they're skating. . . . They'll start skating
'cause it's cool. You know 'cause like, man, Tony Hawk's on TV! And like, he's
a regular guy, I'm a regular guy, you know! I can do a 900 if I practice. And
like, they start skating for the wrong reasons. You know, like I can accom-
plish this, by this time. (Braden, age 15)

In these claims, skateboarders communicate a sense of dissatisfaction with
the current media climate and the importance of sponsorship and commercialism to skate culture. Like Beal and Wilson's participants, the Ann Arbor
skateboarders evidenced a contradictory relationship to commercial culture in which they deemed sponsorship acceptable if it was accompanied
by an inherent love of skateboarding as a practice.[28] The skaters' discontent
with sponsorship and commercialization certainly does not translate into a
rejection of niche skateboarding media and in fact belies most skateboard-

ers' appreciative fandom of the professionals featured in skate videos. Demonstrating their dynamic and contradictory relationship with commercialism, these comments suggest that skaters' reverence for individualism also serves as a strategy through which they can evade developing a definitive critique of commercial culture. Furthermore, the focus on individuality allows skateboarders to continue to regard their culture as authentic even in the face of the extensive media appropriation I have detailed.

Tony Hawk, *The X Games*, *Jackass*, *Viva La Bam*, *Wildboyz*, and other mainstream depictions of skateboarding pose a contradiction to many skaters, who regard the mainstream popularization of their practice to be both promising and problematic. The importance of individuality, the relative lack of concern with the pitfalls of capitalism as an institution, and arguably mainstream producers' skillful appropriation of the heroes and signs of skate culture mitigate skateboarders' concerns with dominant portrayals of their culture. As I discuss in the next chapter, MTV's representation of skate culture draws on its commitment to individuality, pleasure, and youthfulness while also reinscribing skateboarding as extreme and rebellious. The network's skateboarders, furthermore, without question assert American white males' power over women and people of color while mocking the preservation of masculinity via self-inflicted pain.

Listening to skateboarders' passionate descriptions of their practice, I was struck by the boys' devotion to their culture and willingness to express enthusiasm and dedication. More succinctly, I was taken by their evocative and almost poetic language as well as by their poignant mode of delivery. This is not to say that the skateboarders were always thoughtful, constantly emotive, or solely cooperative. In the space of the skate shop, the boys displayed their physical acumen on the skateboarding rail, teased one another mercilessly, and often ignored me. I remained on the boundaries of their culture in part because I was the only woman present, and together this group of boys was able to erect invisible borders that served to exclude me. The skateboarders' expressions and performances of masculinity, then, are always and continuously contradictory. They move easily and seamlessly from rough-and-tumble aggression to thoughtful introspection, they mock one another's skateboarding skills and then offer friendly advice, and they rely on gross-out humor yet elaborate powerfully on grace and beauty.

These contradictions pervade skate life's constructions of masculinity and correspond with the multiply valenced masculinities that saturate mediated portrayals of skate culture. These complex and dynamic codes of masculinity produce skate life's not quite antipatriarchal critique of patriarchal limitations.

"Why is it the things that make you a man tend to be such dumb things to do?"

Never-Ending Adolescence and the (De)stabilization of White Masculine Power on MTV

The highly mediated culture of skateboarding has played a key role in mass-mediated appeals to adolescent boys since ESPN's introduction of *The Extreme Games* in 1995, but it was in 2000 that MTV launched *Jackass*, a television series that served not only as a counterpoint to Tony Hawk's clean-cut athleticism and *The X Games'* competitive focus but also as a consolidated representation of skate culture's irreverent construction of alternative masculinities. Locating its roots in niche skateboarding culture's popular *Big Brother* magazine, the *Big Brother* video series (lovingly titled *Shit, Number Two, Poop,* and *Crap*), and Bam Margera's CKY (within the culture, it is known that "CKY" stands for "Camp Kill Yourself") video series, *Jackass* showcased a former *Big Brother* employee, Johnny Knoxville, subjecting himself and other cast members to a series of pain-inducing pranks and exhibiting a gross preoccupation with bodily fluids. Knoxville, together with professional skateboarder Bam Margera, former *Big Brother* employee Chris Pontius, former clown Steve-O, and a host of other irreverent young men, is now featured in a group of shows developed by producer Jeff Tremaine's (also a former employee of *Big Brother*) aptly named Dickhouse Productions. Spin-offs *Viva La Bam, Wildboyz*, and, more recently, *Bam's Unholy Union* have placed skate culture at the center of MTV's reality show lineup and continue to correspond with skateboarding's simultaneous challenge to and reinscription of dominant masculinities. Each of these shows displays young white men reveling in adolescent humor, taking pleasure in pain, and mocking dominant norms of masculinity, all the while maintaining their power at the expense of women, people of color, homosexuals, and working-class whites. As such, they carry on skate culture's not quite anti-patriarchal critique of patriarchy.

Sean Brayton's smart description of *Jackass: The Movie* reveals the surprising complexity of the Dickhouse narratives, "parod[ies that] provide us with multiple and conflicting depictions of white masculinity that are curiously underscored by an ironic homoeroticism and a working-class disruptiveness."[1] Brayton points to the way in which *Jackass: The Movie* represents white masculinity as abject and thus victimized while at the same time fixing an ironic eye on dominant performances of young masculinity such as jock culture. Highlighting the movie's "ambitious irreverence," Brayton's article demonstrates that MTV's skateboarding texts can both mock and recuperate white masculinity.[2]

In MTV's version of a nature documentary, Steve-O and Chris Pontius morph from *Jackasses* into *Wildboyz*, traversing the world in search of exotic rituals, gnarly wild animals, and opportunities for hypermasculine risk taking, bodily humor, and homophobic/erotic display. In Season 2, these intrepid heroes interact with the Amazon's Mee-Mee Indians. Steve-O and Pontius, wearing their shirts wrapped around their heads, introduce the scene. Steve-O says, "Today, we're gonna become men." Pontius adds, "And it's gonna hurt!" They both dissolve into trademark growling, self-mocking laughter. Steve-O then looks at the camera and asks, "Why is it the things that make you a man tend to be such dumb things to do?" This knowledge, of course, does not preclude the boys from attempting to prove their manhood. After drinking and throwing up some "killer Mee-Mee Indian booze" consisting of fruit chewed up, spit out, and buried for fermenting by Mee-Mee Indian women, the boys take part in "the hand in glove ritual," a "traditional" male initiation in which a boy must wear a glove filled with "the meanest ants in the entire world" and endure the stinging. Pontius wears the glove first, and as he jumps around, screaming in pain, Steve-O asks, "Why don't you take it off dude?" Pontius, smirking, replies, "I wanna be a man!" After Pontius survives the glove, Steve-O takes his turn. With the glove on, he frowns and starts screaming, "I'm gonna pass out! Dude! I do not want to be a man! Get it off! Get it off! Get it off! Okay, I'm a man!" After a Mee-Mee

Steve-O tempts a wolf with meat hanging from his backside in *Wildboyz* during a typical display of macho risk taking and irreverent antics. (Courtesy PhotoFest.)

Indian, dressed in traditional garb, proclaims they've succeeded in becoming men, the boys are shown sitting with topless Mee-Mee Indian women massaging their hands. Pontius smiles, "Oh man that sucked. But being a man is going to be awesome! Heh heh heh." In the next scene, the boys are in the emergency room with swollen hands, pulling down their pants for antibiotic shots.

In this short segment, the Wildboyz demonstrate the multiply inflected, ironic yet sincere mockery and reinscription of masculinity as construction, white dominance over ethnic "others," and men's exploitation of women that pervade *Jackass*, *Viva La Bam*, and *Wildboyz*. Although each of these shows operates in this manner, *Wildboyz* consolidates the nexus of irony;

self-inflicted pain; simultaneous mockery of women, nonwhites, and white men; and adolescent humor that characterize them all. Displacing the overt performance and reinforcement of masculinity onto Amazonian "natives" or "savages" while repeatedly mocking such performances as "such dumb things to do," the Wildboyz demonstrate their knowledge of masculinity as construction while suggesting that they are above such display, particularly because of their whiteness but also because of their confidence as men.[3]

The Wildboyz, then, and their counterparts on *Jackass* and *Viva La Bam*, enact a mode of white masculinity that seems to indirectly align with—or correspond to—skateboarders' mockery of jock masculinity, adherence to cooperation over competition, and core valuation of confident individuality. The intertextual relationships between the Dickhouse oeuvre and the niche media of skate culture establish these similarities, and viewers' extratextual knowledge of these shows' industrial histories—particularly their key personnel's involvement with *Big Brother*—solidifies the significance of skate culture to mainstream appeals to white male youth as well as the intersecting nature of the media's portrayals of young men. Although the show does not exhibit a one-to-one relationship with skateboarder values, its simultaneous critique and reinscription of dominant masculinities certainly demonstrate an affinity with skate culture. The shows' masculine performances also overemphasize the adolescent masculinity frequently on display in niche skateboarding videos.

These shows' representations of masculinity are dynamic and contradictory, relying on multiple axes of identity—age, race, and gender in particular—to continually decodify and consolidate hegemonic masculinity. In playing up and valorizing their adolescent antics, the characters make visible the demands of adult, white, middle-class masculinity to reject bodily or emotional excess and be rational and in control. Their adolescence, then, affords them the opportunity to critique adult masculinity from a safe space. Furthermore, the boys transfer masculine performance onto nonwhite "natives," ridiculing their traditions *while at the same time taking part in them*. As such, the Wildboyz demonstrate the flexibility of whiteness and the tendency of whites to fetishize ethnicity or nonwhite skin in the name of solidifying their coolness while disrupting masculine norms and alerting viewers to the inconsistent and contradictory construction of masculinity.[4] Their renegotiation of masculinity relies on their whiteness.

The versions of skate culture on display on MTV are not the only media texts in which skateboarders depend on their whiteness as a location of power. As David J. Leonard demonstrates, extreme sports video games, particularly the *Tony Hawk* series of video games produced by Activision, showcase white skateboarders playing in urban "ghettos" absent people of color. The virtual skateboarders' forays into these supposedly dangerous spaces construct them as both cool and hypermasculine. What's more, Leonard argues, skateboarding's construction as a white practice means that the adolescent misbehavior often associated with skateboarding (the destruction of property, graffiti, and so on) "not only becomes a 'positive attribute' within extreme sporting cultures, but one without the potential for repression and violence that are often experienced by youth of color who defy societal expectations."[5] Skate media use the whiteness of skate culture to both valorize male skateboarders and challenge dominant ideas about masculinity.

Furthermore, the MTV texts' renegotiation of male norms rests on and reconstructs a new mode of masculine dominance in which men can demonstrate their confidence and power by suggesting that they are "man enough" to ridicule dominant norms of manhood. It is through these contradictions that Dickhouse Productions carries on skateboarding culture's process of criticizing masculinity without being antipatriarchal.

As David Savran points out, the notion that one should "take it like a man," and, I would add, the existence of male initiation rituals,

> seem tacitly to acknowledge that masculinity is a function not of social or cultural mastery but of the act of being subjected, abused, even tortured. It implies that masculinity is not an achieved state but a process, a trial through which one passes. But at the same time, this phrase ironically suggests the precariousness and fragility—even, perhaps, the femininity—of a gender identity that must be fought for again and again and again. For finally, when one takes it like a man, what is "it" that one takes? And why does the act of taking "it" seem to make it impossible for the one doing the taking, whoever that might be, to *be* a man? . . . Why can the one doing the taking only take it *like* a man?[6]

In asking, "Why is it the things that make you a man tend to be such dumb things to do?" Steve-O echoes Savran's thesis, though he uses the irreverent and ironic lingo that characterizes adolescent male culture and the culture of cool. Steve-O's lament simultaneously points out the fragility of masculinity and the centrality of pain to making a man while developing a new mode of hegemonic masculinity. As I have pointed out, hegemonic masculinity is not a stable, ahistoric identity but the mode of masculinity that allows men to remain in power in a particular moment.[7] As such, as dominant expressions of masculinity are critiqued and challenged by social movements, as well as cultural, economic, and social changes, masculinity must shift forms in order to remain powerful. The Dickhouse products can be read as a response to a host of images and movements that send men back to "true masculine" displays such as violence, dominance over nature, and initiation rituals, including, for example, the Promise Keepers, the mythopoetic men's movement, and the film *Fight Club*. Such a response intersects with skateboarders' dissatisfaction with the traditional or institutionalized sporting world, as represented by football, in which young men are celebrated for their adherence to externally defined rituals and ability to enact violence. Furthermore, the shows' mockery seems to rest on skateboarders' irreverent sensibility, suspicion of adult modes of masculinity, and alignment with a culture of cool that takes "irreverence as worldview."[8]

"Tarzan, Schmarzan. You don't see any Janes on this boat, do you?" Irreverence and Irony as Safe Gender Critique

Like so many live action Beavises and Buttheads, Johnny Knoxville, Bam Margera, Steve-O, Chris Pontius, and the rest of the *Jackass* crew revel in adolescent humor in all of its grotesqueness. *Jackass*, *Viva La Bam*, and *Wildboyz* each places on display a boys-only world in which young white men subject themselves to bodily harm, delight in bodily (mal)function, explore and mock homoerotic bonds, and ridicule and dominate the adults in their lives. These three shows clearly rely on a "boys will be boys" mentality that suggests that male misbehavior is simply a product of biology and not the result or demonstration of power. At the same time, however, the bodily humor and harm take on and reimagine masculinities that seek to reinscribe male power via physical dominance, and the experimentation with homoeroticism suggests an awareness of the constructed and slippery nature of sexuality, the problematic nature of the cultural relationship between masculinity and heterosexuality, and, in David Savran's words, "the precariousness and fragility" of masculinity.[9]

What's more, the Wildboyz use Tarzan as an icon of maleness that operates as far more than a cheeky reference or an easy cultural marker of virile masculinity. As Gail Bederman and John Kasson both explain, Edgar Rice Burroughs's famous hero, a British nobleman raised in Africa by apes, represented the apex of masculine physicality in a historical moment when American men were largely moving into white-collar jobs characterized as boring and feminine. Importantly, Tarzan's exaggerated strength and sexuality relied on both his simian upbringing—African apes were aligned with African people—and his "civilized" English background and genetics.[10] As Bederman argues, Tarzan "constructed Africa as a place where 'the white man' could prove his superior manhood by reliving the primitive, masculine life of his most distant evolutionary forefathers."[11] Tarzan, then, represents what bell hooks calls "eating the other," the white appropriation of black cultural markers in the name of experiencing the perceived vitality of blackness.[12] Tarzan's duality—both white and black, "noble" and "savage"—affords him physical dominance, sexual virility, and masculine power. More important, as Kasson argues, it is Tarzan's whiteness that allows him the ability to glean the best from a wild upbringing, a genetic luxury that black Africans simply do not have in the story.[13] Invoking Tarzan, the Wildboyz evoke the power of whiteness to take on blackness, the power of white males to adopt the perceived masculinity of black males while leaving their vulnerabilities behind, and the supposed strong masculinity located in the wilderness and among "savages."

Furthermore, the boys' alignment with Tarzan makes evident the show's function as a response to the recent history of masculinity in the United States, during which Robert Bly's mythopoetic men's movement heralded a return to the wild in the name of upholding masculinity, strengthening men's psyches, and reaffirming men's place in the world.[14] As I will discuss, however, Tarzan is never invoked in full seriousness; from irony to homoerotic play, the Wildboyz never fail to remind viewers that they understand Tarzan as an easy marker of hypermasculinity and seek, in some ways, to disrupt that marker. *Wildboyz* and its predecessors, *Jackass* and *Viva La Bam*, each in its own way says, "Tarzan Schmarzan," throwing off dominant masculine conventions and playing with masculinity's fragility, all the while reminding us that white boys rule.

"God, that's an ugly wiener": Male Vulnerability as Spectacle

Susan Bordo suggests that the 1990s saw a rise, so to speak, in pop culture's obsession with penises. From Lorena Bobbitt to *The Crying Game*, she notes, penises—and their vulnerabilities—were placed on display.[15] Cultural images of the penis embraced its contradictions, valuing "the phallic mythology of Superman masculinity"[16] while simultaneously rallying around everymen in texts such as *Seinfeld* and *There's Something about Mary*. Reflecting further on "this most male of bodily sites,"[17] Bordo demonstrates the contradictions inherent in imagining ultimate masculinity through the penis, arguing that its felicity—its dependence on sexual rhythms and hormones—is contrary to the notion that men rely solely on reason and logic in their actions. For many men, she says, the penis is still aligned with "the ugly, the instinctual, the 'primitive.'"[18] More to the point, "No other part of the body is so visibly and overtly mercurial as the penis, capable of such dramatic transformation from passivity to alertness,"[19] from a hard tool ("jackhammer"), weapon ("torpedo"), or hero ("The Lone Ranger") to "suggest[ing] vulnerability, fragility, a sleepy sweetness."[20]

Such vulnerability shadowed by heroism, Brenton J. Malin asserts, came to the fore in dominant images of masculinity post-9/11. "If the masculine hero of the '90s offered a conflicted blend of hypermasculine toughness and new age sensitivity," he argues, "the September 11 hero is still more profoundly conflicted, eminently heroic and eminently vulnerable."[21] Furthermore, the male hero's—and the United States'—hypermasculine displays of heroism are justified by their concurrent vulnerability.

It is in this climate that *Jackass* and *Wildboyz* in particular send up the contradictions of the penis, male dominance, and homosocial boys' cultures. This mockery is perhaps most concrete in the shows' metonymical abuse of their stars' penises. In the *Wildboyz* series premier, Chris Pontius and Steve-O sit shirtless on top of a van in South Africa watching a group of baboons whose genitals are prominently visible. Pontius cracks, "I was looking at that baboon's wiener and I'm like, God that's an ugly wiener. And then I looked down at mine and I'm like, it looks kind of like mine. Ha ha!"

Aligning his "wiener" with the animal's, Pontius drives home Susan Bordo's suggestion that the penis serves as a source of conflict for men. His remark, however, also simultaneously highlights his animalistic masculinity and the vulnerability—weeniness—of that masculinity. Throughout the series, the Wildboyz turn their penises into jokes, from imagining an anaconda as a snake that is "a little bit bigger than the ones we're used to working with" (Episode 2.2) to asking, "I wonder what animal will bite my wiener off?" while wearing a kilt (Episode 3.4). Steve-O and Pontius's delivery is important to understanding their anxious expressions, for they always end their comments with a gruff "heh heh" and look goofily at the camera. They are, in short, clearly in charge, stars of the show who dominate the television screen and are "man enough" to publicize their masculine anxieties.

At the same time, however, by publicizing and laughing at their own weeniness, their inability to live up to the norms of dominant masculinity—in their body types especially—the men in these shows beat their detractors to the punch. The self-deprecating humor that pervades these shows operates as a rhetorical suit of armor that deflects any criticism of the boys' nonhegemonic masculinity. Such ego defense is also at work in the boys' routine characterization of masculine rituals as "stupid." The mockery of these rituals allows the boys to repel claims that they are unable to live up to the codes of hegemonic masculinity by simply responding that they do not want to live up to them.

The boys in *Jackass* and *Wildboyz* also routinely put their penises at risk. *Jackass*'s constant representation of such risk is perhaps exemplified by the "cup test," which occurs in both *Jackass: The Movie* and Episode 2.1 of the television series. Johnny Knoxville, wearing short jean shorts (what might be called "Daisy Dukes") and a tight red T-shirt, straps a cup over his shorts and says, "I'm Johnny Knoxville, and this is the cup test." He then subjects himself to a series of penile abuses, from children kicking his crotch to a friend dropping a cue ball on the cup from the top of a multistory building. After each test, Knoxville groans, clearly in pain, and at the end of the test he shows the audience the bruises that resulted from abuses that missed the cup and landed on his leg. On *Wildboyz*, Steve-O engages in "some good old-fashioned penis fishing" in Florida. He wraps a string tied to a small fish around his "package," and a close-up shows him pulling the "noose" tight. He then throws the string into the water, and a large tarpon attacks the small fish. Steve-O prances around, screaming in pain, while Pontius and the others on the boat laugh hysterically.

As David Savran argues, such displays of vulnerability are central to the production of masculinity, modern versions of which, he says, are founded in male masochism. This masochism derives from the modern shift from beating to schooling in the production of "civilized" young men. As men learned to police their own "natural" instincts toward rowdy behavior, self-induced pain became part and parcel of middle-class masculinity, and such pain had to be associated with masculine freedom or pleasure. What's more, the experience of pain aligns masculinity with victimhood and feminizes and blackens it while at the same time asserting its power.[22]

The boys' hysterical laughter in the face of self-inflicted pain certainly is suggestive of the masochism central to white male identity. I would add, however, that it also represents disdain for male displays of physical power characteristic of the 1980s action films discussed by Susan Jeffords or the late 1990s *Fight Club*.[23] By raising such masochism to the level of the absurd, these shows suggest that masochistic displays are "stupid," which is to say, unnecessary *or too obvious*. In a culture that valorizes self-reflexivity and irony, the overt display of masculinity—such as that produced through both self-flagellation and hypermasculine physical prowess—in fact reveals that masculinity is at risk, and Savran's deconstruction of the phrase "take it like a man" says as much. I would add that irony and irreverence provide a means by which young men can prove that they are manly without revealing that they are doing so. In other words, they can take the construction of masculinity back underground, making their process of proof invisible by exposing and laughing at the means by which other men demonstrate their manliness. They are, in short, "man enough" to mock masculine proving grounds.

The boys' ever-present irreverence, Steve-O and Pontius's frequent cheeky referrals to demonstrating their manhood, and Johnny Knoxville's pseudo hipster, laid back demeanor all indicate their disdain for dominant masculinities while producing an ironic style through which they can shore up their own masculinity without letting anyone know they are doing so. These men are not the glistening hard bodies of *Rambo, Die Hard*, or *Fight Club;* they are skinny and impertinent adolescents mocking one another, their ugly penises, and their susceptibility to pain. As I discuss next, the boys, over and over again, place on display their physical vulnerability, succumbing time after time to the dominance of nature, other men, and sometimes women.

"Well, if you're asking me if I'm always a pussy, Andre, I probably am": "Taking it like a man" by Admitting Defeat

While *Jackass* and *Viva La Bam* make a point of placing male pain on display, it is *Wildboyz* that most clearly articulates a critique—or at least an awareness—of the cultural construction of this display and its relationship to masculinity. Its relationship to whiteness, of course, goes largely unmentioned. From declaring male proving rites to be "dumb things to do" to characterizing a snake expert who attempts the "kiss of death" with a cobra to be "idiotic" (Episode 1.3), Steve-O, in particular, routinely makes it clear that such dangerous displays of physical dominance are silly and unnecessary. The extremity and absurdity of such displays in *Jackass*—from the skits "Beard of Leaches" (Episode 3.1) to "Extreme Unicycling" (Episode 3.3)—and *Viva La Bam*'s routine reminders that even Bam, the show's alpha male, is afraid of snakes cue the audience that this group of young men is far removed from hypermasculine heroes such as Bruce Willis and Steven Seagal. Still, *Jackass* and *Viva La Bam* never explicitly make fun of such displays in the way Steve-O does throughout *Wildboyz*.

While Steve-O has always been the cast member who most often sends up homoeroticism and masculinity, perhaps it is their presence in the "wild" space of predatory animals and "savage" native peoples that allows the Wildboyz to play with masculinity more freely. That is, their encounters with the animals and their whiteness in the presence of dark native "others" may in fact provide the Wildboyz with a kind of protective shell from which they can critique Western masculinity.[24] Because the show routinely suggests that non-Western men are "crazier" and more grotesque than its white heroes, Steve-O and Pontius are presented as firmly in control and even rational in their knowing mockery of male rituals. So, even while they characterize themselves as irreverent goofballs, they can at least abide by the codes of hegemonic masculinity more easily than the nonwhite natives can. What's more, the non-Western men on display do not live up to the physical norms of hegemonic masculinity. They are frequently presented as shorter and skinnier—and of course, less white—than the American version of the ideal male. The natives' inability to inhabit dominant masculinity makes Steve-O and Pontius appear comparatively "manly" even while they make fun of hegemonic gender norms.

The boys also deploy sarcasm as a kind of protective shell. In the *Wildboyz* series premier, Pontius and Steve-O travel to the Cape of Good Hope's Shark Alley, where the great white shark dominates. Dressed in snorkeling gear and black wet suits and riding in a boat, the boys explain their plan to the audience.

> *Steve-O:* All these seals are doing is waiting to die in the jaws of a great white shark.
> *Pontius:* So we're going to go swim with them. SO stupid!
> *Steve-O:* This is the world's dumbest place to swim.
> *Pontius:* And we don't even like seals.
> *Steve-O:* We hate cold water!
> *Pontius:* We're swimming in Shark Alley right now, with a bunch of seals that are the main food source for the great white shark. And it's starting to get towards sunset, which is the main feeding time. Which makes us pretty stupid.

In admitting the error of their ways, the Wildboyz set up a situation in which their fear of the sharks does not threaten their masculinity. They acknowledge the completely arbitrary nature of their choice—they are certainly not doing it for pleasure—and thereby acknowledge it as an exercise in taking risks for the sake of the hypermasculine performance. By openly mocking themselves, they suggest that they are secure in their masculinity. A "real man" does not need to put his masculinity on display; he does not need to prove himself and can even deride such displays as out-and-out dumb.

This valorization of stupidity upholds the Wildboyz' dominance in another manner. As I have noted, women—particularly white, heterosexual, middle-class women—are constructed as "civilizing" or controlling agents in American culture. They hold the power to rein men in, to bring them under control. In the boys-only world of *Wildboyz*, boys are free to do whatever they please. Such reinforcement of white male power operates in tandem with their critique of traditional male norms.

Steve-O and Pontius also use sarcasm to make fun of their inability to dominate nature. In Alaska, Pontius, Steve-O, and Manny, the show's resident wildlife expert, approach a group of black bears. Steve-O, dressed in a bear costume, proclaims that he will protect Manny should he get into trouble. The bears, he says, will "recognize" him "as one of their own" and listen to him. Pontius chimes in, declaring, "[I'll] cuss to them and . . . swear at them, and if they still won't listen I'll go ahead and give them a taste of my middle finger." The absurdity of this remark is driven home as the bears approach the men. The crew yells nervously that they need to back up. Steve-O, still in his bear costume and floating lazily in an inner tube in the river, solemnly proclaims, "It's not often that a grizzly bear fights a black bear, but if I have to, I will." Pontius says, "Thank God Steve-O's here to protect us." By sending up their clear inability to dominate the bears, the boys make fun of the relationship between dominance over nature and masculine power. They make evident men's relative lack of power and suggest that masculinity need not be proven via dominance over "the wild."

The Wildboyz, however, go beyond making fun of masculine displays to making fun of their own feminized or homosexualized selves. After they dive naked into a shark cage and fearfully jump back out in a matter of seconds, a guide asks, "Do you always look like that when you jump in a cage?" Steve-O replies, "Well, if you're asking me if I'm always a pussy, Andre, I probably am." Such slang displaces Steve-O's fear onto a feminized object while at the same time suggesting that he is confident enough to admit his own fears. Such displacement is also demonstrated on *Viva La Bam*, though in a more conflicted manner. The show has posited snakes as Bam's kryptonite; he is largely in control of himself and others until snakes are introduced. Cast members Ryan Dunn and Johnny Knoxville plot to throw a snake onto Bam, predicting that he will "squeal like a little girl." Bam's response, however, is hypermasculine in its aggression: "Get it the fuck off of me now. . . . I'm serious, get it off! I fucking hate it! . . . Dude, stop it, don't even do it. Dude, PETA's going to come after you if you throw it on me, it's not even worth it." Despite Johnny Knoxville's celebratory proclamation that Bam "screamed just like April" (Bam's mother), Bam's invocation of PETA (People for the Ethical Treatment of Animals), a group that I would argue is feminized in its attention to animal rights (in opposition to the hypermasculine National Rifle Association, for example), transfers his fear of snakes onto fear of the feminized institution. Dunn should back off not because of Bam's fear but because of PETA's requirements (Episode 3.3).

The Wildboyz also enact such confidence when they learn about the World Eskimo Indian Olympics from the world record holder, Carol Pickett. Steve-O explains, "She's going to explain each event and then kick our asses in it" (Episode 1.2). Pickett, who as an Eskimo, a woman, and a guest on the show is darkened and othered, again makes the boys' relative lack of physical prowess evident and reminds the audience that they are far too manly to be threatened by a woman's strength. It is in this contradiction that the Wildboyz produce a new mode of hegemonic masculinity that seems to be a direct response to feminism and Title IX. Male power is predicated on admitting defeat and demonstrating imperviousness to feminine strength.

Wildboyz and *Jackass* take such imperviousness a step farther in their experimentation with homoerotic performances. Although *Viva La Bam* also operates in a boys-only world, the show keeps homoeroticism at arm's length, preferring to remain in the realm of boyish pranks during which the boys certainly have fun with one another, make each other laugh, and even violate each other's bodies with tacks, bees, and other mundane weapons. While this boyish fun does have a homoerotic tint, it never crosses into the type of homoerotic experimentation on display in *Jackass* and *Wildboyz*. What's more, Bam Margera solidified his heterosexuality in his latest show, 2007's *Bam's Unholy Union*, a reality show that depicts Bam and his fiancée as they make their wedding plans. Although Steve-O and Pontius do periodically play their sexuality "straight," they more frequently, and arguably more passionately, "cross that line" into homoerotic performance.

"Oh my God, I think we might have crossed that line. It was an accident!" Performing Homoeroticism and Femininity as Masculine Display

> *Steve-O:* If a big scary jaguar was actually a cute house cat, what would it be?
>
> *Pontius:* It'd be a Margay. We thought this show was getting a bit too macho working with all these jaguars and stuff, so we decided to start working with something a little mar-GAY!
>
> *Steve-O:* What could possibly be margay than this? (*Pontius, wearing only a*

jock strap, sits on Steve-O's shoulders.) So, we worked with the margay, now let's go find the most gay.

Steve-O and Pontius's adolescent wordplay and snickering puns place the complexity of adolescent male identity on display. Conflating "macho" with both the danger of wildcats and heterosexuality, they construct a false dichotomy between dominating modes of masculinity and homosexuality. In the subsequent scene, the boys solidify this dichotomy as they raft down a river wearing only life jackets.

> *Pontius (lisping)*: We're rafting down this bumpy wild river to go swings from some vines.
> *Steve-O:* Tarzan Schmarzan.
> *Pontius:* You don't see any Janes on this boat do you?

The boys lean toward one another, faux kissing, and then dissolve into disgusted laughter. Pontius protests, "Oh my God, I think we might have crossed that line. It was an accident! We hit a bump in the rapids! Our lips touched!" Perhaps to drive home the point, the boys begin to swing from vines. Pontius claims, "I've seen them do this one on Tarzan a million times. It's definitely going to work." Enacting Tarzan's hypermasculinity while sarcastically commenting on the absurdity of vine swinging, Pontius sends up dominant gender roles. The boys further the (self-)mockery later when Steve-O proclaims, "We came to the jungle, we swang on vines, and I think we proved our point." Pontius replies, "Tarzan ain't got nothing on the Wildboyz!" Both yell together, "Yeah!" They start to kiss, and then dissolve into laughter, never fully "crossing that line" (Episode 3.4). As I have noted, Tarzan represents the hypermasculine virility of the "darkened" jungle and whites' power to appropriate that perceived masculinity. Juxtaposing Tarzan with fey homosexuality, the boys demonstrate the instability of the line between the hypermasculine and the homoerotic and between homosocial boys' cultures and homoerotic boys' cultures, lines that create an anxiety deemed "homosexual panic" by Eve Kosofsky Sedgwick.[25] In playing with these lines, the Wildboyz produce a critique of dominant conceptions of masculinity and sexuality usually unseen in adolescent boys' popular culture.

Nevertheless, this critique is immediately mitigated by the Wildboyz laughter, and most of Pontius's homoerotic and/or feminized play—from stripping for a moose and hanging his clothes on the animal's antlers to his *Jackass* persona as Party Boy, in which he prances around in a G-string dancing to techno music—is laced with a mocking irony that could be read as out-and-out ridicule of gay men. Steve-O, on the other hand, tends to play his homosexualized and feminized self "straighter." Commenting on a walking stick, he says, "You can tell that it's a ballerina. Because it does pliés and relevés." Performing some pliés, he goes on, "You can make fun of me all you want for going to dance class. But I know my pliés and relevés" (Episode 2.2). Rather than marking his masculinity with teasing laughter, Steve-O continually reinscribes it by beating potential ridiculers to the punch and suggesting he is confident enough to absorb derision. In fact, Steve-O transfers "taking it like a man" from the physical to the mental domain; the masochism David Savran discusses can be found in his willingness to constantly subject himself to mockery.

Repeatedly approaching "that line," crossing it, blurring it, and playing with it, the *Jackass* and *Wildboyz* cast members demonstrate the relationship between constructions of masculinity and constructions of sexuality while continually upsetting them. The freedom to do so, however, relies not only on their whiteness but also on the constant deployment of irreverence and irony. In this manner, in correspondence with skateboarding culture, these shows and their cast members critique norms of masculinity without disrupting its power and disturb patriarchal constraints without being antipatriarchal. Furthermore, as I will demonstrate, the Dickhouse Productions casts frequently enact patriarchal power over women, nonwhites, and each other.

"It's a jungle out there, and we're Tarzan": Irreverence and Irony as Reinscriptions of Male Dominance

Off the coast of South Africa, the Wildboyz again reference Tarzan. After observing the great white sharks' feeding area, which is teeming with dolphins, Chris Pontius provides the audience with a recap: "So today we had a bunch of dolphins getting hunted down by great white sharks. At the same time, hundreds of kamikaze seagulls tried to stab the dolphins with their beaks. And like three whales trying to eat everybody! It's a jungle out there, and we're Tarzan" (Episode 1.1). Pontius dissolves into his trademark "heh

heh heh" laughter, the camera pans to the sun setting on the ocean, and the sound of "native" chanting rises. Cut to a shot of the "natives" dancing on the waterfront with Steve-O, who is dancing sloppily alongside them and periodically breaking rank to spin in his own way.

The juxtaposition of Pontius's ironic claim on Tarzan—the simultaneously noble and savage he-man—and Steve-O's participation in and mockery of traditional dancing points to the Wildboyz' concurrent mockery of and participation in dominating masculinity. Steve-O and Pontius clearly find Tarzan a funny archetype in his exaggerated masculinity, but at the same time they routinely place themselves in a dominating relationship to themselves, nonwhites, and women. Although such dominance is usually mitigated by irony, it is nonetheless powerful. Even more strongly, the men of *Jackass* and, to a greater extent, *Viva La Bam* place on display an adolescent masculinity impervious to rules, disrespectful of parents and other adults, and superior to just about everyone. Although *Jackass* and *Viva La Bam* also play their power with humor, the repeated assertion that their boyish pranks are acceptable reveals the sense of power the cast members share.

"What will he do next? Whatever the fuck I want": Bam Margera's Total Domination

Without question, *Viva La Bam* exhibits the most explicit claims to male dominance in the Dickhouse oeuvre. From the show's credit sequence, in which a voice-over asks, "What will he do next?" and Bam responds, "Whatever the fuck I want" before appearing to jump off a multistory building with his skateboard in hand, *Viva La Bam* places Bam in charge of his parents, his friends, and the community of Westchester, Pennsylvania. The ultimate alpha male and the leader of the multiple male minions who took part in producing the CKY skateboarding videos, Bam routinely performs the superiority of white adolescent males over women, people of color, adults, and even his other white male friends.[26] I would argue that the trait allowing Bam to dominate other white males is his athleticism. The only skateboarder of the bunch to be a well-known professional—he is featured in one of Tony Hawk's Activision video games—Bam positions himself as the reason for the other boys' success on the show. Although the superiority of male adolescents over adult men does correspond to the critique of adult masculinity in niche skateboarding videos, the show's overt displays of dominance and Bam's clear level of power over his friends depart from the values espoused by many skaters.

Much of *Viva La Bam* is predicated on Bam's unusual relationship with his parents, April ("Ape") and Phil, who represent caricatures of contemporary parents unwilling to place limits on their children. From routinely waking them up abruptly in the middle of the night—in one memorable moment, Bam's obese friend Preston crawls into bed next to April, replacing Phil without her knowledge—to ironing hamburger decals onto all of Phil's shirts, Bam and his friends absolutely torture April and Phil. While Phil allows most of these pranks to roll off his back, April responds to Bam with high-pitched, hysterical screams. They get angry but have absolutely no control over Bam, who can, after all, "do whatever the fuck [he] want[s]." Leading the crowd and making his parents a mockery, Bam highlights the power of his youth.

Phil's brother Don Vito also serves as a constant source of laughter. Obese and largely unintelligible, Don Vito represents a working-class white male grotesque, the picture of excess. In the series' third episode, Bam places his father and Don Vito's working-class family on display for absolute mockery during a family reunion. After asking his friend to replace the family home's front door with a drawbridge that will allow appropriate space for his reportedly obese relatives, Bam travels to his grandmother's house with Phil. There he makes fun of her living room rug, her old-fashioned values, and her clear frustration with her family and their drinking habits. Bam summarizes his father's family as such: They all "grew up next to this gnarly power plant in Lynwood, PA, and I have a feeling that all that radiation just fucked with my whole family because everybody's nuts!"

Characterizing his father's family as the product of radiation, Bam solidifies his own power, indirectly characterizing himself and his friends as "not nuts," that is, not irrational, not grotesque, not old-fashioned. Although Bam does not use the term *white trash* to describe Phil's family, the reference to the power plant, the family members' excess weight, the grandmother's out-of-date rug, and their excessive beer consumption all serve as markers of it. As John Hartigan Jr. explains, "[W]hite trash . . . materializes a complicated policing of the inchoate boundaries that comprise class and racial identities in this country."[27] That is to say, the invocation of these markers of

Bam Margera demonstrates his dominance over his parents, Phil and April, in a promo for *Viva La Bam*. (Courtesy PhotoFest.)

white trash sets up Bam as incontrovertibly powerful in his mode of white masculinity. Compared to Phil's family, Bam and his friends are rational and in control. By framing his father's family as excessive, Bam mitigates his own adolescent excesses, thus maintaining the power of white masculinity's association with reason and control while rejecting the hyperrational, uptight, bureaucratic image of adult middle-class masculinity. Furthermore, by placing himself in opposition to his white trash—and therefore lazy— family, Bam can highlight his own vitality, energy, and enterprise. Unlike Don Vito, who supposedly spends much of his day eating and drinking beer, Bam and his friends take great strides to build elaborate clubhouses and skate parks and formulate pranks. Using their young, middle-class, white vigor, Bam and his friends showcase American mores of hard work without subscribing to traditional models of employment. In this way, this show aligns with Dickhouse Productions' ongoing critique of white masculine norms and subscription to white male power.

Beyond asserting his dominance over working-class adults, Bam continually suggests that he and his friends are far more rational and in control than his mother. Phil Margera contributes to this representation. While Phil is calm, April is a shrieking, hysterical shrew. As Bam and his friends begin to break down the family home's front door with a sledgehammer, April screams at them to stop. Phil stands idly by, and April turns to him, wailing, "How are you watching them chop our door up? Any? Any? Hello-o?" Phil just chuckles and looks on (Episode 1.3). April is placed in the role of the "mother who must civilize," the calming influence on a group of men, but she routinely fails at this role. By Season 3, Bam asks, "Ape, do you just bitch all day, is that what you do?" and institutes "Ape's 24-hour Bitch-No-More Marathon," challenging his mother to abstain from complaining for an entire day, during which, of course, he and his friends work to torture her (Episode 3.3). Although April protests, "Bam, I am not bitchin' all the time, it's just that you do so much shit that's bad," Bam is clearly represented as rational, in control, and in the right while April must "dig deep" to find the self-control necessary to make it through the day. While April seems irrational and out of control, Phil functions as a grown-up who has not fallen prey to norms of adult white masculinity.[28]

By casting adult family members as objects of ridicule, Bam and his friends can indeed do whatever they want without suggesting that they are out of control or excessive. Although they may run through a grocery store dressed as Vikings (Episode 1.3), fill the Margera house with soapsuds (Episode 3.3), purposely fail or sabotage a host of jobs from baker to farmer (Episode 4.3), and saw a "moon roof" into Bam's Lamborghini (Episode 5.2), Bam and his friends appear to be in control in comparison to the adults on the show. As I discuss later, people of color, particularly "Compton Ass Terry," a black skateboarder, also serve as irrational foils to the CKY crew.

Although in some ways *Viva La Bam* continues the mockery of traditional masculinities characteristic of *Jackass* and *Wildboyz*, the show's premise valorizes white adolescent male dominance and exhibits an explicit mockery of the working class, women, and people of color. In this way, the show represents the low point of Dickhouse Productions, as it fails to produce even the contradictory critique present in *Jackass* and *Wildboyz*.

"A well-groomed woman's undercarriage": Irreverent Sexism and "Straight" Heterosexuality

My criticism of *Viva La Bam* should not imply that *Jackass* and *Wildboyz* are without fault. As I have made clear, both of these series serve to uphold patriarchal power while at the same time ridiculing traditional modes of masculinity. Despite (or perhaps because of) their relatively frequent blurring of boundaries between homosexuality and hegemonic masculinity and between homosexuality and heterosexuality, the cast members of both shows exhibit blatant sexism and play their heterosexuality "straight." That is to say, the characters on both shows largely drop their sarcastic and irreverent tones when discussing heterosexual encounters, instead picking up an adolescent tenor that suggests a fascination with sexuality and a sense of awe at their ability to express their sexuality freely. After attempting the numerous events in the Eskimo Olympics, for example, Steve-O asks their female instructor who makes the better Eskimo. As she is deciding, Pontius proclaims, "What we really want to find out, though, is which is the better lover, because Carol's hot!" (Episode 1.2). Although Pontius never operates in full seriousness, his sense of glee in proclaiming "Carol's hot!" is palpable, and it is this glee that solidifies his heterosexuality. Always joking, Pontius plays his heterosexuality straight.

The men also speak irreverently as they toss off sexist comments, and

their irreverence in this case serves to shore up their power in that it acknowl-
edges the absurdity of sexism without ever abandoning it. Dressed in an
Uncle Sam suit, Pontius proclaims, "The Bald Eagle. Not only our national
symbol, but also the nickname of a well-groomed woman's undercarriage.
God bless 'em all. Heh heh heh" (Episode 1.2). Though the conflation of a
national symbol with such sexist slang does demonstrate the slippery and
constructed nature of symbols, the sexism coupled with Pontius's gruff and
somewhat aggressive chuckle places him in a location of dominance. Free
to judge and objectify women—even while laughing at either himself or the
slang—he solidifies his power as a white male.

Although women, in the rare instances when they are present on *Jackass*,
Viva La Bam, and *Wildboyz*, serve as either irrational foils (April Margera)
to the boys' adolescent but controlled irreverence or as sexual objects, it is
people of color and indigenous groups who truly serve to maintain the boys'
power in spite of their mockery of masculinity. Although they seem capable
of negotiating various masculinities and mocking, reimagining, and remold-
ing masculine rituals, the cast members of these shows do so on the backs
of the various people of color who periodically appear on the three shows.
Furthermore, as I have mentioned, their adolescent irreverence seems to
break from the rational and enterprising construction of whiteness highlighted by Richard Dyer, but in defining the actions of various people of
color as "crazy" or "out-of-control" the shows mitigate the "wildness" of the
Wildboyz and their crew.[29]

"This is some freak show crap": White Western Dominance

Homi Bhabha has noted that colonialist discourse relies on "fixity" in the
construction and representation of indigenous peoples' identities. Such representation, he argues strongly, "connotes rigidity and an unchanging order
as well as disorder, degeneracy and daemonic repetition."[30] In contrast, as
Dyer notes, whiteness is characterized by flexibility in its representation
and derives much of its power from that flexibility. Whiteness, he contends,
is "everything and nothing." Although it is frequently tied to rationality and
enterprise, it also enjoys freedom of movement and metamorphosis.[31] The
white male adolescents of *Jackass*, *Viva La Bam*, and *Wildboyz* delight in
this flexibility and use it to perform alternative modes of white masculinity,

as I have discussed throughout this chapter. But their maintenance of white male power in the face of these negotiations is dependent on fixed images of indigenous peoples and American people of color in two ways. First, hypermasculinity is displaced onto people of color, particularly indigenous people in *Wildboyz*, allowing the shows' stars to take part in hypermasculine display while simultaneously mocking it. Second, the cast members' irreverent, over-the-top actions are played in relationship to the others' actions, and people of color are routinely characterized as "crazier" than the regular cast members. The boys, then, are able to walk a line between serious modes of dominant masculinity and absurdist antics; they can be "everything and nothing," both critical of hypermasculinity and adherent to norms of "civility" in comparison to the darkened others. In comparison to the "natives'" crazy antics and nonnormative bodies, the white heroes of these shows appear relatively dominant, and from this position of power they are able to make fun of dominant gender codes. Furthermore, the natives' participation in hypermasculine displays of masculinity discloses their need to prove their manliness and thus suggests that they are not *truly* manly. It is this relationship that contributes to the Dickhouse crew's ability to enact a critique of patriarchal norms that is neither antipatriarchal nor antiracist.

In the first episode of *Wildboyz'* second season, Steve-O and Pontius travel to Jipur, India, which, the voice-over explains, is "home to a number of bizarre street performers." Having made their way through South Africa, where they swam with great white sharks; Alaska, where Steve-O mixed salmon semen and eggs—directly from the source—in his mouth; and a host of other locations that presented numerous opportunities for the boys' silly pranks, daredeviltry, and gross-out humor, the boys introduce Jipur's street performers as "some freak show crap" (Episode 2.1). The "freaks," Indian men who Pontius describes further as a "crazy bastard" and "creepy guy," eat light bulbs and walk on broken glass. Steve-O remarks, "Where we come from, playing with broken glass is totally frowned upon. But, as you can see, in Jipur it's cool!" The boys laugh, delighting in their discovery of such crazy men.

Positioning himself and Pontius as "we," Steve-O implicates the Indian men as "they," a group that is positioned as being more irrational and pushing the boundaries of civility farther than the Wildboyz ever would. Though light bulb eating is certainly shocking, it pales in comparison with the extent of bodily harm and disgust to which Steve-O subjects himself repeatedly. It is through this positioning that the Wildboyz secure their own normality or their relative sense of rationality or even civility at the expense of the Indian men. *Viva La Bam* makes a similar move when the African American skateboarder, Compton Ass Terry, appears on the show. Again, although the show is driven by Bam and his friends' adolescent antics, Terry is characterized as "wild and out of control" by Bam. Furthermore, Bam suggests that his desire for excitement is driven by Terry's presence. Preparing for his family reunion, he declares, "I can't just have some boring-ass dinner. I gotta do something cool because Compton Ass Terry's here." His declaration of desire, which can certainly be read as an assertion of Terry's naturalized knowledge of "cool" as a black man, is followed by a shot of Terry wearing ski goggles and speaking something unintelligible. The episode is punctuated throughout with images of Terry dancing to hip-hop, and shows him losing control while driving an all-terrain vehicle (ATV) and crashing into an Audi. Although Bam routinely loses control of this ATV, Terry's mishap is characterized as a result of his "wild and out of control" nature. Bam is purposefully daring and irreverent; Terry seems to have no choice.

Beyond characterizing Terry as crazier and cooler than Bam and his friends, the show others him. Introducing Terry to his parents, Bam says, "I seriously made a wrong turn off the 405 and I ended up in Compton. I met this dude. Look at the bling-bling shit he has." His story suggests that Bam, save for a wrong turn, would never be found in Compton, and Terry is positioned as a novelty brought in from a strange land. Terry is even employed to teach Phil about bling, accompanying him to Philadelphia to get an Elvis pinky ring. Phil asks Terry, "Do you gotta tell him that you have it [bling], or do you just let them see it?" Terry, in other words, is positioned as a cultural tour guide, leading Phil and Bam through the culture of bling. Phil and Bam are the norm; Terry is a novelty.

Beyond mitigating their own irreverence and craziness, which is to say, their chosen distance from mainstream norms of behavior, by displacing such transgressions onto people of color, the boys on these shows also transfer hypermasculine displays onto people of color. This dual displacement positions the boys in a location in between, from which they critique masculinity while maintaining their power. In Florida, Steve-O and Pontius meet William Cypress, a Seminole Indian wearing traditional dress. With

Cypress, the boys participate in "the traditional party dances of the Seminole Indians," dancing around a fire, jumping around, and humping the
ground. Steve-O declares, "So you could say that the Seminole Indians are
the original Wildboyz of Florida." In this statement, Steve-O aligns himself
with native peoples, an action not dissimilar from Robert Bly's mythopoetic men's movement, while at the same time suggesting that it is Seminole
Indians, not the white Wildboyz, who participate in masculine displays in
all seriousness. They do the same with the male initiation ritual described
at the beginning of this chapter and in India, where after walking through
coals Steve-O proclaims, "If us three didn't just prove that we're the most
badassed dudes in India, then you've got to be an absolute idiot!" Although
the boys have participated in this performance, they've also repeatedly
characterized the Indian men as creepy. As such, they can perform hypermasculinity while mocking such performance.

The Dickhouse boys' whiteness serves as a cultural shelter from which
they can safely play with dominant norms of masculinity while maintaining
its power. Positioning people of color as both irrational and hypermasculine—characteristics that are antithetical in dominant codes of gender—the
shows suggest that the boys' actions are normative or at least purposefully
transgressive. In this manner, the shows also place on display the willful
othering characteristic of much of skateboard culture. Possessing the freedom to operate within or without dominance, these white male adolescents
can pick and choose those elements of mainstream culture they deem worthy. Although the Wildboyz, in particular, mock performances of masculinity
in a manner suggesting their knowledge of the constructed nature of gender
identity, their clearly produced dominance over people of color operates
to maintain systems of white male power. This contradictory relationship
to power and critique certainly corresponds to skateboarding culture's not
quite antipatriarchal critique of patriarchal norms.

"Does it look cool? You guys suck so bad":
Performance on Display

Dickhouse Productions' *Jackass*, *Viva La Bam*, and *Wildboyz* cannot be
discussed as clear appropriations of skateboard culture. In fact, only Bam
Margera has suggested a measure of thievery and exploitation in the devel-

opment of these shows, telling *Entertainment Weekly* that Johnny Knoxville stole material from his CKY video series to use in *Jackass* without acknowledging or paying the CKY cast. Margera's somewhat whiny complaint is interesting given his subsequent success as an MTV reality star, Knoxville's history in the skateboarding industry, and the CKY cast's presence both on the *Jackass* television show and in its movies.

In fact, the Dickhouse Productions oeuvre is far more appropriately read in correspondence with skateboard culture. Not so much an appropriation as a series of documents in correspondence with and corresponding to the values of skateboarding, and related intertexually to skate media, *Jackass*, *Viva La Bam*, and *Wildboyz* each align in some way with skateboarding's reverence for male adolescence, discomfort with dominant masculinities, and willingness to explore and play with alternative masculinities. The complexity and contradictions of these correspondences are made evident by skateboarders' responses to the shows, most of which demonstrate a level of appreciation for both the shows' humor and the stars' success while at the same time suggesting that at times the shows misrepresent skateboarders.

> I watch *Viva La Bam*. And I guess *Jackass*, it's really funny sometimes and sometimes it's just really stupid. Like when I see them do stuff it's really funny, but I'd never do it, really. It's just like stupid. But the fact that someone would go do that is kind of funny. And *Viva La Bam* has a lot of skateboarding in it, so I like watching it. But when it doesn't have skateboarding, it just has Bam being himself, doing whatever he wants, so I watch it to see skateboarders. (Adam, age 11)

> The shows are giving skateboarding a bad name. They're doing stupid stuff while they're representing skateboarding. Like they talk shit to older people or something just because they think that like, 'cause they went and saw some Bam show and they're like, that's what Bam would want me to do. But actually that dude was pretty smart. He doesn't, he just does that shit 'cause like, MTV pays him and like, he usually, if you notice, doesn't harm other people. He just does stupid shit to himself. But all these kids see it, and they're like, "Man, that's what I need to do to become popular." (Joe, age 19)

I actually like *Viva La Bam*. But, uh, its funny 'cause I think, like, a lot of people, like get this idea of that's what skaters are like. Which is true, you know, a lot of, you know, a lot of us are, I don't know, some people are like, I don't know, just goofy like that. But other people are goofy that don't skate. But like, I don't, that's what a lot of people think skateboarding is like. These like CRAZY kids, doing CRAZY stuff, you know? But that's not all true, you know. But, uh, I think it's funny, there's no doubt about it, there's some funny stuff that goes on on those shows, you know. You just gotta like, um, deevolutionize yourself to, like take a step back in evolution to like, enjoy that humor, you know, but there's nothing wrong with it. It's funny. (Matthew, age 21)

Those guys, are cool, you know, but Bam, Bam's cool. He sold out, a little bit. Like, I don't know, not really. Like he's makin' movies and stuff. He's collectin' his checks. I've got respect for that. He's been doin' that, that's him, you know. He's been doin' that for years and years. That's his straight up thing. He's lucky he can sell it, you know. I mean I wish I could sell my life. . . . But *Jackass* . . . it'd be cool if they just kept the skateboarding out of it. If they did everything else, and not have, um, skateboard involved I'd be happy. . . . People, like have said to us, "This isn't *Jackass*" or something like that. I'm like, "Oh, OK. Sorry! We're out to be jackasses, to look cool you know?" (Braden, age 15)

The skateboarders' contradictory responses to *Viva La Bam*, in particular, demonstrate the shows' active and inconsistent correspondence with skateboarding culture as well as the complex nature of that culture and its multiple takes on commercialism. Eleven-year-old Adam actually quotes *Viva La Bam*'s opening sequence and implies that it demonstrates his authenticity: "[I]t just has Bam being himself, doing whatever he wants." For Adam, Margera is not a persona constructed for media culture; he is authentically presented. Braden also invoked Margera's authenticity—"that's him, you know"—while admitting, "He sold out, a little bit." The skaters also all suggested that at times they act like the characters on these shows while at the same time critiquing others for doing so and bringing a bad name to skate culture. Here, again, we can see that a straightforward discussion of mainstream appropriation of subcultural forms does not do justice to the relationships among these varied expressions of skateboarding culture, nor does such a discussion adequately explain skate media's varied and multiple expressions and understandings of masculinity, race, sexuality, and class.

I want to conclude this chapter by drawing attention to the notion of performance. Much of these shows' critique of masculinity is made clear by the overt nature of the cast members' performances. That is, the boys on these shows remind the audience that it is watching the performance and production of multiple modes of white masculinity. In India, Steve-O interacts with an Indian face piercer, who pierces his cheek every day with a long needle. Steve-O, of course, chooses to pierce his own cheek. Moaning and yelling in pain, he pushes the needle into his cheek while the cameraman tells him to turn his head so that he can get a better view of the process. Steve-O moans, "Is it cool?" The cameraman eggs him on, and Steve-O goes bug-eyed. "Does it look cool?" he asks again. "You guys suck so bad." Having given up his face in the service of this hypermasculine display of "native" daring and the shocking and television-worthy exoticism so mundanely deemed cool, Steve-O makes explicit the ongoing construction of masculine identities and cultural cool. In the same moment, he has also constructed himself as willing to reveal his susceptibility, man enough to take such pain and white enough to take on the Indian man's ways. It is in such multiply inflected performances throughout the Dickhouse oeuvre that whiteness, masculinity, and sexuality are all destabilized, demonstrated to be tenuous and malleable. Concomitantly, however, these identities' boundaries are reinforced as they are placed in relationship to blackness, homoeroticism, and the working class. As I have noted, these contradictory relationships are present throughout skateboarding culture, particularly in the niche videos I examine in the following chapter.

"It's just what's possible"

Imagining Alternative Masculinities and Performing White Male Dominance in Niche Skateboarding Videos

Fiddling with a cup of coffee as he stared pensively out of Starbucks' window at the groups of university students walking down the street, a 16-year-old skateboarder, Jack, reflected on the pleasures of watching skateboarding videos.

> It just kind of inspires you like, I don't know, just seeing what [the featured skateboarders] do, during the cold winters and stuff, just to see their style. How it's so effortless and graceful, and beautiful. You just look at it. It's just like, I don't know, it's just like watching people who are really, really good at skating, it's just like, you know, like what's possible, you know. It's just fun. Better than TV!

Jack's comments, delivered with quiet emotion and conveying a sense of awe, exemplify skateboarders' devotion to the myriad industry and independently produced skateboarding videos that highlight professional and local skateboarders' skills, document their everyday lives, and offer a sense of their personalities. More, his tone stands in stark contrast to the irreverence of the Dickhouse productions. Invoking grace and beauty, as well as physical talent and aspiration ("what's possible"), Jack's passionate explanation brings to light the multiple pleasures that skate videos produce. While physical prowess and achievement are certainly part of dominant codes of masculinity, an appreciation for grace and beauty are not. In this way, skateboarding videos open space in which boys can give expression to types of pleasure that are normatively off-limits. Skateboarding videos are not how-to videos, "greatest hit" compilations, or taped coverage of skateboarding contests. Rather, they are videos produced by niche skateboarding companies to highlight the skills and lifestyles of skateboarders. Numerous and widely varied in their aesthetics and tone, they are highly similar in form. Each 30- to 60-minute video is segmented into song-length montages of individual skateboarders skating through numerous public and private spaces throughout the "developed" world: parking lots, city parks, loading docks, city sidewalks, and skate parks.[1] Using a variety of lenses and film formats, multiple camera angles, and jump-cut and continuous editing, the montages operate to define each skateboarder's—and company's—sense of "style," which loosely refers to his or her identity and attitude toward skateboarding or the world at large.[2] A skater's—and a video's—style can take a variety of forms: expressive, artistic, aggressive, laid back, and so on. As Michael Nevin Willard explains in his ethnographic study with professional skateboarder Rodney Mullen, "the 'feeling' of a video is crucial . . . [as] when there aren't as many contests to differentiate skaters," style serves to individualize and distinguish their personalities.[3] Most skateboarding videos also include "slam scenes" (images of the skateboarders falling), as well as "skits" and "lifestyle scenes," which are scripted and caught-on-tape images of the skateboarders when they are not skating that are meant to represent the skateboarders' personalities and styles.

Although skate videos are produced by the skateboarding industry as promotional materials for their products, they are widely regarded by skateboarders as "authentic," and their representation of individual skateboarders' various identities signifies this authenticity for the audience. In fact, the videos are so firmly regarded as a "true" element of skateboarding culture that many amateur skateboarders produce their own short versions of skate videos (approximately 3 to 10 minutes long) as representations of their "unique" identities. Often called "sponsor-me tapes," a moniker signaling the fact that the amateur tapes are sometimes sent to skate companies as auditions for employment as professional skaters, these videos are usually just shown to friends in the relative privacy of their own homes or the skate shops.[4] Sometimes operating as stand-alone documents of individual skaters' skills, the "footage" is also contributed to local skate shops' composite videos.[5]

Taken together, these videos comprise what I call "documents of iden-

tity," which define the boundaries of skateboarding culture and the individuals participating in it. A central element of the culture, skateboarding
videos mediate the personae of both professional and amateur skateboarders, exhibit the generally accepted and sometimes celebrated practices of
skateboarders both on and off their boards, highlight the cultural forms and
styles associated with skateboarding culture, and display the aesthetic pref-
erences of the culture. Stated more simply, skateboarding videos work to
define skateboarding culture; they tell skateboarders who they are. Sponsor-me tapes are developed in dialogue with skate videos and operate to
define individual skateboarders and claim individual skaters' identity and
place within the larger skateboarding culture and community.

Skateboarding videos and skateboarders' responses to them reveal that
this culture contends with identity, particularly notions of masculinity, in a
highly contradictory manner that both challenges and upholds hegemonic
masculinity. Specifically, both skate videos and skateboarders reject the
identity norms and responsibilities associated with middle-class, white,
adult men and uphold a highly individuated ideal of masculinity purportedly
open to multiple forms or expressions of it, including expressions that are
emotionally sensitive and expressive, centered on corporeal pleasure, or
noncompetitive. In actuality, skateboarding videos actively work to exclude
nonheterosexual expressions of masculinity and use nonwhite masculinity
to uphold the power of white masculinity.

Sean Brayton has made a similar argument in his analysis of skateboarding media, though he focuses on skateboarding magazines. Arguing that
"skateboard media repudiates middle-class whiteness only to replace it with a
rejuvenated heteromasculinity that is often informed by a black other," Brayton compares skateboarding texts to beat narratives such as Jack Kerouac's
On the Road, which celebrate the joys of independence over the banality of
suburban conformity.[6] He posits that "a physical and symbolic flight from
conformity is predicated on a departure from middle-class whiteness."[7] His
work skillfully reveals the way in which skate culture both critiques buttoned-
up images of middle-class whiteness and basks in the privileges it affords to
move through public space free of harassment, to engage in leisure activities,
and to rebel without fear of violent recrimination.

Skateboarders, in the images of the videos, either never grow up or grow
up to support heterosexual families via fulfilling and creative work. These

content videos

images position skateboarders against a highly traditional conceptualization of white, middle-class, adult masculinity characterized in the 1950s by the organization man and represented today in images of cubicle apathy in *Dilbert, Office Space, Fight Club,* and *The Office.*[8] Brayton notes that "skateboard texts often parody the perceived emasculation of middle-class white men by the corporate world."[9] This is the image of the responsible, middle-management individual working simply to support his family, suffering daily through mindless work, clueless bosses, and neurotic coworkers.[10] Implicit in the rejection of organization men and the endorsement of individual, multiple masculinities is a critique of traditional images of white masculinity as hyperrational, aggressive, physically dominant, and emotionally reticent. In opposition to this image of adult masculinity, skateboard videos and skateboarders present two alternatives: the perpetual Peter Pan and the independent entrepreneur and family man.

Skateboarding videos' critiques of hyperrational and controlled masculinity, however, do not translate into the practice of producing amateur videos. Rather, skateboarders approach this process with a great deal of care, carefully considering the formal norms portrayed in professional videos and rigorously choosing appropriate footage and accompanying music. Many southeastern Michigan skateboarders have high-level digital video and editing equipment at their disposal either in their own or friend's personal computers or at work or school. This equipment affords skaters the opportunity to produce professional-level videos. Rather than adopting the cut-and-paste, do-it-yourself (DIY) aesthetic found in the "micromedia" of punk culture, for example, skateboarders use this equipment to make videos that can blend almost seamlessly with those that are industry produced.[11]

Documents of Masculinity: Individualized Collectivity, Hegemonic Masculinity, and Perpetual Peter Pans

Unlike the advertising industry and mass media, which generally represent skateboarding as a competitive sport or the domain of slacker/stoner male teenagers, skateboarding videos render the practice and culture as an individualized collectivity in which young men may reap the rewards of hegemonic masculinity while at the same time rejecting those norms of masculinity deemed restrictive, unappealing, or inauthentic. Highly homosocial documents, these videos actively exclude women and girls while simultaneously suggesting that male skateboarders, *as long as they are heterosexual,* can choose to perform any identity and inhabit any space they wish. Skateboarding videos construct a fantastic world in which white male adolescents can live as perpetual Peter Pans, mocking bourgeois norms of white masculinity as embodied by adults and in turn living lives unencumbered by limitations of hegemonic whiteness and masculinity or male and female adult authority. What's more, skateboarding videos' content and form strategically suggest that the world depicted on the screen is a world available to skateboarders everywhere.

Individualized Collectivity and Multiple Masculinities

Montages of both individuals and groups of skateboarders are the central form in skate videos. By both highlighting the individual style of each skateboarder and blending them together in group montages, the videos suggest that skateboarding is a culture that highly values individuality while at the same time promising the benefits of cooperation and inclusion in a larger group. As I have noted, southeastern Michigan skateboarders value this individualized collectivity in their everyday lives, pointing to skateboarding's cooperative nature and its acceptance of varied forms of masculinity as part of its appeal. Strongly valuing individuality, skate life comprises an idealized space for the individual that also ignores larger social concerns and the ways in which society is structured by various economic, educational, and social institutions. That is, skateboarding videos echo and reinforce skate culture's rather apolitical concentration on individual skateboarders' well-being to the detriment of a more broad-based cultural, political, or social critique.

It is through this highly individualized form that skateboarders respond to their nascent critiques of hegemonic masculinity as restrictive, overly competitive, and lacking in emotional and bodily expression. Despite the utter absence of structural critique or organized protest, it is important to take seriously these boys' burgeoning dissatisfaction with traditional masculinity, for it reveals the changing standpoint of young men as well as the ways in which hegemonic masculinity may reassert itself. As R. W. Connell reminds us, a particular cultural moment's expression of hegemonic masculinity—the mode of masculinity that maintains men's power—constantly shifts in response to criticism.[12] Furthermore, by taking these boys' ideas seriously we can reveal the changing modes of what subcultural theorists call "resistance." As I have argued, subcultural theorists too often take resistance for granted, defining it very loosely without examining the particular modes of resistance or identifying the particular objects of resistance taken on by particular subcultures. Here, I assert that skateboarders are resisting hegemonic masculinity in a manner that does not disrupt men's power but shifts the demands of adolescent masculinity.

As I have noted, each skate video features individual and group montages and lifestyle scenes. While the individual montages and scenes highlight individual skateboarders' personalities and lifestyles, the group montages and particulars of the individual montages suggest that the differences between individuals are vastly unimportant and sublimated by the norms of the group. In fact, only the highly trained eye can discern individual skateboarders during each montage, and even individual skateboarders' montages frequently include guests. The videos' focus on the practice of skateboarding, with their low camera angles (often focused on the feet and board) and quick segments, draws the viewer's eye away from the distinguishing features of each skateboarder. As such, viewers must be accustomed to an individual skateboarders' style, as well as highly familiar with his appearance, in order to accurately and consistently identify him.

This is not to suggest that the videos fail to distinguish between skateboarders. As I have noted, each individual on a skateboarding team is highlighted at some point during the video, and during their individual sections skateboarders' names are displayed on title screens. Even the uninitiated viewer is given a sense of each skater's personality via the lifestyle scenes. For example, in Enjoi skateboarding company's *Bag of Suck*, an industry-produced video, professional skateboarder Caswell Berry's part is introduced with a montage of him jumping into the air and landing sitting down on his skateboard. In many of these segments, Berry breaks his board, but in the final section the board does not break, and he yells "Bastard!" The video then segues into his skateboarding, which is set to the relatively aggressive tone of Dead Prez's song "Hip Hop." In contrast, professional skater Louie Barletta's segment in the same video opens with a reverse-edited shot of him jumping onto his skateboard, which breaks and then miraculously fixes itself. Barletta then falls off his board and laughs hysterically. The next scene shows him at a house party wearing a smart grey suit and mugging for the camera. "Hey, I'm Louie. I'm a Taurus!" he introduces himself in a goofy voice. Even a cursory reading suggests that Caswell Berry is being presented as an aggressive skateboarder while Louie Barletta is to be perceived as a silly, fun-loving guy. Despite their different personalities (and arguably different approaches to masculinity), these two skateboarders are presented as equally important members of the team.

Although an individualistic collectivity may be present in many representations of sports, particularly as sports coverage moves to a focus on individual players,[13] notions of personality and lifestyle are preeminent in skateboarding. The skateboarders wear apparel provided by their sponsoring companies, but they do not wear uniforms that designate them as members of a team, and their success in the sport does not contribute to the success of a team in the quantifiable manner that a particular basketball player's ability to sink baskets does. Although the skateboarders "need" their sponsoring companies in order to make a living, they do not need their teammates as other sports enthusiasts do. Furthermore, the development of personae for individual skateboarders is couched as absolutely natural; because of the subcultural requirement for authenticity, any hint of a manufactured persona is detrimental to a skateboarder's popularity. As identity, personality, and persona blur in the representation of individual skateboarders in the videos, it seems as if skateboarders can adopt a wide variety of masculinities—aggressive, artistic, serious, or silly—while maintaining their acceptance in the culture. In a culture where personality rules, such acceptance is a critical element.

Authentic Individuals

As identity documents in a corresponding culture that sometimes prides itself on its difference from a monolithic "mainstream," skate videos must be situated incontestably within the "authentic" boundaries of the culture. They cannot, that is, appear to be created in the name of anything but the advancement of skateboarding as a practice or the pure pleasure of it. Skate videos cannot be overtly about making money, asserting dominance, or showing off; they must be of the culture and for the culture.

Skateboarding videos employ a variety of signifiers of authenticity in their portrayal of an individualistic collectivity. While the skateboarding montages are highly produced, the lifestyle scenes simulate home video or "caught-on-tape" footage. Depicting skateboarders in their "natural" settings—hanging out on the sidewalk, in skate shops, at home, and at parties—these images are often shaky, poorly lit, and feature ambient noise that overpowers the audio track. It is nothing new to suggest that these unprofessional qualities signify "reality" to viewers; however, these realities are authentic for skateboarders only in relation to the videos' other signifiers of authenticity.

Throughout most skateboarding videos, one can hear skateboarders cheering during their friends' successes and moaning in pain during their failures. We also see skateboarders engaging in seemingly spontaneous pranks, dumping flour on a sleeping friend's head, for example, and bursting into peals of laughter. These scenes also include "man on the street" encounters in which skateboarders are depicted chatting with various characters they meet while skateboarding. These characters are often homeless men, street performers, or children, and the professional skateboarders talk with them, giving them a chance to expose their eccentricities, and frequently burst into laughter. These encounters serve two key purposes: (1) they shore up skateboarders' power, authority, and superiority; and (2) they suggest that everything that happens in the videos is spontaneous and could happen to anyone. In other words, these encounters are meant to evoke the experiences with public and street figures that many skateboarders have had while playing in public. Professional skaters, then, seem to be everyday people engaging in skateboarding culture in much the same way that all skaters might.

Most of the images in skateboarding montages are in stark contrast to the lifestyle scenes. Highly professional, the montages are characterized by professional lighting, complex camera angles, steady-cam footage, and seamless editing. Though such professional-quality work could signify that the practice of skateboarding is solely a performance for the camera—and thus inauthentic—the combination of images and music is compelling enough to easily draw the viewer into the world of the featured skater: they bring the viewer along for the ride. The videos visually assert the joys of skateboarding, and so even these professionally edited montages are about the individual experience of pleasure rather than the outwardly directed performance of physical skill. The frequent use of the fish-eye (extremely wide angle) lens reimagines public spaces in a curvy, almost carnivalesque manner. These spaces become playful, open, and new through the camera lens. Furthermore, regular low-angle shots draw the viewers' eyes up and into the action of the skateboarder, making the viewer feel as if he is experiencing what is on the screen.

Not all of the videos employ such high production values. Some skateboarding montages make the process of production evident. The crew sometimes uses handheld cameras, which skateboarders crash into, and we sometimes see other camera operators in the scenes. These videos, in other words, do not work to maintain the "fourth wall" of fictional, narrative-based television and film. The very fact of letting the production gear show heightens the reality effect and the comprehensibility of these videos; the spectators "get it" and can imagine making such videos on their own. This belief, in turn, allows viewers to imagine the production of skate videos as an authentic element of their own lives. In their own way, that is, these images draw the viewer into the world on the screen and proclaim that world's authenticity.

Most skate videos include "slam montages" or "slam scenes" in which the skateboarders are depicted falling. These scenes work to several ends. First, they highlight the difficulty, the challenge, of skateboarding, demonstrating that skateboarders take bodily risks that might be described as "gnarly," aka "tough" and "manly." Many videos include skateboarders thrusting bloodied hands toward the camera, showing off dislocated fingers, and grimacing at temporarily deformed knees. Second, the slam scenes make it clear that the skateboarding on the screen is real, that it has not been produced using stunt performers or trick photography, and that the skateboarders have had to work hard to achieve the level of skateboarding depicted. Closely related to this last point is the third: slam montages present professional skateboarders as real and fallible. They are not supermen of the skateboarding world; pro skaters simply work hard, endure physical pain, and try and try again to achieve their skating prowess. They are, in sum, just like us.

Finally, pro skaters move through knowable space. The locations depicted on skate videos range from the mundane to the mythic, but they are always "real," recognizable locations that are often archetypal and always nominally accessible to all. Pros engage in skateboarding in parking lots, near schools, in front of courthouses, on loading docks, in front of businesses, and in their homes. They also utilize skate parks, some of which are "famous" within the skateboarding world, and go to locations famed for their perfect obstacles and cool scenes. One such location is Love Park in Philadelphia, the home of Robert Indiana's iconic "Love Stamp" monument.[14] This mythic space is revered by skateboarders for its once permissive attitude toward their practice, its host of engaging obstacles, and the number of skateboarders in the park. When depicted on the screen, it signals viewers, inviting them into a knowable and accessible world.

Borrowed Legitimacy: "Multiculturalism" and Skateboarding's Culture of Cool

Most professional skate videos feature multicultural casts that include white, African American, Latino, and Asian skateboarders. Although these casts may be a product of both skateboarding's international scope and its primary location in California, they also serve to construct skate culture as modern, hip, and dynamic. Because of the highly varied nature of skate videos' content, it is impossible to produce a definitive analysis of their representation of race. However, in the following paragraphs I offer a discussion of two videos that can be thought of as opposite ends of the spectrum. The first, *The DC Video*, produced by the DC shoe and apparel company, a subsidiary of Quiksilver, draws on "ghetto" imagery to shore up its characters' coolness. The second, *Hallowed Ground*, produced by Hurley International, presents a thoughtful tour through Brazilian culture that nonetheless uses that culture to reinforce the authenticity of the skaters on the screen.

The differences between the videos can be read as artifacts and signifiers of their producers' brand identities, which are presented most clearly through the personae of their star skateboarders. As a company, DC has taken on a fairly mainstream status, sponsoring major events such as the X Games and advertising on MTV, but it manages to maintain some of its subcultural credibility. The brand presents itself as urban, and its shoes and clothing retain some signifiers of urban sporting culture, such as oversized jerseys and overstuffed white sneakers. The brand's primary personality, professional skateboarder Rob Dyrdek, has gained recent mainstream attention in the MTV show *Rob and Big*, which was spun off the personae developed in *The DC Video*. Rob Dyrdek is aligned closely with hip-hop music and culture, adopting hip-hop (read black) *and* working class signifiers such as heavy gold chains, oversized clothing, "trucker" hats, and scruffy facial hair. He exhibits the flexibility of whiteness in his adoption of black and working-class signifiers.[15]

Hurley International has not developed the clearly identifiable brand identity possessed by DC, though it has recently acquired mainstream status due to its sale to Nike. Originally a surfing company, Hurley products can readily be found at popular suburban malls in stores that capitalize on subcultures such as Hot Topic. Still, like DC, it has managed to maintain some credibility. Its public celebrity, professional skateboarder Bob Burnquist, dominates the *Hallowed Ground* video, and the video can be read as an expression of his persona rather than a particular identity attributable to Hurley's image. Burnquist is a white Brazilian who immigrated to the United States in order to pursue his career as a professional skateboarder (he was "discovered" in Brazil). Although he does not enjoy the same mainstream recognizability as Tony Hawk, Burnquist has become a recognizable character within the niche culture of skateboarding that includes *The X Games* and MTV's *Cribs*. Burnquist has constructed himself as an environmentalist and family man. Along with his wife, the professional skateboarder Jen O'Brien, Burnquist owns an organic farm and is raising a young daughter, Lotus. Burnquist and O'Brien also founded the Action Sports Environmental Coalition in order to promote environmentally sustainable practices in action sports events such as the X Games. His Brazilian heritage is well known, and we are meant to understand that he is a skater with a social conscience. Clearly, the elements of this persona have worked their way into *Hallowed Ground.* The video does not make explicit that as a white Brazilian Burnquist probably enjoyed a relative level of cultural mobility not available to all Brazilians. Both Burnquist's persona and *Hallowed Ground*'s tone, then, portray cultural, racial, and class difference while smoothing over the issues of power crucial to understanding such difference.

The DC Video attempts to present skateboarding culture, and the DC brand in particular, as "hip" to hip-hop culture and, perhaps more insidiously, urban, working-class culture. That is, *The DC Video* suggests that skateboarders experience discrimination by authority figures that is quite similar to the discrimination felt by black teenagers, particularly young black men. Like an advertisement for skateboard wheels analyzed by Sean

Brayton, this video "relies on references to street culture in general and the 'ghetto' in particular to signify the skater's distance from middle-class sensibilities."[16] The video's representation of black skateboarder Stevie Williams begins with a montage of scenes from North Philadelphia, including run-down townhomes and garbage-strewn streets. At the end of his skateboarding segment, Williams punches his fist toward the screen to reveal a DC pinky ring and then juts his chin toward the camera. Clearly, the viewer is meant to conclude that Williams is a product of the Philadelphia underclass who has a street-smart, aggressive attitude. Whether or not this conclusion is accurate, it may convey two important ideas. On the one hand, it attempts to present a black skateboarder as a product of authentic black culture. On the other hand, particularly given the absence of other black skateboarders on the screen, it simply reinforces stereotypes of African Americans as aggressive products of the ghetto.

The DC Video also presents African Americans as employees of white skateboarders. After a long montage during which skateboarders are portrayed clashing with various security guards and policemen, Rob Dyrdek turns to the camera and says, "I'm sick of cops, I'm sick of security guards. Okay, from here on out, I'm bringing a security guard to deal with security guards, cops, I'm over it." Dyrdek carries out his promise by hiring an African American man simply called Big Black. The video then features a skit during which Big Black is "interviewed," telling the audience, "I do the dirty work." The interview and accompanying montage of images suggest that Big Black works to make skateboarding more convenient for Dyrdek, not only fending off security guards but also preparing concrete curbs with skateboarding wax, shooing away autograph seekers, and acting as Rob's friend and confidant.[17] Dyrdek not only adopts the accoutrements of hip-hop culture—frequently wearing oversized DC sports jerseys and large white sneakers while listening to hip-hop music—but he also adopts a "Big Black" friend who operates to bring Rob both physical security and cultural authenticity.

Between Rob Dyrdek and Stevie Williams, then, DC aligns its privileged, corporate identity with an underprivileged and disenfranchised—but still street-smart and cool—image of black culture. In this way, the video suggests that skateboarding culture is authentic and worthy of attention. That is, according to this logic, skateboarding culture is not the development of a corporate world interested only in profit; rather, it is a group of oppressed individuals simply trying to make their way in a hostile world. By adopting images and signs of the "ghetto" or black culture, *The DC Video* legitimates itself via the borrowed authenticity of cultural subordination. Whether or not it is represented at all, the life of African Americans becomes a series of stylistic signifiers rather than a location where relationships of power must be examined and critiqued. By letting its spectators off the hook—by allowing the audience to experience black culture as a lifestyle choice—the videos' adoption of black culture, what bell hooks would call "eating the other," serves to shore up the power of white masculinity.[18] That is, white spectators can continue to choose various modes of masculinity, including black masculinity, in the "supermarket of bodies" and personae made available through skate videos.[19] White spectators, then, can bask in the freedom of choice and accept the borrowed legitimacy of blackness while ignoring racial inequality and subordination.

Hallowed Ground, on the other hand, presents a more sympathetic and rounded image of racial difference, though, somewhat unsurprisingly, this difference is filtered through its international scope and differences in nationality seem to trump differences in race. Because Bob Burnquist, who hails from Rio de Janeiro, reads visually as white and aurally as American, his "difference" can only be signified via culture and so can be signified at will.

Hallowed Ground's title screen presents it as "A Hurley International skateboarding documentary." The video offers itself as a trip through its skateboarders' histories, a glimpse into their personal and family lives. As such, it makes great use of confessional lifestyle scenes that employ documentary images of the skateboarders' hometowns. For example, when the Brazilian skateboarder Lincoln Ueda is introduced, his voice-over intones, "It's always good to go back home, back to Brazil. Because, uh, now that I have a nephew, it's a totally different feeling of life. I remember skating three to four different ramps, that's it. And all cement." The montage of black and white and color images depicts Ueda hugging his father, women in a small sewing factory, and Ueda holding a child's hand. We also see a large half-pipe ramp covered with graffiti in the middle of a field with a large puddle in it. These images convey not only a sense of poverty (particularly the women sewing and the graffiti-covered ramp) but also a sense of familial happiness. Despite his poverty, these images suggest, Lincoln Ueda grew up in a close-knit, happy family. Although it is not made clear in the video, the director's comments on the DVD reveal that the women are employees of a small sewing factory owned by Ueda's mother and that his father owns a motor repair shop. While such ownership may not make his family upper class, it is clear that they are not in poverty. Such knowledge makes the implied poverty of the images that much more disingenuous.

Later, as a different skateboarder moves through Brazil eating a tostada, a voice-over marvels, "There's too many things that can go wrong, growing up where he did. And if you don't have an exit, an escape, you really end up just going down a path that you shouldn't follow. It's really amazing and it shows a lot of personality on his part and I am very proud of him. I thank God for skateboarding." This skateboarder, moving through the sites of his upbringing, is presented as a member of the Brazilian underclass who was lucky enough to have found a way out. The specter of poverty and a life of crime or worse ("a path that you shouldn't follow") serves not to examine the social inequalities producing such circumstances but to invest the skateboarder with authenticity. Although *Hallowed Ground* attempts to present the nuances of a particular culture and to imagine nationality and class as determining factors in its skateboarders' histories, it still utilizes these histories to trumpet the authenticity of skateboarding culture and professional skateboarders.

As I have noted, George Yudice has suggested that men in profeminist groups end up resorting to assertions of oppression in an attempt to justify their claims on identity.[20] Still, Yudice asserts, "The argument that men are donning the mantle of victimhood for the sake of maintaining hegemony, however, is not fully explanatory, especially in the case of progressive, profeminist men."[21] Arguably, skateboarding videos use claims of difference to instill their brands and skateboarders with an authentic and recognizable identity, and for all we know these skaters did experience poverty and were otherwise deprived of the power enjoyed by white, American, middle-class, straight men. Although skateboarders do not present themselves as profeminist (and, in fact, far from profeminist, their culture serves to exclude women), I would also contend that the maintenance of hegemony is not fully explanatory. Rather, this adolescent subculture's valorization of authenticity, paired with the authenticity (or legitimacy) bestowed on subordinated groups and American culture's denial of unequal power relations, operates to make such claims understandable. As Robert Goldman and Stephen Papson note, "Middle-class culture defines authenticity as a state of individual, social, and cultural integrity originating from the conditions of existence in everyday life," and as such the economic strife of working-class and black cultures serves to make them commodifiable as authentic.[22] Of course, race and class have been dissolved into decontextualized signifiers through this process; the histories and power relations associated with these identities are never addressed, particularly in *The DC Video*.

Although they operate somewhat differently, taken together the videos' erasure of racial identity and the strategic employment of difference as authenticity in an individualized collectivity suggest that identity is constructed through lifestyle, that lifestyle—and culture—can be put on and taken off at will, and that it is acceptance and tolerance of these differences that reign supreme rather than a collective examination of structural differences in power. Again, such a highly individualistic stance serves to create a location of choice for white heterosexual skateboarders while ignoring the relations of power that subordinate nonwhites. As I have noted, such individualism is somewhat unsurprising in twenty-first-century American youth culture in that it aligns easily with American culture more generally; however, what is interesting are the ways in which these videos present themselves as an alternative to mainstream ways of thinking.

Skate videos' individualized collectivity is important because it permeates them and operates as the ethos under which they document masculine identity. In other words, while the videos mock some tenets of hegemonic masculinity and subscribe to others, they more generally suggest that anything goes, that skateboarders can be any type of men they wish as long as they do not impose their views on others or force others to occupy a particular masculinity. As such, although skateboarders assert in a rather opaque way that a central tenet of skateboarding is respect for multiple masculinities, their culture and cultural products make this claim in an individualistic, apolitical manner. This is not about social change but about finding a space in which individual idiosyncrasies and multiple masculinities are accepted, though within certain boundaries.

Homosocial Heterosexuality and Hypermasculinity

Although it is generally left unstated and even denied, the most crucial boundary for the exploration of various masculinities is a subscription to homosocial heterosexuality. Homosocial heterosexuality is characterized by a boys-only culture wherein boys sometimes interact with one another through playful touch while actively asserting their heterosexuality and masculine dominance through the exclusion and mockery of homosexuality and women. To be clear, this claim is not meant to suggest that female and gay skateboarders do not exist, nor that all gay skateboarders are closeted. Rather, I wish to assert strongly that skateboarding culture operates systematically to exclude, or at least make entry difficult for, most women and most homosexuals. Furthermore, these exclusions operate to produce an exclusionary modality of masculinity; that is, despite their denial of such exclusions, it is clear that skateboarders are expected to assert their dominance over women and their suspicion of homosexuality in order to maintain their place in the culture. In fact, although the videos seem to allow multiple expressions of masculinity, the images in them frequently revert to hypermasculine representations that operate to mitigate the more introspective or artistic representations of the culture. Taken together, homophobia and hypermasculinity serve to shore up the heterosexuality of skateboarding culture even in a homosocial context where homoeroticism is sometimes allowed and even encouraged.

Skateboarding videos generally represent a culture from which women are absent and men are revered. Only one of the five professional videos I analyzed included a female skateboarder, and her presence lasted less than the length of one song and was confined to one individual montage of her skateboarding. In contrast, the male skateboarders in these videos usually enjoy the exposure of at least one song-length montage as well as highlights throughout the videos. The lone featured female was Alexis Sablone in *P. J. Ladd's Wonderful, Horrible Life* (2002). Notably, *Hallowed Ground*, which devotes much of its time to the prominent skateboarder Bob Burnquist, also includes in its footage professional skateboarder Jen O'Brien. Rather than being presented as a pro skater, however, Jen is only defined as Bob Burnquist's wife and his child's mother. She is portrayed holding their young daughter, Lotus, while she sits on a skateboard at the top of a ramp. We never see O'Brien riding on her skateboard let alone performing the tricks of which she is capable. Only extratextual knowledge reveals her professional status.

Although women in general are excluded from the videos, they may make a rare appearance as authorities (teachers or mothers) or sexual objects. Skateboarder Caswell Berry's title screen in *Bag of Suck* features a shot of him lying on a bed, torso bared, with a woman on each side of him. One woman holds a cigarette in his mouth while the other uses a container of whipped cream to finish spelling his name on his body. An image of total male heterosexual decadence, the absurdity of this sketch also works to mock such hypermasculine images. In fact, at the end of the film an outtake features the two women smearing the whipped cream all over Berry and laughing; this scene is decidedly not sexual but silly. The women are laughing loudly, not giggling flirtatiously, and they are frenetically smearing the whipped cream on Berry, not lovingly caressing his chest. *Bag of Suck* also concludes with a small drawing of a woman, blue in the face from choking herself and wearing a sweatshirt that reads "Hairdiaper Cameltoe." This misogynistic mockery of a woman's genitals, paired with the woman's self-inflicted oxygen deprivation, actively works to exclude women in its violence and cruelty. Furthermore, it suggests to skateboarders that such misogynistic imagery is funny, harmless, and worthy of inclusion in representations of their culture. Skater boys, then, are encouraged to participate in such humor and to position themselves in opposition to women.

The videos are also homophobic, although the expressions of homophobia are not as explicitly violent as the expressions of misogyny and are presented in a more seemingly banal, playful manner. Given their propensity toward gross-out humor, their misogyny, and their hypermasculinity, the use of the epithet *fag* is notably absent from the five videos I review here, but this absence should not imply tolerance for homosexuality. Furthermore, the videos do assert what Adrienne Rich has famously deemed "compulsory heterosexuality."[23] From *Hallowed Ground*'s reverence for skateboarders' families and procreation to the focus on the phallus in both *P. J. Ladd's Wonderful Horrible Life* and *Bag of Suck*—at various moments, the skateboarders and cameramen hold their skateboards and camera equipment to their crotches—the videos present heterosexuality as the desired norm.[24] *The DC Video* mocks the possibility of a sexual relationship between skateboarder

Rob Dyrdek and his "security guard" Big Black, who jokes, "We went to the movies last week. We watched that new Kate Hudson flick. *Ten Things I Miss about You* or something like that. We wanted to go check that out. We go to a lot of movies. Share a slurpie." The "chick flick" and the seemingly innocent sharing of the slurpie (and its attendant sexual—though adolescent—overtones) present Rob and Big as a couple, and Big's goofy, off-the-cuff remark makes it clear that homosexual relationships (or even boys' outings that can be too easily construed as a date) are decidedly effeminate. Not overtly or violently homophobic, this remark nonetheless privileges heterosexuality and uses even implied homosexuality as a source of laughter.

Beyond these attempts to characterize their same-sex relationships as social and nothing else, the videos are careful to valorize hypermasculine images. Their expressions of gender and sexuality are inextricably linked: homophobia, hypermasculinity, and misogyny work hand in hand to uphold the skateboarders' normative identities and place limits on the range of masculinities acceptable within the culture. *Bag of Suck* opens with the adage "Pain is weakness leaving the body" and features several shots of skateboarders or cameramen holding cameras as phalluses next to their crotches. *P. J. Ladd's Wonderful Horrible Life* frequently represents its skateboarders wrestling with one another and giving each other "wedgies" (pulling one's underwear over his head) and "swirlies" (dunking one's head in toilet water and flushing). A young fan in this video takes such physical hypermasculinity to the next level, telling the camera, "I want them to attempt something so dangerous, something so cool that it would threaten their life." In *The DC Video*, skateboarding star Danny Way tells the audience, from his hospital bed, "It's not the glorious life you think we all live. . . . Gotta pay to play."

Each of these scenes is accomplished with a level of irony that suggests the boys know that they are engaging in hypermasculine behavior designed to prove both their gender and their sexuality. Like Steve-O and Chris Pontius, the skateboarders frequently follow their hypermasculine remarks with knowing glances at the camera and self-deprecating laughter. Extratextual knowledge of skate life also suggests that claims such as "Pain is weakness leaving the body" are to be mocked, as I have demonstrated repeatedly. Although skateboarding is a physically demanding and pain-inducing activity, skateboarders constantly make fun of masochistic rituals designed to shore up masculinity. Danny Way's tone of voice—dry and mocking—and his facial expression, complete with rolling eyes, imbue his "glorious life" remark with sarcasm. Way's presentation is particularly interesting; shot in a hospital bed here, he is usually portrayed as fearless and physically unstoppable.

Skateboarders do participate in hypermasculine displays, and skate videos suggest that the boys can do whatever they want whenever they want. *The DC Video*, in particular, presents the life of the skateboarder as epic. In this video, "big air" skateboarder Danny Way demonstrates his prowess on a larger-than-life skateboarding ramp by breaking two world records: the longest jump on a skateboard (75 feet) and highest air (23.5 feet). Aerial shots of the ramp demonstrate its impressive size, and the images make it seem as though Way is skateboarding on it all by himself out of pure dedication rather than for adoration. Low and high angles, sweeping shots, and slow motion all make his skateboarding appear heroic. In other words, the camera functions to objectify Way as larger than life, to inspire awe, and to magnify the displayed feats of physicality. More than silly boys participating ironically in hypermasculine shenanigans, these images suggest, skateboarders are heroic men cut out for daring physical feats.

Most of the skateboarders did not discuss the portrayals of gender and sexuality in skate videos with one notable exception. Nineteen-year-old Jeff, who is openly gay and works in the skate shop, provided valuable insights into skate culture's identity politics. After I asked him, "What do you think skateboarding videos say about young men?" he responded:

Sometimes kind of negative. Some things bug me. Some attitudes in skateboarding that are somewhat diminishing but not fully diminishing—that I don't care for. Until recently, magazines had antigay attitudes and things like that. It's gotten a bit better. A magazine recently printed something like, "You can be any race, gender, or sexual orientation, and be a skateboarder. Just don't be an Insane Clown Posse fan." There's a gay issue of [the skate magazine] *Big Brother*. It's kind of like *Will and Grace*. They'll bring the topic up, but not like you think they should, but still positive in some way. Might be stereotyping, but not saying "gay" and "fag" and stuff like that. I've put the veto on that in the skate shop. I don't want to hear that or for customers to say that. It can be a touchy subject. . . . There's definitely some jock mentality in skateboarding—calling out things you're going to do. "Oh man, watch this one!" Aggression, completion of a task rather than just doing it for the fun of it. *King of the Road* videos represent the jock mentality. They make out with a girl who's like 5 years older, 10 years older, 25 years older. There's definitely a heterosexual pervasiveness. Hubba Wheels has an image of a kid with his teeth on a girl's thong. It's a by-product of guys being guys, and most guys are straight. It's a guys' culture, and that's what's gonna happen.

I quote Jeff at length because his discussion of identity politics reveals the contradictions that pervade skate culture. Skate culture is generally homophobic, but some publications have begun to push against that homophobia, though not in an entirely meaningful way. Skateboarders repeatedly proclaim that they are not jocks, but their actions still demonstrate masculine and heterosexual dominance. Still, Jeff does not seem to even see the possibility for systemic change; in fact, he characterizes skate culture's homophobia and sexism as natural: "It's a guys' culture, and that's what's gonna happen."

Notably, one of Jeff's favorite videos is *Bag of Suck*. Although I have showcased its heterosexism, Jeff characterized the video as a friendly portrayal of skateboarders with excellent (and nonnormative) music choices such as Etta James, a Sonic Youth cover of the Carpenters, and "Coma Girl" by Joe Strummer and the Mescaleros. This music deviates from the punk, hip-hop, heavy metal, and rock usually present in skate videos. Moreover, he said, the video has "a friendly vibe" and "they seem nice, like they're a close-knit group, which can just make a great addition to the overall cohesiveness of a skate video." Although Jeff is critical of the politics of skate culture as a whole, he still deems *Bag of Suck* "one of the best videos ever."

Perpetual Peter Pans

At the same time that they elevate the physical prowess of hegemonic masculinity, skateboarding videos present skateboarders as perpetual Peter Pans wary of the norms of white, adult, suburban masculinity. As such, the videos showcase skateboarders' discomfort with the hegemonic demands of adult, suburban masculinity as well as their adherence to norms of identity that serve to maintain white male power. Skateboarding videos portray urban and suburban space as a never-never land where boys can be perpetual Peter Pans, never growing up to face the responsibilities and demands of adult masculinity.

All of the videos reviewed present their featured skateboarders firmly in the realm of childhood at some point. *P. J. Ladd's Wonderful, Horrible Life,* for example, features a skateboarder asking his mother for laundry and then ironing a slice of pizza. But it is Enjoi's *Bag of Suck* that does so most consistently. In particular, a skit introducing the skateboarder Jason Adams works overtime to highlight the absurdities and hypocrisies of white, suburban, adult masculinity.

Adams's section of the video begins with a caught-on-tape lifestyle scene during which the other featured skateboarders are swinging on a playground swing set. "Push me, Daddy!" yells one of them, and the camera pans to reveal Jason Adams dressed in an Elvis wig, a Henley shirt, and large pants pulled up to his waist. As Presley's "Love Me Tender" plays in the background, Jason looks at the camera and then his friends with discomfort. This lifestyle scene marks Jason as a suburban father oblivious to the fashions of the day, and he makes it clear that he feels uncomfortable playing this role.

The following skit elevates Jason's discomfort with suburban father-hood to an indictment of the absurdity of postwar myths of suburban utopia. In this skit, Adams, dressed in striped Bermuda shorts, a polo shirt, white loafers, black socks, and a hat with a brim, plays a white suburban father. He and a young girl, perhaps five years old, dressed in a striped sundress, white cardigan, white tights, black mary janes, and white gloves and wearing her hair in a bun with a tiara, move into the shot simultaneously. Adams, mowing the lawn with a nonmotorized push mower, stops briefly to take a swig of beer while the little girl approaches the camera to "serve" a tray of cookies to the audience. The set's suburban ranch house, 1950s car, pink lawn flamingos, and Elvis crooning in the background all signify postwar suburban aspirations while at the same time making it clear that Jason and his friends harbor no illusions about the joys of suburbia. In fact, by the end of this section of the video the father (Adams) is passed out on the lawn with Miller Light bottles strewn around him.

We can align this father with the organization man, the figure that William H. Whyte, as I have noted, characterized as a middle-management automaton trapped in a meaningless job in 1956.[25] This is the organization man aware of his entrapment and finding escape only in drinking to excess. As the clip makes fun of this suburban father, it suggests that white male adulthood is a limited, stifling identity to be avoided if possible. Simultaneously, the image of the little girl in a cute dress and white gloves serving fresh-baked cookies to the audience sends up postwar images of domestic femininity. While such femininity is mocked in passing, white male adulthood represents a mode of masculinity against which skateboarders define themselves.

Although the organization man version of white adult masculinity operates as a model of dominant masculinity against which skateboarders position themselves, skateboarding videos prescribe very particular boundaries within which this nascent critique may take place. As I have made clear, skateboarding videos valorize hypermasculinity and heterosexuality while excluding women and homosexuals, and they present a world in which young men can perform heroic feats of the body. At the same time, however, they do suggest that some variation in masculine expressions is acceptable, and they work as documents of identity that open more possibilities for artistic or emotional expression than traditional images of sporting contests and masculine competition. In the next section, I consider skateboarders' responses to these videos and the ways in which the videos operate as locations of escape from the demands of adult masculinity.

Back to Life: The Pleasures of Skate Videos

As Jack's quote at the beginning of this chapter exemplifies, skateboarders take lasting, profound, and multifaceted pleasure in watching skate videos. Taken as a mode of inspiration and documents of lifestyle and identity, skateboarding videos promote skateboarders' vicarious identification with the featured skaters and prompt skateboarders to experience a host of emotions, including excitement, awe, and admiration. Such identification provides a space in which skateboarders can experience pleasures normally off-limits to white males, pleasures of the body, mind, and spirit.

Vicarious Identification and Inspiration

Over and over, skateboarders raved about the videos' ability to inspire them to go skateboarding. This inspiration often derived from skaters' vicarious identification with the practice of skateboarding as featured on the videos. In other words, they repeatedly reported that they could identify with the skateboarding that was being done on the screen: the way it might feel to the featured skaters and the sense of accomplishment and freedom it might supply. After he told me that skateboarding videos are "better than TV," I asked Jack, "So, do you feel like it kind of makes you, makes you want to go out skating more?" He replied with certainty, "Yeah! I watch, you know, certain things you just watch and you get a spark! And then might as well go out and skate!" When asked why they watch skateboarding videos, others echoed Jack's excitement.

I watch [skate videos] all the time. I love watching 'em 'cause it always makes me want to skate. I've grown to love 'em even more because when you start seeing things that you can do, it makes you feel really good. You're like, "Oh! I did that yesterday! Some pro just did it." And it's just awesome 'cause no matter who you are when you skateboard and it's in a video, I love to watch it. (Joe, age 19)

And it's just kind of a really fun thing to watch, especially with the music. It makes you excited and like, makes you want to go out and skate. It's amazing to see, like if you watch somebody do something really hard, you believe that it's possible, and then you kind of like, I don't know, when I watch skating, like sometimes like, I actually felt the trick happen as I was watching it. (Timmy, age 20)

Jeremiah (age 21): But when you watch professionals you get a better understanding of what you actually need to do with your feet and your body. And it's amazing when you watch it, some of the things people can do.
Yochim: It's a source of inspiration?
Jeremiah: Yeah, it really is. It can really get you excited about skating.

The skateboarders' enthusiasm about skateboarding videos reveals that much of the pleasure of watching the videos derives from their ability to echo or evoke the pleasures of skateboarding as a practice. As the quotations make clear, vicarious identification and inspiration are very closely tied to one another; the videos' ability to inspire is frequently reliant on skateboarders' identification with the screened experience. Such identification takes several different forms, from Timmy literally "feeling" the trick to Joe seeing his abilities on the small screen authenticated because "some pro just did it," and Jeremiah applying learned knowledge from the screen to his everyday life. Skateboarding videos may prompt a vicarious experience of pleasure; as Timmy admitted, "I actually felt the trick happen as I was watching it." With some embarrassment and a series of linguistic qualifiers traditionally deemed feminine (note the "you kind of like, I don't know . . . like sometimes, like" in the full quote), Timmy articulates an absolute relation to the life on screen. Watching the video here becomes a physical experience reminiscent of actual engagement in the mediated practice. Even when the videos do not provoke such direct identification with the text, they almost always encourage skateboarders to recall the pleasures associated with skateboarding. In other words, seeing skateboarding on the small screen, skateboarders imagine and desire the experience of skateboarding in real life.

Pleasure and the Power to Escape

The level of absorption and devotion in which skateboarders engage with skate videos is a mode of audience reception frequently coded in popular culture as feminine. Although skateboarders do not regularly identify themselves as fans in the way that fan communities surrounding cult television series such as *Star Trek* and *Buffy the Vampire Slayer* do, their communal viewing practices, repeated viewing, and vast array of knowledge about skate videos and skateboarding culture more generally echo such communities' viewership. As Henry Jenkins notes, fans are typically perceived as antisocial and linked with "religious and political zealotry, false beliefs, orgiastic excess, possession, and madness."[26] Male fans are labeled "de-gendered, asexual, or impotent" while female fans are over-sexed and crazy.[27]

Arguably, skateboarders' fandom may be closely allied with the traditionally masculine mode of sports fandom, which, as Jenkins makes clear, enjoys far more status than other fandoms. Not only coded as masculine, sports fans are engaged with "reality" rather than fiction. As such, in hierarchies of taste, they are sanctioned.[28] Sports fans are revered and courted by mainstream media and marketers. Importantly, such marketable fandom is centered on the competitive sphere; fans are depicted as coming out to support "their" teams, competing along with the players by both cheering them on and participating in small- and large-scale gambling such as Final Four tournaments and Fantasy Football. Sports fans, then, engage with sports through competition. They also participate as fans via record keeping and the acquisition and display of knowledge about the intricacies of sporting statistics, as well as knowledge about sports' celebrities, following the careers of the likes of Michael Jordan and working to predict upcoming successes and failures.[29]

Although sports fandom does carry a certain amount of cultural cachet, skateboarders actively reject defining their fandom as sports centered, noting frequently that skateboarding is neither competitive nor team based. Skateboarders have not defined skateboarding in opposition to sports without some help from the skateboarding media; outside of the limited sphere of *The X Games*, skateboarding is rarely conceived as a traditional sport. It carries few statistics, is noncompetitive, and does not rely on scoring. Although skateboarding, as a practice and a mediated sport, does not possess a magical resistance to normalization within the mainstream sporting world, its wider sphere of practice and portrayal diverges significantly from that of traditional sports. As I have made clear, the primary media of skateboarding culture position it as a lifestyle or an expression of personality, not as a competitive sport. Further, the reception of these videos bears little resemblance to traditional modes of sport spectatorship.

In fact, skateboarders' viewing practices align more closely with the reception of fictional media. Scholars have suggested that fans of "women's media" such as romance novels, soap operas, and melodramas use these texts to soothe the anxieties and boredom endemic to "women's work" in the home,[30] to quiet fears and disenchantment with patriarchal relationships and romance,[31] and to imagine a life where choices are abundant, simple, and easily made.[32] In short, such viewership can be defined as a mode of escape from everyday life and the pitfalls of being female in a patriarchal, postfeminist world. Ien Ang encourages us to take such fantasy seriously, understanding fictional texts as presenting a range of possibilities in terms of gender identification and "modes of femininity" while also remembering that such fantasy often takes place at the level of emotional involvement rather than "realistic" identification. Such involvement, for Ang, is vital.

[T]he pleasure of fantasy lies in its offering the subject an opportunity to take up positions which she could not do in real life: through fantasy she can move beyond the structural constraints of everyday life and explore other situations, other identities, other lives. It is totally unimportant here whether these are realistic or not.[33]

Skateboarders, indeed, claim a high level of emotional involvement in skateboarding videos. At the basic level of affect, skateboarders' descriptions of the depiction of skateboarders in videos as "amazing" and "awesome" and skateboarder Mike's assertion that watching videos "fills you with EVERY emotion" suggest that watching skating on the small screen is a moving experience. What's more, skaters claim to physically feel the screened experience. Unlike the fantasies encouraged by fictional "women's" texts, however, skate videos seem to provide skateboarders with a portal through which they can escape *to* life rather than *from* it. That is, skateboarding videos, rather than providing skateboarders with emotional experiences they cannot find in their everyday lives, evoke the emotions and feelings the boys get while skateboarding. While the texts' status as nonfiction certainly invites viewers to believe that they, too, can experience the fantasy depicted on the screen, the skateboarders' willing and optimistic belief that they can transfer the screened experience to a lived experience suggests the particular level of agency these mostly middle-class, mostly white, adolescent boys have in their lives. The simple fact that they can enact the free and awe-inspiring practice of skateboarding requires that they possess not only the money to purchase the necessary equipment but also the leisure time to develop the requisite skills to feel free while skateboarding. Such monetary and temporal capital is surely more available to middle-class adolescent males than to, for example, the working- and middle-class mothers discussed by Janice Radway.[34] The practice of skateboarding also prefigures a particular mode of engagement with public space that involves moving quickly through space, appropriating civic and private monuments as obstacles on which to perform tricks, and sometimes running from the authorities. It also requires a high level of risk taking in terms of bodily injury.[35] In these ways, the ability to experience this type of fantasy in real life is a privilege endowed to only particular populations.

As other scholars and I have noted, skateboarding works to actively exclude everyone but adolescent males. In particular, although skateboarders frequently declare that more young women should participate in the activity, the boys' club nature of skateboarding communities presents a challenge to adolescent girls interested in the practice. As Becky Beal reports, male skateboarders frequently see the lack of females in their culture as a result of "natural" differences between the sexes. Girls do not want to skate, Beal's interviewees suggested, because they do not want to risk getting hurt or dirty. Furthermore, Beal notes, the boys regarded female skateboarders as "Skate Betties," meaning that the girls were only skateboarding to get the boys' attention or to fit into the group. Girl skateboarders, then, were defined from the start as "posers" uninterested in the "true" pleasures of the practice.[36] Beyond the fact that skateboarding is a practice that requires economic and leisure capital, the skateboarding community has developed further barriers to entry in its delineation of authentic modes of participating. As Natalie Porter points out, female skateboarders have responded to this exclusion by creating their own, "girls-only" skate culture, including competitions, magazines, and videos.[37]

Still, the escape to life remains an escape, and as such it is not about everyday norms of living. Skateboarders, when they imagine skateboarding, are imagining escape to a particular part of life where they are unencumbered by the everyday demands of the workplace, school, home, and family. Skateboarders imagine and experience skateboarding as a practice through which they can experience their authentic or true selves unmediated by responsibilities or the pressure to obey or conform to rules or social norms. As 29-year-old Brian explained:

> I'm just disengaging from, 'cause when I'm skating, my mind's somewhere else. It's not, it's all about the skating; it's not about like, "Oh I wonder if the puppy needs to go to the bathroom, or did I feed the cat, or did I iron this shirt." You know, none of that stuff even comes into play.

Analogously, 32-year-old Jason told me, "It's a freedom! I feel free when I'm skateboarding, and I can forget about everything that's bothering me for that hour or two of the day. It's liberating, so it's kind of like therapy, as well." Listing the mundane responsibilities of everyday life, Brian suggests that skateboarding is truly an escape to a freer mind-set. More than everyday life, though, Brian is referencing domestic life, which is generally coded as feminine. The responsibilities he escapes are traditionally women's responsibilities. Moreover, this type of domesticity is associated with white, middle-class, suburban family life.

It is unsurprising that Brian would reference the responsibilities of suburban life in his discussion of escape, or, as he puts it, "disengagement," as his whiteness, masculinity, and middle-class status locate him in this space. It is important to note that he explicitly discusses the responsibilities and rule-bound nature associated with not only domestic life but also working life, particularly when he refers to ironing his shirt. Although ironing is stereotypically "women's work," the need to have one's shirt ironed is linked to the appearance required for either white- or pink-collar work or middle- to upper-class leisure pursuits. Moreover, the requirement that one's shirt be ironed for these activities symbolizes the restrictions associated with them: the requirement to present oneself in a particular manner and to look "put together" rather than wrinkled and relaxed. The ironed shirt is decidedly not the purview of adolescent masculinity during leisure time. To engage fully in responsible, *adult* masculinity, then, requires an ironed shirt or its equivalent: rules, restrictions, and responsibilities. Skateboarding, for Brian, is an escape from this domain.

Women are also associated with such grown-up, responsible masculinity. Garry Whannel argues that women (and mothers in particular) have a "civilizing and rounding impact" in "the transition from carefree youth to family responsibility."[38] The stereotypical gender roles that skateboarders escape while skateboarding, then, are not only those of women but also those of adult men.[39] The struggle with identity that so many skateboarders imply in their discussions of skateboarding's pleasures suggests not a simple understanding of gender as male versus female but a conceptualization of gender that is imbued and intersects with notions of race, class, and, most important, adulthood. Skateboarders' opposition to and discomfort with both adult masculinity and feminine authority reaffirm Robert Hanke's assertion that masculinity is not a cohesive "discourse" defined solely as the reverse of femininity but a system of sometimes contradictory meanings "articulated" in various ways with other systems of meaning and power.[40] In this case, skateboarders' masculinity is defined via the superiority of youth over adulthood. Youth comprises an identity category that plays a key role in the construction of gender, and our understanding of the politics of gender should examine how youth inflects the construction of identities.

On one hand, skate life's mode of adolescent authenticity works to shore up masculine power. Despite their refusal of the status obtained in adulthood, the male adolescent can sometimes enact his adolescence by refusing accountability and suggesting that he can do whatever he wants. The simple portrayal of skateboarders moving through public and private spaces suggests that they believe they are entitled to dominate these spaces, that they can do whatever they want wherever they want. As Cathy Schwichtenberg argued of the men in the television series *Miami Vice*, the movement of men through space, particularly when combined with music, creates "a sensualization of movement . . . linked to a romanticized notion of male freedom of movement within the public domain."[41] Skateboarding videos certainly make male movement sensual, and the skateboarders' responses to these videos make it clear that they experience these portrayals as sensual.

On the other hand, the rejection of male adulthood suggests that it represents a position of inauthenticity, limitations, and restrictions. Couching adult white masculinity as inauthentic, these tropes critique hegemonic masculinity and whiteness, particularly their association with rationality and disassociation from the pleasures and comforts of the body. In contrast, youthful masculinity is constructed as a space in which boys can experience corporeal pleasure while at the same time enjoying the power endowed on middle-class white males. Presenting a critique of some aspects of hegemonic masculinity and whiteness while at the same time ignoring inequalities between men and women and the power of masculine expressions of physical prowess and technical acuity, skateboarders engage in a highly individualistic form of resistance.

Although skateboarders' resistance has been associated with adult masculinity, they still believe that they can live an adult male life authentically. Taking professional skateboarders and local skate shop owners as their models, skateboarders dream of growing up to be entrepreneurs. Young skateboarders imagine that they can be successful adults in charge of their own lives as owners of skate shops, producers of skate apparel, or professional skateboarders. That is, skateboarders reenvision adult masculinity in opposition to the organization man, imagining an adult life characterized by independence and freedom.

Producing Videos, Producing Masculinity

The culture of skateboarding is appealing in part because it allows for the enactment of the multiple forms of masculinity displayed in the videos. This perceived freedom in terms of personality extends through the practice of skateboarding, which skateboarders characterize as boundless, spiritual, expressive, and cooperative and thus characterized by multiple expressions of masculinity as creative and passionate rather than aggressive and hyperrational. Although the mode of skateboarding shifts from individual to individual, and aggressive homophobia and misogyny characterize parts of the videos, the pleasures evoked by the videos still contradict such hypermasculine codes. Unlike skateboarding, though, the practice of producing sponsor-me tapes is rule bound, formulaic, and precise.

To produce their videos, which they usually "film" on digital video cameras, skateboarders use the video-editing suites available on many home computers—iMovie on Macs and Windows Media Maker on PCs—as well as, when available, more sophisticated programs such as FinalCut and Adobe Premier. Many of the skaters are self-taught in both filming and using the editing suites. Jeff relayed that he learned to use Windows Media Maker after his computer crashed and he realized he could reinstall the program. Other skateboarders learn to use these programs in classes in high school or college and pass the information on to their friends. Although the videos are made with a larger audience in mind—from a sponsoring company to the local skateboarding community—they are usually only shown within small friendship groups, sometimes at home, and sometimes on the TV at the skate shop.

Sponsor-me tapes and the videos produced by local skate shops follow professional videos very closely in their form. They usually last the length of one or two songs and generally show a montage of an individual skater performing tricks in multiple urban and suburban spaces. One montage made for Launch Board Shop video, for example, included tricks performed in parking lots; in front of houses, warehouses, and university buildings; in public parks in Detroit; and in skate parks. These spaces are not foregrounded in the videos—close and medium shots on the skateboarders relegate the space itself to the background, and one must look very closely in order to discern familiar locations. The skaters make a wide variety of choices in terms of the accompanying music, but they make them carefully in order to showcase another aspect of their personalities. In other words, the skaters view music choice as representative of their identities. What's more, Jeff suggested that highly skilled skaters have greater leeway in song choice; they may choose a more unconventional (and perhaps even more "feminized") song. As Jeff put it, "if you use more of an emotional song, you definitely have to come through with your skating." Although most videos use punk, hip-hop, or rock, Jeff's montages for Launch included a song by the alternative band Metric, which has a female lead singer, and Bing Crosby's "White Christmas."

Ann Arbor skateboarder Tom's sponsor-me video was representative of many such tapes. His video, set to heavy metal music, featured clips of him skateboarding in urban space in Detroit and on the University of Michigan campus. Many of the scenes are shot with a low-angle camera held by a filmer on a moving skateboard. These "skateboard's-eye view" shots do not benefit from the steady-cam technology that anchors many professional shots, and so they are quite shaky. Although most of the footage simply shows Tom performing tricks on his own, there are some interactions with other people. For example, at one point he performs a trick on what appears to be a raised sidewalk. He brushes past a garbage can, accidentally tipping it over, and then skates dangerously close to two older men walking on the sidewalk. The men glance at him suspiciously and walk away. Later Tom grabs onto a pole (perhaps a light pole) and swings around it. The video portrays Tom as a skilled skateboarder and a somewhat aggressive young man with a sense of humor and play. Most of the locally produced videos follow this format, though to different effects. Different music choices, for example, might convey a more artistic, emotionally sensitive tone.

Skateboarders often discuss the practice of filming with some sense of contradiction. They note that they like to capture video and try to "film" as frequently as possible, but at the same time filming can make skaters appear to be interested in the performance of skateboarding rather than the experience itself.[42] As Matthew, age 21, told me:

We're videotaping for the Launch video right now, but it's just us going out and goofing around. We try to get stuff on videotape but it's not like top priority at all, you know. Some of these kids just get too, like, "When am I gonna get sponsored? How am I gonna get sponsored?" This, that, and the next thing. I don't remember ever having that mentality. I just went out and did it and had fun.

In other words, the practice of filming can make the skateboarding seem inauthentic, as if it is done to "get sponsored" rather than for pleasure.[43] The seemingly rational end of earning money for skateboarding is derided in the name of pleasure. Again, we can see that responsible, rational pursuits—such as those in which adult men may take part—are deemed suspicious or inauthentic. The process of filming, then, may be antithetical to the image of the perpetual Peter Pan operating solely in the interest of fun.

Furthermore, the process of editing videos is vastly different from the practice of skateboarding due to its rather superficial focus on display and its requirement for precision. As I have noted, the availability of professional-level editing suites—at home, school, or work—allows skateboarders to strive for high production values that are vastly different from the DIY aesthetic of 1970s—or even 1990s—punk culture. Making their sponsor-me tapes, some skateboarders spend countless hours perfecting the editing, choosing music, and aligning the music with the motion on the videos. What's more, the process of creating a sponsor-me tape is a process of representing the self and, in the case of composite videos, representing a community or group of people. Rather than evoking an inherent feeling of pleasure, the practice of editing videos produces a high level of anxiety for many skaters.

Kiran explained editing as "very formulaic," discussing what he called a "hierarchy of tricks" and a generic formula for each video. Jeff, with some anxiety, discussed the process of creating videos: "It's just, it's gotta be really well edited. There can't be too much nonskating, and there can't be too much of a serious attitude if the skating's not there." Jeff has recently taken on the task of creating a video for Launch, his local skate shop. The skateboarders who work at Launch have been telling me for the last five years that they would soon be releasing the Launch video; however, it has yet to be finished. Jeff recently told me, "I'm somewhat happy with the way the montages look, but yeah, there's lots more work to be done before a video can ever be done. It seems like to make a good video would take about a year more, even though it's always getting pushed back." Jeff revealed that he spent six hours working on one several-minute montage for the video; clearly, video making is an enormous undertaking in terms of time and effort. Although both the practice and the portrayal of skateboarding reveal it to be an unbounded and expressive culture, the process of creating skateboarding videos involves precision, perfectionism, and rules, precisely those elements of adult white masculinity against which skateboarders position themselves.

To conclude, skateboarders' DIY videos comprise a space for the exploration and expression of masculine identity. Appearing on the videos, skateboarders situate themselves within the larger culture of skateboarding, align themselves with professional skateboarders, and place multiple modes of masculinity on display. At the same time, the process of creating the videos is highly contradictory, placing skateboarders at risk of appearing inauthentic and requiring attention to detail, formulas, and rules. Working through these tensions, skateboarders wrestle with what it means to enact or refute the cultural, institutional, and social power of hegemonic masculinity.

As documents of identity, skate videos and the sponsor-me tapes modeled after them situate the authentic boundaries of skateboarding culture and instruct skateboarders in its norms and values. As they talk about these videos—to me and one another—skateboarders reveal and express an appreciation for self-expression and beauty that they also draw on when explaining the pleasures of skateboarding. At the same time, the videos are almost relentless in their mockery of women, people of color, homosexuals, and adult men. Skateboarders rule in these videos; their expressions of dominance mitigate their more gentle expressions of emotional and spiritual fulfillment.

Taken together, these contradictory ideas reveal that skateboarders have constructed an unarticulated lay theory of masculinity that imagines white adult men as the embodiment of the limitations of patriarchal structures. Simultaneously, this lay theory constructs youthful masculinity as an identity characterized by freedom, corporeal pleasures, and authenticity. In their ability to escape to never–never land, skateboarders enact and use masculine power while at the same time thinking through and pushing against traditional norms of white, adult masculinity.

"You do it together, and everyone just does it in their own way"

Corresponding Cultures and (Anti)patriarchal Masculinity

Nineteen-year-old Joe, reflecting on his reasons for skateboarding, told me, "You go around and meet people that enjoy the same thing you do, and love something just as much. And you do it together, and everyone just does it in their own way. So like, there's no way it can't be fun, you know, it's what you love to do." Joe's claim explicates skateboarding as a corresponding culture. He suggests that through skateboarding he is able to find others whose affinities and interests align with his own while at the same time providing a space in which he is able to express his individuality: "*You do it together, and everyone just does it in their own way.*" Toggling between group and individual identification, skateboarders produce and reproduce their identities in relation to the culture of skating.

The notion of a corresponding culture not only captures this relationship but also opens up opportunities for discussing the multiple ways in which skateboarders—and arguably a variety of youth cultures—might negotiate with both mainstream constructions of identity and power relationships between independent and corporate cultural producers. From Stuart Hall's "negotiated readings"[1] to Dick Hebdige's "bricolage"[2] to Michel de Certeau's "making do" and "cultural poaching," scholars have posed numerous conceptualizations of the interaction between cultural producers and cultural consumers.[3] I would contend that skateboarders engage in each of these practices. In fact, 16-year-old Jack inadvertently channeled de Certeau when he explained the history of skateboarding as one of "making do" with inadequate equipment and terrain.

[Early skaters] just took some . . . roller skates and put 'em on a two-by-four. Which is like super ghetto, and like, they didn't even use bolts, they just nailed and screwed 'em on. And like, that's making do with what you have! And it just keeps going on and on and on like that. . . . You just make do with what you have, because it's not like a basketball court where there's like nets put up and everything. You know, a skate park's just stuff that came later. But for the original, like art that skateboarding is, there's nothing, there's nothing there. So you just had to make do with what you had.

For Jack, part of skateboarding's creativity derives from its reuse of public space, and the lack of a court or field signifies skating's openness, the ways in which it provides opportunities for self-expression. As another skateboarder explained, "It's like, the play is in your head, you make it up. Um, that's part of the art of it, too, it all just comes from your soul and your heart."

The multiple media comprising skate life and skaters' principles of engagement with these media operate as a nexus through which skateboarders deconstruct norms of white masculinity while maintaining its power. Venerated by, used by, rejected by, and reinvented by the dominant society, skateboarders also venerate, use, reject, and reinvent the mainstream. In constant correspondence with many representations of skate life—from FedEx's commercial to MTV's *Wildboyz* to Enjoi skateboarding company's *Bag of Suck*—skateboarders persistently explore constructions of masculinity. Explaining, "this is how I think," the skaters lodge their complaints with the demands of dominant codes of masculinity: its preoccupation with competition and physical dominance; its rejection of the emotional, spiritual, and mental pleasures of self-expression and exploration; and its obligatory rationalism and stoicism. These complaints, however, do not preclude skateboarders from expressing their dominance over women, gay men, non-Westerners, men of color, and working-class folks. Although skate life—both in and outside of the mainstream media—sends up the constructed nature of white masculinity, it does so without questioning power relations.

Skateboarding's (anti)patriarchal revelations regarding the codification of dominant masculinities demonstrate not only the staying power of white male power but also the need for a theoretical stance that can account for the ways in which constructions of identity and power relations are both inextricably related *and* operate independent of one another. The scholarship on masculinity and whiteness has suggested that in exposing the constructed nature of these identities we may denaturalize them and consequently strip them of some of their power. Although such exposure does destabilize identity, it does not necessarily eliminate its power. R. W. Connell has made perhaps the most useful contribution to this dilemma in defining hegemonic masculinity as highly contingent. Hegemonic masculinity, he argues, is the mode of masculinity that at a given historical moment is most able to uphold patriarchy.[4] Scholars of identity and popular culture would greatly benefit from a broader theory that captures the fluidity of identity and power and explains why alternative—or even radical—constructions and performances of identity might not be sufficient for remaking power relations. Such a theory would certainly help to establish the importance of popular culture's representation of identity as well as its relationship to the many everyday practices that are infused by power.

The notion of corresponding cultures begins this discussion by creating a conceptual space in which we can think of the interactions between multiple media and individuals as dynamic, constantly in progress, and generally mutable. As Joe's description of "do[ing] it together" while "do[ing] it in your own way" suggests, individuals carry some independence in their interactions with culture and society, but that independence is decidedly limited. One step toward elaborating on these ideas would be to offer a more indepth examination of the corresponding culture's relationship to the public sphere. In skate life, for example, we might explore the relationships among portrayals of skate parks in Tony Hawk's Activision video games; the rhetoric of the Tony Hawk Foundation, which supports the construction of local skate parks; and the grassroots activism of a skateboarding community attempting to erect a skate park in its locale. We might ask, how do corresponding cultures and counterpublic spheres intersect and interact?

As skateboarding becomes more and more entrenched in American culture—a California man recently established a skateboarding league for high schoolers that will operate like a club sport and be sponsored by Nike—its racial and gender borders, as well as its notions of identity, may expand and be transformed.[5] The emergence of the "skate pimp" not only exemplifies how cultural phenomena are discovered and commodified by mainstream media but also points to the ways in which such commodification redraws the lines of cultural forms. Embodied by hip-hop artists Pharrell Williams and Lupe Fiasco, the skate pimp is a hip-hop skater. Although hip-hop and skateboarding have a long history of confluence within skateboarding culture, the mainstream construction of this image highlights continuing conflicts about race, lifestyle, and the blurring and crossing of racial boundaries. An analysis of these figures would speak to the ways in which racial identity and cultural style intersect in the construction of masculinity as well as to the ways in which signifiers of authenticity shift across lines of race and culture. Do Pharrell Williams and Lupe Fiasco enact the same critiques of masculinity as Bam Margera and Chris Pontius? Does the fact that Williams and Fiasco might be regarded as authentic by skateboarders impact their hip-hop credibility or vice versa?

Professional skateboarder and Olympic snowboarder Shaun White's recent catapult into celebrity also exposes the solidification of skateboarding's space in mainstream culture. After winning a gold medal at the 2006 Winter Olympics, White, whose long red hair, pale skin, and skinny body defy the norms of athletic masculinity and physical dominance, was featured on the cover of *Rolling Stone* with an American flag draped around his shirtless torso. This cover, which deemed White "the coolest kid in America," presents a seemingly unlikely confluence of signifiers: youthful cool, patriotism, and alternative masculinities. How do these signifiers work together to reimagine white American masculinity? Why was such a negotiation effective in this particular cultural moment? How do the Olympics' desire for cultural cachet, White's charisma and talent, and contemporary concerns about masculinity and dominance intersect to make White, the "Flying Tomato," resonate?

Skate life and extreme sports culture certainly resonate throughout youth media, and this book has only analyzed a few key pieces of it. Tony Hawk's line of Activision video games is on its ninth installment, with the latest iteration, *Proving Ground*, acting as a key element in a cross-promotional effort involving Jeep, *Rolling Stone*, and Sirius Radio (on which Hawk has his own show). As an icon and brand, Tony Hawk traverses mediascapes and simultaneously presents himself as a grown-up family man and a youthful troublemaker.[6] In 2006, MTV's *Rob and Big* debuted, featuring professional skateboarder Rob Dyrdek and his "bodyguard," Chris "Big Black" Boykin, and in 2007 MTV released *Scarred*, which showcases home videos of terrible extreme sports accidents and the resulting injuries. These two series place skateboarding front and center and complicate some of the norms I have discussed here. Dyrdek's appropriation of hip-hop culture and his interactions with Big Black upset notions of whiteness, and *Scarred*'s fetishization of male pain appears to be a darkly serious version of the "boys will be boys" masochism on display in *Jackass*. How might adolescent males who do not define themselves primarily as skateboarders respond to these media? Do skateboarding's multiple constructions of masculinity reverberate in broader youth cultures? Do they challenge male youths' understanding of masculinity?

Skate life's mockery of male proving rituals, which is on display in *Wildboyz* but also permeates skate culture, deserves to be analyzed more fully in terms of the contemporary cultural moment. During the years when I got to know the Michigan skateboarders and started to pay close attention to skate media, American culture was increasingly criticized for its hypermasculinity. In the months leading up to the 2008 presidential election, cultural discourse portrayed the United States as getting far too big for its britches. Hummers and McMansions have run up against the mainstreaming of environmentalism and the "green" movement (which has now been fully commodified), and key criticisms of the Bush administration revolved around the arrogance of its foreign policies, particularly in the use of preemptive strikes. A 2007 *Newsweek* article trumpeted the rise of "beta males—losers who are winning." Noting the popularity of nonnormative men—actors such as Steve Carrell and characters such as Shrek—and the downfall of such hypermasculine icons as Don Imus, Mel Gibson, and Donald Rumsfeld, the article suggested that self-deprecating, nonaggressive men are coming to power. *Newsweek* does not suggest that this shifting image will substantially change power relations, though it did note the (then) possibility of a first gentleman.[7] This article prompts a variety of questions. Can we think of Johnny Knoxville and his cohort as precursors to the beta male? Could the beta male provide space for more egalitarian gender relations? Why are all the beta males white? How might skateboarders respond to various images of the beta male? The answers to these questions would help to further explain the shifting nature of hegemonic masculinity, the ways in which power and images of identity work separately and in tandem with one another, and the extent of skate culture's correspondence with mainstream culture.

As I write this chapter, Barack Obama is in his third week in office. He has just issued an apology for Tom Daschle's withdrawal from consideration for secretary of health and human services, saying, "I screwed up."[8] *Ms.* magazine depicted Obama on the cover of its special inauguration issue ripping open his white button-down shirt to reveal a black T-shirt reading "This is what a feminist looks like." In the image, Obama is decidedly masculine—head held high, shoulders thrust back, and chest puffed out—but it seems that he's proud in his feminism. More, Obama has signed into law the Lily Ledbetter Fair Pay Act; he has signed executive orders ending torture and closing the prison at Guantánamo Bay; and he has declared U.S. support for the United Nations Population Fund. Although the president certainly does not determine dominant ideologies about gender, Obama's presence in office surely will change the culture in which young men wrestle with masculinity. It remains to be seen how (and if) relations of power and notions of hegemonic masculinity will shift over the course of this new administration.

Throughout its history, skateboarding has occupied a liminal space in which it has been defined as both decidedly American and decidedly countercultural. Perceived as a childhood pastime, the rebellious destruction of property, an athletic pursuit, and a cool lifestyle, skateboarding functions in multiple ways to uphold, disrupt, and consolidate dominant masculine codes. In January 2009, the *New York Times* reported that an Australian man was working to open a skateboarding school in Afghanistan called Skateistan. The school, with 120,000 dollars in funding from the governments of Norway, Canada, and Germany, would, he hoped, be "a way to woo students into after-school activities like English and computer classes, which are otherwise reserved for the elite." Far from a culture of rebels, the *Times* depicted skateboarding as a meaningful childhood pastime. The Australian, Oliver Percovich, said of the Afghan children, "They just haven't been given the same opportunities. They need a positive environment to do positive things for Afghanistan and for themselves."[9] Clearly, images of skate life continue to oscillate between nonthreatening pastime and extreme rebellion.

Both the practice and culture of skateboarding correspond with skaters' seemingly authentic desires, values, ideas, and dreams, and this corresponding culture provides an open space through which they experience emotional, mental, intellectual, and spiritual pleasures that they believe could not be derived from other youth cultures, including institutionalized sports. The skaters' individual desires and pleasure are tied closely to their negotiations of dominant modes of masculinity and constitute a nascent critique of hegemonic masculinities without reimagining power relationships or relinquishing the power of white masculinity.

As they told me their stories and escorted me through their culture, skateboarders taught me the norms for engaging in skate life. But the skaters didn't simply teach me; many of them became my friends, and I have worked hard in my writing to convey both rigorous, critical analysis and warm respect for their culture. After reading the book, Kiran told me, "I can definitely tell that you appreciate our culture, which is cool. It's not often that you see someone outside of skateboarding do such an in-depth study surrounding it." My skateboarder husband, who is an engineer, has always had a skeptical attitude toward cultural analysis, preferring to think of skateboarding as simply a fabulous pastime. Still, he has always wholeheartedly believed that skate culture is a space in which boys can be creative and sensitive while at the same time maintaining their cool. His experience of being mocked for skateboarding in the late 1980s and early 1990s permeates this book, and together he and I have noted the tremendous change in depictions of skateboarding since the advent of *The X Games*. In short, Chris has experienced the contradictions of skateboarding that this book discusses, but, more important, he has communicated to me in ways both profound and banal that skateboarding was a space in which he could push against normative notions of manliness.

Proclaiming skateboarding to "come from the heart," demonstrating the feelings evoked while watching skate videos, and struggling with their analyses of mainstream representations of skateboarding, the boys elaborated the credos and directives that provide a paradigmatic template for multiple social situations and mediated constructions. Skateboarders' discussions of skate culture and their interactions in the skate shop and in front of the television operated to indoctrinate me, as well as each other, into the rituals of skate life. Knowing how to watch skate media, how to speak about the practice, and how to be a skater in everyday life, the skateboarders operate as a corresponding culture that informs their impressions of self and identity more generally. Telling me and one another the tenets of engagement in skate life, skateboarders correspond with multiply mediated representations and elaborate their culture's and their own correspondence with alternative masculinities: "You do it together, and everyone just does it in their own way"; "The play is in your head"; "You just make do with what you have"; "This is how I think." Skate life opens a space for alternative masculinities: "This is how I think."

Method

Much of the data for this project were derived from interviews conducted, starting in May 2002, with southeastern Michigan skateboarders, including skateboarders from Ann Arbor and surrounding areas (Brighton, Flint, Novi, Howell, and Milan). The skateboarders were contacted via flyers posted at the Launch Board Shop and the now defunct Modern Surf and Skate in Ann Arbor as well as through a snowball sample wherein I asked interviewees to recommend friends to be interviewed. The interviews were conducted in local restaurants over meals I provided in return for the skateboarders' time and lasted between 60 and 90 minutes.

Skate Life also depends on participant observation with this community conducted in the summers of 2002, 2004, and 2006. My observations were surely aided and otherwise affected by my point of annunciation, which perhaps most significantly derives from my experiences as a skateboarder's girlfriend and wife. I first entered the Launch Board Shop when my husband Chris was shopping for skate apparel, and I frequently told Michigan skaters about my husband and his attempts to teach me to skate. Arguably, this relationship gave me some credibility with the skateboarders and situated me in a position that many women in this culture inhabit, that of the girlfriend. I could quite easily blend in as a "typical girl" when sitting on the sidewalk watching the boys skate. Chris attended several of the boys' skate sessions with me, and so I was easily able to fit into this community. This personal history also means that over the past decade I have observed a variety of skateboarders behaving in immature and sexist ways while I have also become quite attached to skateboarders who are kind, generous, and politically engaged. I report this information to better explain my entry into this community as well as to acknowledge that my personal history has some relevance in my interpretation of the data.

I spent an average of four hours a week at the Launch Board Shop for approximately two months each in the summers of 2002, 2004, and 2006. During this time, I engaged in whatever activities the skateboarders were engaged in: watching skate videos on the shop's small television, hanging around the counter talking, or just sitting around. Skateboarders came and went during this time; consequently, I spent the most significant amount of time with the shop's employees, all skateboarders. When skateboarders invited me along, I attended skateboarding sessions in Ann Arbor, Brighton, Detroit, and Toledo. These sessions were more difficult to attend as they are often spontaneous. I have also developed a more extensive relationship with two skateboarders and have attended a concert, gone out to dinner, and "hung out" with them on numerous occasions (e.g., shopping; walking around Detroit and Ann Arbor; participating in a photo session for a college class; attending graduation parties; and meeting girlfriends, parents, and siblings). Finally, I have participated in Milan skateboarders' ongoing fund-raising efforts for a skate park in Milan.

Interview Guide

1. How did you get into skateboarding?
2. Why do you skate?
3. If someone asked you to define skateboarding, what would you tell them?
4. Describe your group of friends. Describe a typical weekend.
5. What is a stereotypical skater? How true is the stereotype?
6. What perpetuates the stereotype?
7. Is there anything that you see in the media that portrays skater culture accurately?
8. Is there anything that you see in the media that is a poor representation of you and your friends?
9. Do you play the skating video games (e.g., ProSkater)? What do you think of them?
10. Are there any "must go" skater events?
11. Tell me about your favorite skate video.
12. How can you pick a skater out of a crowd?
13. If you could control the future of skateboarding, what would it be?

Notes

Introduction

1. In this analysis, I define *mass media* as media directed toward a large demographic such as males age 18 to 34. Although these media are niche oriented in that they do not aspire to the old "least common denominator" formulation for attracting the largest segment of the population possible, this strategy is less specific than the lifestyle-oriented approach that many American magazines take. Niche media are media designed to attract a segment of the audience via both demographic and lifestyle considerations. Such media may be more readily available in specialized distribution areas such as skate shops. Videos produced by skateboarding companies and magazines comprise niche media in this project. Local or "community" media are those designed by skateboarders using equipment and materials developed for personal use.

2. Iain Borden, *Skateboarding, Space, and the City: Architecture and the Body* (New York: Berg, 2001).

3. Ocean Howell, "The 'Creative Class' and the Gentrifying City: Skateboarding in Philadelphia's Love Park," *Journal of Architectural Education* 59, no. 2 (2005): 33.

4. Kyle Kusz, *Revolt of the White Athlete: Race, Media, and the Emergence of Extreme Athletes in America* (New York: Peter Lang, 2007).

5. Belinda Wheaton, "Introduction: Mapping the Lifestyle Sport-Scape," in *Understanding Lifestyle Sports: Consumption, Identity, and Difference*, edited by Belinda Wheaton (New York: Routledge, 2004), 16.

6. Skateboarders' opinions about skate parks are highly contradictory; while they frequently lobby local governments for a sanctioned space in which to skate, they also find skate parks, as enclosed places with safety rules and sometimes fees, to be too limiting and organized. These contradictions symbolize just one of the ways in which skate culture's relationship to mainstream entities is highly contingent and dynamic.

7. Bicycle motocrossing (BMX) biking is a sport in which participants ride small, one-speed bikes on ramps similar to skateboarding ramps. Participants perform a variety of tricks, flipping their BMX bikes in a manner similar to skateboarders' use of skateboards.

8. Deirdre M. Kelly, Shauna Pomerantz, and Dawn H. Currie, "'You Can Break So Many More Rules': The Identity Work and Play of Becoming Skater Girls," in *Youth Culture and Sport: Identity, Power, and Politics*, edited by Michael D. Giardina and Michele K. Donnelly (New York: Routledge, 2008), 113.

9. Becky Beal and Charlene Wilson, "'Chicks Dig Scars': Commercialisation and the Transformation of Skateboarders' Identities," in *Understanding Lifestyle Sports: Consumption, Identity, and Difference*, edited by Belinda Wheaton (New York: Routledge, 2004).

10. Michele K. Donnelly, "'Take the Slam and Get Back Up': *Hardcore Candy* and the Politics of Representation in Girls' and Women's Skateboarding and Snowboarding on Television," in *Youth Culture and Sport: Identity, Power, and Politics*, edited by Michael D. Giardina and Michele K. Donnelly (New York: Routledge, 2008).

11. My phrase "culture of cool" is inspired by the title of Thomas Frank's *The Conquest of Cool: Business Culture, Counterculture, and the Rise of Hip Consumerism* (Chicago: University of Chicago Press, 1998).

12. Fuse Marketing, http://www.fusemarketing.com/fuse.php, accessed December 1, 2005.

13. Laura Petrecca, "Going to Extremes," *Advertising Age*, July 24, 2000, 16, http://search.epnet.com/login.aspx?direct=true&db=ufh&an=3357939.

14. "Going to Extremes," *American Demographics*, June 1, 2001, 26, accessed online, General BusinessFile ASAP.

15. Joan Raymond, "Going to Extremes," *American Demographics*, June 1, 2002, n.p., accessed online, General BusinessFile ASAP. Soccer has been more successful, having experienced a 48 percent increase in "frequent participants" between 1987 and 2000 according to the Sporting Goods Manufacturing Association. The National Sporting Goods Association reported 12.5 million soccer players in 1995 (*Pediatrics*, March 2000, 659).

16. "The WWD List: Going to Extremes," *Women's Wear Daily*, December 13, 2004, 110S, accessed online, General BusinessFile ASAP.

17. "1995 Summer X Games," Skatelog.com, edited by Kathie Fry, http://www.skatelog.com/x-games/1995/summer/.

18. Jeff Jensen, "Vans Readies $25 Mil Brand Blitz," *Advertising Age*, March 3, 1997, http://search.epnet.com/login.aspx?direct=true&db=ufh&an=9703134485.

19. Paul Hochman, "Street Lugers, Stunt Bikers, and—Colgate Palmolive! Spokesmen with Nose Rings," *Fortune*, November 22, 1999, accessed online, General BusinessFile ASAP.

20. Wheaton, "Introduction," 13.

21. Laura Petrecca, "Going to Extremes" (2000). Dropping the *e* from *extreme* sub-

tly moved the word away from its use as an indicator of a relatively narrow range of characteristics toward a branding device that could be attached to any range of products from cheeseburgers to hair color. This shift arguably marks the moment of sedimentation in marketing when a phrase becomes an empty signifier of "cool."

22. Kim Cleland, "Action Sports Form Fabric of Generation," *Advertising Age*, April 16, 2001, accessed online, General BusinessFile ASAP.

23. Ibid. See also Louis Chunovic, "X Games Score Big with Advertisers," *Electronic Media*, August 13, 2001, 2.

24. Raymond, "Going to Extremes." See also Theresa Howard, "Being True to Dew," *Brandweek*, April 24, 2000, 28.

25. Lea Goldman, "From Ramps to Riches," *Forbes*, July 5, 2004, 98, http://proquest. umi.com.proxy.lib.umich.edu/pqdweb?did=657165491&sid=1&Fmt=3&clientId=17 82&RQT&VName=PQD. More than a very talented skateboarder, Tony Hawk, like Michael Jordan, has become a brand. His name is attached to various products in order to convey Hawk's aura and his authentic relation to skateboard culture.

26. Wheaton, "Introduction," 1.

27. Petrecca, "Going to Extremes" (2000).

28. Laura Petrecca, "Going to Extremes," *Advertising Age*, October 11, 1999.

29. Raymond, "Going to Extremes," 29.

30. Hochman, "Street Lugers."

31. Marie Case, managing director, Board-Trac, personal communication, December 24, 2008.

32. Funding Universe, "Hot Topic, Inc.," http://www.fundinguniverse.com/company-histories/Hot-Topic-Inc-Company-History.html.

33. "Fortune 100 Best Companies to Work for, 2006," *Fortune*, http://money.cnn. com/magazines/ fortune/bestcompanies/snapshots/637.html.

34. "Retailer Doubles Earnings," *New York Times*, May 11, 2004, http://query. nytimes.com/gst/fullpage.html?res=9907EEDD133CF932A25756C0A9629C8B63.

35. *Jackass*, *Viva La Bam*, and *Wildboyz* are all "reality" shows aired during MTV's Sunday night "Sunday Stew," a lineup aimed at teenage boys that also includes Ashton Kucher's *Punk'd*. *Jackass* and *Viva La Bam* feature professional skateboarders and their friends engaged in pranks, including launching innumerable objects at each others' groins and building skate parks in their parents' homes. *Wildboyz*, a spin-off of *Jackass*, showcases the skateboarders' friends in various "exotic" locales wearing loincloths and botching local activities such as wrestling alligators. *Made* remakes its participants. For example, in one episode a blonde, thin, teenage girl interested in makeup and clothes asked to be made into a skateboarder. She was introduced to a coach and had to practice skateboarding for five weeks. She also learned to participate in its culture by wearing the right clothes, becoming sufficiently irreverent, watching skate videos, and so on.

36. In 2004, New York passed a law requiring skateboarders under the age of 14 to wear helmets while skateboarding in public places. California has a similar law. Al

Baker, "Law Requires Children to Wear Helmets While Skateboarding," *New York Times*, November 25, 2004, B9.

37. For example, in response to a San Francisco city supervisor's proposal to legalize skateboarding on all city sidewalks, Bob Planthold, cochairman of the Senior Action Network's Transportation and Pedestrian Safety Committee, asked council members to consider the safety of blind pedestrians and elderly citizens who find it difficult to avoid quickly moving skateboarders. He complained, "We can't see how the city can authorize night skateboarding. . . . Why do kids need to skateboard at night? Why can't they be home doing their homework? Or doing laundry? We'd be happy to help them lobby for more skateboard parks, but this is the wrong solution." Carolyn Jones, "Supes Ponder Plan for Greater Access for Sport on Sidewalks," *San Francisco Chronicle*, April 1, 2005, F1.

38. See, for example, Jean Laquidara Hill, "Skateboards at Town Hall Mean Trouble," *Worcester Telegram and Gazette* (MA), August 16, 2000, B1.

39. For example, one individual said, "We're kind of treating those kids who want to roller blade or skateboard like they're dealing drugs downtown," and another said, "Before we take space away from the kids we should have a place for them to go." George Barnes, "Althol Bans Skateboards Downtown," *Worcester Telegram and Gazette* (MA), May 16, 2000, B2.

40. Damien Cave, "Dogtown, U.S.A.," *New York Times*, June 12, 2005.

41. Frank, *Conquest of Cool*.

42. Mike Davis, "On-line interview with *Escape Velocity*," 1995, quoted in Neil Campbell, *American Youth Cultures* (New York: Routledge, 2004), 21.

43. Robert E. Rinehart, "Exploiting a New Generation: Corporate Branding and the Co-optation of Action Sport," in *Youth Culture and Sport: Identity, Power, and Politics*, edited by Michael D. Giardina and Michele K. Donnelly (New York: Routledge, 2008), 73.

44. Ibid, 83.

45. Michael D. Giardina and Michele K. Donnelly, "Introduction," in *Youth Culture and Sport: Identity, Power, and Politics*, edited by Michael D. Giardina and Michele K. Donnelly (New York: Routledge, 2008), 2.

46. Ibid.

47. Belinda Wheaton, "After Sport Culture: Rethinking Sport and Post-subcultural Theory," *Journal of Sport and Social Issues* 31, no. 3 (2007): 298.

48. Ibid.

49. Ibid.

50. Although the construction of nations and nationality is not a central focus of this volume, skateboarders' and extreme sports texts' constructions of masculinity are infused with American values of independence, individuality, and freedom. Throughout my investigation, I return to the particularly American nature of extreme sports' masculinity.

51. Sunaina Maira and Elisabeth Soep, *Youthscapes: The Popular, the National, the Global* (Philadelphia: University of Pennsylvania Press, 2005), xvii.

52. Ibid., xxv. The quote is from Néstor García Canclini, *Consumers and Citizens: Globalization and Multicultural Conflicts* (Minneapolis: University of Minnesota Press, 2001), 20.

53. Dick Hebdige, *Subculture: The Meaning of Style* (London: Methuen, 1979). See also Paul E. Willis, "Culture, Institution, Differentiation," in *The Subcultures Reader*, edited by Ken Gelder and Sarah Thornton (New York: Routledge, 1997), 121–29; and Angela McRobbie and Jenny Garber, "Girls and Subcultures," in Angela McRobbie, *Feminism and Youth Culture: From "Jackie" to "Just Seventeen"* (London: Macmillan Education, 1991), 1–15.

54. John Clarke, Stuart Hall, Tony Jefferson, and Brian Roberts, "Subcultures, Cultures, and Class: A Theoretical Overview," in *Resistance through Rituals: Youth Subcultures in Post-war Britain*, edited by Stuart Hall and Tony Jefferson (London: Hutchinson, 1976; repr., New York: Routledge, 2000), 47, emphasis in original.

55. Ken Gelder, "Introduction to Part Two," in *The Subcultures Reader*, edited by Ken Gelder and Sarah Thornton (New York: Routledge, 1997), 87.

56. David Muggleton and Rupert Weinzierl, eds., *The Post-subcultures Reader* (New York: Berg, 2003). This moniker unfortunately suggests that subcultures as theorized by the Birmingham School did at one time exist. While the editors never make this claim explicitly, and in fact their contributors frequently refute the idea of traditional subcultures without hesitation, the implication is unavoidable given the temporal nature of the term *post*. Muggleton's previous work also has this implication as his analysis is located in the postmodern era. That is, he implies that post-subculturalists came into existence as part of postmodernity, and so the reader may infer that subculturalists populated the modern era. Such bifurcations are questionable at best. Perhaps it would be more useful to use the term *post-Birmingham*.

57. Ibid.

58. Oliver Marchart, "Bridging the Micro-Macro Gap: Is There Such a Thing as a Post-subcultural Politics?" in *The Post-subcultures Reader*, edited by David Muggleton and Rupert Weinzierl (New York: Berg, 2003), 83–97.

59. Angela McRobbie and Jenny Garber, working at Birmingham, first critiqued the malecentric nature of the CCCS's work in 1980. See McRobbie and Garber, "Girls and Subcultures," 1–15.

60. See, for example, Doreen Piano, "Resisting Subjects: DIY Feminism and the Politics of Style in Subcultural Production," in *The Post-subcultures Reader*, edited by David Muggleton and Rupert Weinzierl (New York: Berg, 2003), 253–65.

61. Wheaton, "After Sport Culture," 286.

62. Geoff Stahl, "Tastefully Renovating Subcultural Theory: Making Space for a New Model," in *The Post-subcultures Reader*, edited by David Muggleton and Rupert Weinzierl (New York: Berg, 2003), 27–40.

63. Sarah Thornton, *Club Cultures: Music, Media, and Subcultural Capital* (Cambridge, UK: Polity, 1995), 203.

64. Ibid.

65. Stahl, "Tastefully Renovating Subcultural Theory," 2003.

66. Theresa M. Winge, "Constructing 'Neo-tribal' Identities through Dress: Modern Primitives and Body Modifications," in *The Post-subcultures Reader*, edited by David Muggleton and Rupert Weinzierl (New York: Berg, 2003), 119–32. The notion of neotribes, as Belinda Wheaton points out, has been critiqued for ignoring struggles for power. See Wheaton, "After Sport Culture."

67. Joshua Gunn's analysis of the production of goth identity is one exception. Highlighting the importance of mainstream meanings of subcultures to the subcultures themselves, Gunn argues that goth identity is constituted in the interstices of subculture and mainstream, in the tension between mainstream conceptualizations of goth (e.g., the much maligned "Trenchcoat Mafia" to which Columbine shooters Eric Harris and Dylan Klebold belonged) and subcultural definitions. Such subcultural statements as "Marilyn Manson is not goth," Gunn notes, are crucial to subcultural goth identity. Gunn's discussion prompts certain questions: how do mainstream cultural understandings of a subculture change subcultural identity and are subculturalists always in opposition to dominant culture? See Joshua Gunn, "Marilyn Manson Is Not Goth: Memorial Struggle and the Rhetoric of Subcultural Identity," *Journal of Communication Inquiry* 23, no. 4 (1999): 408–31.

68. Belinda Wheaton and Becky Beal, "'Keeping it Real': Subcultural Media and the Discourses of Authenticity in Alternative Sport," *International Review for the Sociology of Sport* 38, no. 2 (2003): 156.

69. Wheaton, "After Sport Culture," 288.

70. Robert E. Rinehart, "ESPN's X Games: Contests of Opposition, Resistance, Co-option, and Negotiation," in *Tribal Play: Subcultural Journeys through Sport*, edited by Michael Atkinson and Kevin Young (Bingley, UK: JAI Press, 2008).

71. Wheaton and Beal, "Keeping It Real," 158.

72. Beal and Wilson, "Chicks Dig Scars," 33.

73. Stuart Hall, "Encoding/Decoding," in *Culture, Media, Language*, edited by Stuart Hall, Dorothy Hobson, Andrew Lowe, and Paul Willis (London: Hutchinson, 1980), 105.

74. David Muggleton, *Inside Subculture: The Postmodern Meaning of Style* (New York: Berg, 2000), 167.

75. Matt Wray and Annalee Newitz, eds., *White Trash: Race and Class in America* (New York: Routledge, 1997).

76. For a discussion of the invisibility of class on American television and American women's subsequent difficulty in articulating class differences, see Andrea L. Press, *Women Watching Television: Gender, Class, and Generation in the American Television Experience* (Philadelphia: University of Pennsylvania Press, 1991).

77. Wray and Newitz, *White Trash.*

78. Joanne Kay and Suzanne Laberge, "Mapping the Field of "AR": Adventure Racing and Bourdieu's Concept of Field," *Sociology of Sport Journal* 19, no. 1: (2002): 26.

79. Ibid.

"The mix of sunshine and rebellion"

The quotation in the chapter title is from Kate Betts, "The Whoosh of What You'll Be Wearing," *New York Times*, May 5, 2002, 6.

1. Michael Brooke, *The Concrete Wave: The History of Skateboarding* (Los Angeles: Warwick, 1999), 14.

2. Ibid.; James Davis, *Skateboarding Is Not a Crime: 50 Years of Street Culture* (Buffalo: Firefly, 1999); *Thrasher: Insane Terrain* (New York: Universe, 2001).

3. See, for example, Sarah Pileggi, "Wheeling and Dealing," *Sports Illustrated,* September 1, 1975, 22; Mary Alice Kellogg, "Rebirth of the Boards," *Newsweek*, June 21, 1976, 56–57; and Frank Deford, "Promo Wiz in Kidvid Biz," *Sports Illustrated*, February 7, 1977, 30–33.

4. "The New Teens Market" (Packaged Facts, 1995).

5. Michele K. Donnelly, "Alternative and Mainstream: Revisiting the Sociological Analysis of Skateboarding," in *Tribal Play: Subcultural Journeys through Sport*, edited by Michael Atkinson and Kevin Young (Bingley, UK: JAI Press, 2008).

6. *Dogtown* won both the audience and directors awards for documentaries at the 2001 Sundance Film Festival as well as the IFP/West Independent Spirit Award for best documentary. See Beth Pinsker, "Personal Documentaries Are New Form of Marketing," *New York Times*, April 15, 2002, 12.

7. Arjun Appadurai, "Disjuncture and Difference in the Global Cultural Economy," in *The Phantom Public Sphere*, edited by Bruce Robbins (Minneapolis: University of Minnesota Press, 1993), 269–95. Appadurai uses the notion of a "scape" to connote "the fluid, irregular shapes" of these "deeply perspectival constructs," (275). By employing his terminology, I point to the dynamic and interactive nature of the various media in which skateboarding is portrayed and constructed as an appeal to teen boys.

8. Sunaina Maira and Elisabeth Soep, *Youthscapes: The Popular, the National, the Global* (Philadelphia: University of Pennsylvania Press, 2005). As I noted in the introduction, Maira and Soep's extension of Appadurai's "scapes" usefully illustrates the complexities of the numerous groups with which youths associate.

9. Kyle Kusz, "Extreme America: The Cultural Politics of Extreme Sports in 1990s America," in *Understanding Lifestyle Sports: Consumption, Identity, and Difference*, edited by Belinda Wheaton (New York: Routledge, 2004), 197. See also Kyle Kusz, *Revolt of the White Athlete: Race, Media, and the Emergence of Extreme Athletes in America* (New York: Peter Lang, 2007).

10. Kusz, "Extreme America," 203.

11. Kusz, *Revolt of the White Athlete*, 95.

12. Kusz, "Extreme America," 198.

13. Angela McRobbie, "Second-Hand Dresses and the Role of the Ragmarket," in *The Subcultures Reader*, edited by Ken Gelder and Sarah Thornton (New York: Routledge, 1997).

14. Brooke, *The Concrete Wave*.

15. Consider, for example, early radio boys. See Susan J. Douglas, *Listening In: Radio and the American Imagination* (New York: Times Books, 1999).

16. Brooke, *The Concrete Wave*, 18.

17. *Thrasher*, 8.

18. Ibid, 12.

19. Leerom Medovoi, *Rebels: Youth and the Cold War Origins of Identity* (Durham: Duke University Press, 2005), 3.

20. Although it is beyond the scope of this study to discuss the movement of surfing from Polynesian cultures to California—and its subsequent whitening—it is important to suggest that the exoticism imagined in the islands most likely follows in our cultural imagination of surfing. Note, for example, the markers of Hawaiian culture that are frequently attached to surf culture such as leis, tropical flowers, and hula dancing.

21. *Thrasher*, 12.

22. I want to note here that in the wake of the September 11 attacks and the war in Iraq, benevolent images of America as resilient, energetic, adventurous, and pioneering have been both shored up and critiqued. While it is beyond the scope of this study to fully analyze changing images of the nation, my discussion of the post-9/11 media representation of skateboarding will surely take this into account. For now, I submit that while the foundational myths of the United States—the centrality of the Pilgrims, the pioneers, and westward expansion more generally—may come under scrutiny, they endure as fundamental characteristics of what it means to be American.

23. "Skateboard Skiddoo," *Newsweek*, May 10, 1965.

24. "The Week in Review," *Los Angeles Times*, June 14, 1959.

25. "The Week in Review," *Los Angeles Times*, July 12, 1959.

26. Gene Early, "Skateboard Ban Drive Growing," *Los Angeles Times*, April 29, 1962, SG14.

27. Ibid.

28. "*Surf Crazy* Advertisement," *Los Angeles Times*, May 19, 1964, B3; "Santa Monica Civic Shows Surfing Movie," *Los Angeles Times*, May 19, 1964, B4.

29. George Garrigues, "Skateboard Ban Plea Puts Burbank in Spin," *Los Angeles Times*, May 21, 1964, G1.

30. For an illuminating discussion of the role of rebels in postwar American culture, see Medovoi, *Rebels*.

31. For example, one man cautioned that the nurse treating him for an arm broken

while skateboarding said that she had seen four broken arms over the course of one week. The letter implies that the fractures were due to skateboarding but does not say so outright (Philip T. Allen, "Letter to the Editor: Sidewalk Surfers," *Los Angeles Times*, November 14, 1964). Another reader warned that skateboarders were "either spilling into the sidewalk or into the street" (Janet L. Holt, "Letter to the Editor: Sidewalk Surfers," *Los Angeles Times*, November 14, 1964). Several articles that year reported skateboarders either injured or killed while riding. See, for example, "Boy Avoids Bad Injuries as Car Runs over Chest," *Los Angeles Times*, September 21, 1964, E7; and "Skate-Board Rider Dies after Crash," *Los Angeles Times*, September 1, 1964, C8.

32. "A New Sport or a New Menace?" *Consumer Reports*, June 1965, 273–74.

33. "Skateboarding: Hazardous New Fad for Kids," *Good Housekeeping*, August 1965, 137.

34. Thomas Plate, "Snap Goes the Skater," *Washington Post*, September 1, 1965, A3.

35. Bill Gold, "The District Line," *Washington Post*, November 8, 1965. On June 17, 1966, the *Washington Post* declared, "Last spring skateboards caused an epidemic of fractures and injuries which hit hardest at boys in the 10- to 12-year-old-age bracket" (Joan Beck, "Transfusion New Aid for Unborn Rh Babies," *Washington Post*, June 17, 1966, D6).

36. "Sidewalk Plan Hits Obstacle," *Los Angeles Times*, October 21, 1965, SG1.

37. "Skateboards: Fun but Dangerous," *Consumer Bulletin*, August 1965, 13.

38. Ernie Bushmiller, "Nancy," *Los Angeles Times*, July 27, 1965, A7.

39. "Ban on Skateboards Enacted 'Reluctantly,'" *Los Angeles Times*, June 22, 1965, 23.

40. "Pepper . . . and Salt," *Wall Street Journal*, November 2, 1965, 18.

41. Jerry Doernberg, "Skateboarders Near Thin Ice," *Los Angeles Times*, May 24, 1965, SG8.

42. "Skateboard Skiddoo," 45.

43. Ibid.

44. Katharine Davis Fishman, "Danger: Children at Play," *New York Times*, September 25, 1966, 286.

45. "Business Bulletin," *Wall Street Journal*, May 27, 1965, 1.

46. "Skateboard Award," *Los Angeles Times*, July 22, 1965, WS2.

47. "Ban on Skateboards Enacted 'Reluctantly,'" 23.

48. For example, Sierra Madre, California's Parks and Recreation Commission, contemplated declaring a Skateboard Day after banned skateboarders complained ("Glendale Police Chief's Edict Bans Skateboarders," *Los Angeles Times*, June 23, 1965, SG9). The city also instituted a Skateboard School, which offered six weeks of instruction over the course of the summer ("Sierra Madre Plans Skateboard School," *Los Angeles Times*, July 5, 1965, SG8).

49. Stern Brothers advertisement, *New York Times*, August 29, 1965, 101.

50. "A 'Good Skate' Competes Above Board," *Los Angeles Times*, October 19, 1964.

51. "Winning Form," *Los Angeles Times*, August 29, 1965, WS2; "Skateboarders in Action," *Los Angeles Times*, August 25, 1966, WS2; "Good Skates," *Los Angeles Times*, August 26, 1966, A1.

52. "84 Compete in Skateboard Tournament," *Los Angeles Times*, January 3, 1965, WS13; "Skateboarders Wheel around in City Finals," *Los Angeles Times*, August 27, 1965, SF8.

53. "Skating Dog," *Los Angeles Times*, August 15, 1964, B8; "Skateboard Award," WS2; "New Skateboarder," *Los Angeles Times*, June 14, 1965, 27. Lucy and the other girls from the 1966 CBS special *Charlie Brown's All Stars* also had skateboards. J. M.C., "'Peanuts' on TV," *Christian Science Monitor*, June 10, 1966, 4.

54. Brook, *The Concrete Wave*, 21–31.

55. "Movies," *New York Times*, http://movies2.nytimes.com/gst/movies/movie.html?v_id=138604.

56. Bosley Crowther, "Who Says There Is No Talent?" *New York Times*, December 4, 1966, X5.

57. Kevin Thomas, "Film Short Is Long on Artistry," *Los Angeles Times*, March 15, 1966, C11.

58. Charles R. Donaldson, "Few Youths Entering Skateboard Contests," *Los Angeles Times*, August 14, 1966, C8. See also "Skateboards on the Way Out? Not in This Generation," *Los Angeles Times*, August 29, 1966, SF9.

59. Marylin Bender, "Advertising Heeds the Eloquent Call of Fashion," *New York Times*, August 16, 1966, 30.

60. McCandlish Phillips, "Family Visit Is Happy Day in Life of a Plebe," *New York Times*, May 26, 1966, 31.

61. Lawrence Laurent, "Johnny Carson Knows His Job," *Washington Post*, May 4, 1966, B17.

62. Brooke, *The Concrete Wave*, 15.

63. C. W. Kirk, "Around the Beltway," *Washington Post*, March 28, 1968, F2.

64. Kellogg, "Rebirth of the Boards."

65. Pileggi, "Wheeling and Dealing," 22. See also "Wheel Crazy," *Time*, October 27, 1975.

66. Pileggi, "Wheeling and Dealing"; Tony Hiss and Sheldon Bart, "Free as a Board," *New York Times*, September 12, 1976, 40; Judi R. Kesselman, "The Skateboard Menace," *Family Health*, August 1976, 34–35, 76; David F. Salisbury, "Skateboarding: From Fad to Sport," *Christian Science Monitor*, September 3, 1976, 6; Mary McHugh, "Skateboards Are the Hottest Thing on Wheels," *New York Times*, June 6, 1976, 101. The *Washington Post* offered a prehistory of this story, describing the scientist Vernon Heightfield, who at his sons' behest used the urethane with which he was experimenting to make skateboard wheels. According to the *Post*, Frank Nasworthy

worked at Heightfield's factory and began marketing his own wheels after working there. Dave Scheiber, "Science Comes to Skateboards and the Sport Is Booming," *Washington Post*, August 11, 1977, D9.

67. William K. Knoedelseder Jr., "Skateboarding: A Story," *Los Angeles Times*, October 16, 1977, T99.

68. See, for example, Lynde McCormick, "Skateboards Come Back with Fresh Set of Antics," *Christian Science Monitor*, August 27, 1975, 19; Joe Helberger, "Skateboards Scoot Up in Popularity," *Washington Post*, October 5, 1975, 9–10; Jon Nordhiemer, "Skateboards Make Comeback as Older Boys and Girls Join In," *New York Times*, October 9, 1975, 46; Kellogg, "Rebirth of the Boards," 56.

69. Richard O'Reilly, "Skateboard: Personal Rapid Transit, Southern California Style," *Los Angeles Times*, June 2, 1975, OCA1.

70. "Sidewalk Surfin'," *Washington Post*, June 8, 1975.

71. Nordhiemer, "Skateboards Make Comeback as Older Boys and Girls Join In," 46.

72. Tony Kornheiser, "Whoosh! Skateboards Zip Back into Big Time," *New York Times*, June 19, 1976, 35.

73. William Knowlton Zinsser, "Super Rad Means O.K., Dad," *Sports Illustrated*, April 24, 1978, 36.

74. McCormick, "Skateboards Come Back with Fresh Set of Antics," 19.

75. Pileggi, "Wheeling and Dealing," 24.

76. Kellogg, "Rebirth of the Boards," 56.

77. Hank Burchard, "Riding the Skateboard Wave," *Washington Post*, August 5, 1976, D7.

78. Knowlton Zinsser, "Super Rad Means O.K., Dad," 38.

79. Kellogg, "Rebirth of the Boards," 56.

80. Jerry Belcher, "Georgia's 'Colonial Dream' Wins Top Prize for Floats," *Los Angeles Times*, January 2, 1975, A1, 4; "Blood Transfusion Ordered for Youth," *Los Angeles Times*, June 12, 1975, OC5; "Skateboard Fall Fatal to Youth," *Los Angeles Times*, May 6, 1975, OC1.

81. Hiss and Bart, "Free as a Board," 8; Kesselman, "The Skateboard Menace," 35; Kellogg, "Rebirth of the Boards," 56.

82. Kesselman, "The Skateboard Menace," 35.

83. Phyllis C. Richman, "Try It!" *Washington Post*, September 26, 1976, 276; Kellogg, "Rebirth of the Boards," 56.

84. Salisbury, "Skateboarding," 6.

85. McHugh, "Skateboards Are the Hottest Thing on Wheels," 35.

86. ". . . No List," *Washington Post*, November 16, 1975, 75.

87. Judith Martin, "Tagging Toy Prices," *Washington Post*, December 5, 1975, D1.

88. "CHP to Ticket Skateboarders for Speeding," *Los Angeles Times*, March 30, 1975, SE2.

89. Patricia A. Bayley, "Skateboards," letter to the editor, *Los Angeles Times*, July 7, 1975, C6.

90. "Christmas Eve a Time of Fear for Young Burglar," *Los Angeles Times*, December 26, 1975, 3.

91. Tom Gorman, "Playing Santa Can Be Tough Sledding," *Los Angeles Times*, December 14, 1975, SE7. For more examples of such associations, see "Robbers Flee on Skateboards," *Los Angeles Times*, August 3, 1975, SFA2; and Leslie Berkman, "Swap Meet at Fairgrounds Raided by 130 Law Officers," *Los Angeles Times*, February 3, 1975, 6A.

92. Tom Newton, "104 Arrested in Tujunga after Street Melee," *Los Angeles Times*, June 10, 1975, A3.

93. Kesselman, "The Skateboard Menace," 35.

94. Deford, "Promo Wiz in Kidvid Biz," 33.

95. "Manhattan Will Apply Brakes to Skateboarding," *Los Angeles Times*, January 19, 1975, CS4; Doug Smith, "Lorenzen Seeks Law to Regulate Skateboard Use," *Los Angeles Times*, May 11, 1975, SFA1; "City Will Study Skateboarding," *Los Angeles Times*, June 5, 1975, OCA10; "Peninsula Cities Get Tough on Skateboards in Streets," *Los Angeles Times*, August 7, 1975, CS2; "Skateboarding Ordinance Ok'd," *Los Angeles Times*, December 15, 1975, D2.

96. "Safety Series on Skateboards," *Los Angeles Times*, July 13, 1975, WS5; "41 Groups Plan Safety Exhibits," *Los Angeles Times*, September 4, 1975, SE5; "All-Day Safety Program Slated at Laurel Plaza," *Los Angeles Times*, November 13, 1975, SF14.

97. McHugh, "Skateboards Are the Hottest Thing on Wheels," 35.

98. Ibid.

99. Scott Moore, "Skateboarding Industry Rolling to Success," *Los Angeles Times*, September 18, 1977, OC1.

100. "Glendora Will Prohibit Skateboards Downtown," *Los Angeles Times*, April 27, 1975, SG5.

101. Hiss and Bart, "Free as a Board," 40.

102. Lynn Darling, "Skateboard: Status Symbol for the Young in Suburbia," *Washington Post*, November 13, 1977, 36.

103. Earl Gustkey, "Skateboarding May Be Kids' Stuff but It Pays," *Los Angeles Times*, September 22, 1977, E1.

104. Leo C. Wolinsky, "Skateboarding the Next Pro Sport?" *Los Angeles Times*, June 23, 1977, CS1.

105. Pileggi, "Wheeling and Dealing," 22. See also Hiss and Bart, "Free as a Board," 81. A sporting goods store owner in New York City told them, "It's not going to be a fad this time. . . . This time it's going to be a sport."

106. Catherine Coyne, "Family Guide to Weekend Events," *Los Angeles Times*, May 8, 1975.

107. "Vacation Events Set for Children," *Los Angeles Times*, December 19, 1975, U16.

108. "5,266 Raised for MS," *Los Angeles Times*, April 17, 1975, SG4.

109. Hiss and Bart, "Free as a Board," 40.

110. "With Money on the Line, Coast Skateboards Roll," *New York Times*, September 7, 1976, 14.

111. Kornheiser, "Whoosh!" 35.

112. Hiss and Bart, "Free as a Board," 83.

113. "With Money on the Line," 14.

114. Ibid.

115. Penelope McMillan, "Top Skateboarders Spin Their Slicks," *Los Angeles Times*, September 26, 1977, B3.

116. Salisbury, "Skateboarding," 6.

117. Elliott Almond, "Skateboarding's New Young Pros," *Los Angeles Times*, September 18, 1977, OC1.

118. Deford, "Promo Wiz in Kidvid Biz," 30.

119. Ibid., 32.

120. Gustkey, "Skateboarding May Be Kids' Stuff but It Pays," E1.

121. Ibid., E1.

122. Korneiser, "Whoosh!" 35.

123. Hiss and Bart, "Free as a Board," 81. While this quote points to the changing availability of skateboarding to the working class, it also invokes, like accounts of skateboarding's earliest history, the boys who tinkered with radio equipment. See Douglas, *Listening In*.

124. Moore, "Skateboarding Industry Rolling to Success," OC1.

125. Ibid.

126. Ibid., OC5.

127. Gustkey, "Skateboarding May Be Kids' Stuff but It Pays," E8.

128. Knoedelseder, "Skateboarding," T99.

129. "With Money on the Line," 14.

130. Deford, "Promo Wiz in Kidvid Biz," 32.

131. "With Money on the Line," 14.

132. Ibid.

133. McCormick, "Skateboards Come Back with Fresh Set of Antics," 19.

134. Kesselman, "The Skateboard Menace," 35.

135. Deford, "Promo Wiz in Kidvid Biz," 43.

136. Darling, "Skateboard," 36.

137. McMillan, "Top Skateboarders Spin Their Slicks," B3.

138. Ibid.

139. Ibid.

140. Elliott Almond, "Skateboarder Means Business," *Los Angeles Times*, August 13, 1976, D8.

141. Gustkey, "Skateboarding May Be Kids' Stuff but It Pays," E8.

142. While this law did a number of things, the most well-known is its requirement that schools provide equal opportunity for both male and female athletes.

143. Deford, "Promo Wiz in Kidvid Biz," 33.

144. Leo C. Wolinsky, CS1.

145. McMillan, "Top Skateboarders Spin Their Slicks," B3.

146. Ibid.

147. Almond, "Skateboarding's New Young Pros," OC1.

148. Ibid., OC8.

149. McMillan, "Top Skateboarders Spin Their Slicks," B3.

150. Moore, "Skateboarding Industry Rolling to Success," OC1.

151. Judy Mann, "Skateboard Fever," *Washington Post*, May 25, 1979, B9.

152. Edwin McDowell, "Roller Skates: 300,000 Pairs a Month," *New York Times*, May 13, 1979, F13.

153. Henry Allen, "The New Fad Afoot," *Washington Post*, March 29, 1979, D1.

154. Ibid.

155. David J. Blum, "U.S. Makers Confident of Victory in Trade Battle with Cheap Skates," *Wall Street Journal*, April 6, 1981, 25.

156. Scott Ostler, "Some Things Will Just Never Be the Same," *Los Angeles Times*, October 5, 1983, D3.

157. Jura Koncius, "Video Games: Regulating America's Latest Craze," *Washington Post*, October 8, 1981, VA1.

158. Lynn Myking, "New Wheels Help Spur Revival," *Los Angeles Times*, February 6, 1979, SD_A4.

159. On safety, see, for example, "The Week in Review," June 14, 1959, SG2; Annette Rick, "Fifty-Four Hours," *Los Angeles Times*, July 21, 1983, G8; "Views and News," *Los Angeles Times*, November 26, 1963, 48; and Mayerene Barker, "Law, Order Become Part of Curriculum," *Los Angeles Times*, June 4, 1981, SG8. On bans, see Barry M. Horstman, "Shrinking Territory Upsets S.D. Skaters," *Los Angeles Times*, March 8, 1982, SDA1. On events, see "Santa Monica Civic Shows Surfing Movie," WS6; Debora Robinson, "Good Scouts Get Together to Show Off Their Skills," *Los Angeles Times*, November 15, 1982, OC4; Marc Appleman, "Celebrations, Color Will Mark Easter," *Los Angeles Times*, April 1, 1983, SDA1; "Sierra Madre Plans Skateboard School," N2; and Don Snyder, "Skateboarder Plunges Feet First into Routines," *Los Angeles Times*, April 15, 1979, GB1.

160. Ellen Hume, "Sharks Circling, Hayakawa Concedes," *Los Angeles Times*, July 5, 1981, A8.

161. Liz McGuinness, "Cities Ponder What's in a Game," *Los Angeles Times*, August 16, 1981, D1, 16–17; Sharon Launer, "Ah, the Sounds of Summer," *New York Times*, July 12, 1981, L120.

162. Brooke, *The Concrete Wave*, 45.

163. Mike Granberry, "At 21, Top S.D. Skateboarder Is Sport's Old Man," *Los Angeles Times*, April 25, 1985, SDC25.

164. Brooke, *The Concrete Wave*, 95.

165. Karl Taro Greenfeld, "Skate and Destroy," *Sports Illustrated*, June 7, 2004.

166. Ibid.

167. Brooke, *The Concrete Wave*, 96.

168. Granberry, "At 21, Top S.D. Skateboarder Is Sport's Old Man," SDC1.

169. Ibid., SCC24.

170. Ibid., SCC25.

171. Dick Wagner, "Hanging 10 at 36," *Los Angeles Times*, October 31, 1985, LB8.

172. Currently deemed "the Michael Jordan of skateboarding," Hawk has been tapped for numerous marketing endeavors by manufacturers of teen and "tween" products such as Bagel Bites, has played a key role on *The X Games* as both a competitor and an announcer, and has made appearances as himself or fictionalized versions of himself in media texts as diverse as *The Simpsons*, *CSI: Miami*, and *XXX*.

173. Armen Keteyian, "Chairman of the Board," *Sports Illustrated*, November 24, 1986.

174. Ibid.

175. Ibid.

176. Nancy Ray, "Scouts to Save Skateboard Park," *Los Angeles Times*, October 27, 1985, SDA4.

177. Jack Cavanaugh, "Towns Cite Safety Cares as Skateboarding Gains," *New York Times*, May 10, 1987, CN15. Although Grigorian certainly has a vested interest in encouraging skateboarding, his comment still speaks to the controversies surrounding the practice's image.

178. Rich Levine, "Curbing Teen Violence," *American Health*, April 1989, 108.

179. Richard Bienvenue, "A Little Bit of Noise but a Whole Lot of Fun," *Washington Post*, July 28, 1990, A18.

180. Dennis Hevesi, "Parents Vow to Protest AIDS Student," *New York Times*, September 16, 1990, 34.

181. Michael Gross, "A Club Scene Just for Teen-Agers," *New York Times*, August 1, 1987, 56; Elaine Louie, "In Schools, Fashion Is Whatever Is 'Fresh,'" *New York Times*, September 22, 1987, C11; Brenda Fowler, "Teen Taste: Like, Trendy," *New York Times*, November 6, 1988, EDUC7; Deborah Hofmann, "Clothes for Beach (or Mall or Main Street)," *New York Times*, August 6, 1989, 44.

182. Jene Stonesifer, "Kids' Fashion Cuts," *Washington Post*, April 23, 1992, 15.

183. R. Rugoff, "Get Big! Fashions Worn by Skateboarders," *Vogue*, September 1992, 191.

184. Ibid., 194.

185. Ibid., 207.

186. Ibid., 212.

187. Beastie Boy Adam Yauch told the *New York Times* in 1992, "'I never go any-place without my skateboard." Penelope Green, "Absolute Necessities," *New York Times*, October 18, 1992, SMA94.

188. Tamar Lewin, "Hey There, Dudes, the Kids Have Grabbed a Network," *New York Times*, October 21, 1990, H35.

189. Susan Reed, "From Homemade Chutes to Steep Streets, San Francisco's Thrashers Just Love Riding for a Fall," *People Weekly*, December 3, 1984.

190. Derek Raser and John McCoy, "Over Board," *Los Angeles Times*, July 31, 1985, VB13.

191. Jane O'Hara, "Trouble in Paradise," *Maclean's*, April 6, 1987, 48.

192. Jay Cocks, "The Irresistible Lure of Grabbing Air: Skateboarding, Once a Fad, Is Now a National Turn-On," *Time*, June 6, 1988.

193. Peter Carlson, "Ragin' on the Ramp," *Washington Post Magazine*, February 25, 1990, W23.

194. Ibid., W25.

195. John Berger, *Ways of Seeing* (London: Penguin, 1972). Notably, the description of these young women echoes my own early experiences with skateboarders.

196. Peter Watrous, "Pop Turns the Tables—with Beefcake," *New York Times*, February 10, 1991, H27.

197. Jim Schaefers, "Why Boys Have More Fun," *Seventeen*, July 1989, 68.

198. Ibid., 69, emphasis in original.

199. Garry Whannel, "From Pig's Bladders to Ferraris: Media Discourses of Masculinity and Morality in Obituaries of Stanley Matthews," in *Sport, Media, Culture: Global and Local Dimensions*, edited by Alina Bernstein and Neil Blain (Portland, OR: Frank Cass, 2003).

200. Susan Faludi, *Backlash: The Undeclared War against American Women* (New York: Crown, 1991).

201. S. Enfield, "Boy Talk," *Gentlemen's Quarterly*, September 1991.

202. Patrick Phillips, "Boy Wonder Gets the Purple Crayon," *New York Times*, May 7, 1995, 59.

203. Watrous, "Pop Turns the Tables."

204. Mary-Kate Arnold, "Skater Babes: Asexual or Not?" *Sassy*, December 1992, 46–47.

205. Esther D'Amico and L. Maxine Sanford, "Pint-Size Purchasers," *Home Office Computing*, October 1994, 98.

206. Jennifer Steinhauer, "Lulu and Her Friends Are, Therefore They Shop," *New York Times*, April 29, 1998, G6.

207. Petrecca, "Going to Extremes," *Advertising Age*, October 11, 1999, 37.

208. Michael Hiestand, "Going to Extremes," *TV Guide*, June 24–30, 1995, 32.

209. Ibid., 33. See also Robert E. Rinehart, "ESPN's *X Games:* Contests of Opposition, Resistance, Co-option, and Negotiation," in *Tribal Play: Subcultural Journeys through Sport*, edited by Michael Atkinson and Kevin Young (Bingley, UK: JAI Press, 2008).

210. Hiestand, "Going to Extremes," 34.

211. Michael Burgi, "Don't Try This at Home," *Mediaweek*, June 12, 1995, 24.

212. Hiestand, "Going to Extremes," 35. See also Stuart Chirls, "Extreme Gear," *Popular Mechanics*, May 1996.

213. Stuart Elliott, "*The X Games:* Going to Extremes in an Effort to Tap a Growing Segment of Sports," *New York Times*, June 21, 1996, 6.

214. Robert E. Rinehart, "Exploiting a New Generation: Corporate Branding and the Co-optation of Action Sport," in *Youth Culture and Sport: Identity, Power, and Politics*, edited by Michael D. Giardina and Michele K. Donnelly (New York: Routledge, 2008), 84.

215. David Winzelberg, "Skateboarding, a Big Business, Seeks More Venues on L.I.," *New York Times*, October 27, 1996, LI13.

216. Burgi, "Don't Try This at Home," 24. See also Rinehart, "ESPN's *X Games.*"

217. Elliott, "*The X Games*," 6.

218. J. Seabrook, "Tackling the Competition," *New Yorker*, August 18, 1997, 47.

219. Karl Taro Greenfeld, "A Wider World of Sports," *Time*, November 9, 1998, 81.

220. Peter Spiegel, "Gen-X-Tremist Pitchmen," *Forbes*, December 14, 1998, 188.

221. Ibid.

222. Dan Gordon, Brannan Johnson, Dennis McCoy, Carey Hart, and Chris Edwards, "Future Shock," *Sport*, September 1999, 93.

223. Zina Moukheiber, "Later, Skater," *Forbes*, November 29, 1999, 108.

224. Rob Givens, "Skateboarding's Best Seller," *New York Times Upfront*, December 11, 2000, 21.

225. L. Goldman, "From Ramp to Riches," *Forbes*, July 5, 2004. Apparently, department store prices also demonstrate Hawk's authenticity, for, she went on, "You won't ever find a Hawk T shirt for $5 in the discount bin. It ain't gonna happen."

226. Lea Goldman, "Going to Xtremes," *Forbes*, April 3, 2000, 140. See also Terry Lefton, "Alt-Sports: Popular, Yes, but No Salvation for Licensing," *Brandweek*, February 7, 2000, 32.

227. Arlene Weintraub, "Chairman of the Board," *Business Week*, May 28, 2001, 96.

228. Rinehart, "ESPN's *X Games.*"

229. Alex Wilkinson, "Bob Burnquist," *Rolling Stone*, June 10, 1999, 105.

230. Ibid., 108.

231. "Skateboarding: Hazardous New Fad for Kids," 33.

232. Susan Pearsall, "Soaring Teen-Agers at the Skate Park," *New York Times*, October 11, 1998, CT19.

233. Petrecca, "Going to Extremes" (2000), 36.

234. Jennifer Steinhauer, "Feet First into the Clubs," *New York Times*, May 22, 1994, V1.

235. Frank DeCaro, "Forgotten, but Not Yet Gone: French Blue, Platforms, and Pierced Navels," *New York Times*, July 19, 1998, ST2. See also Amy M. Spindler, "Flip-Flop: The Runway Leads the Street," *New York Times*, September 19, 1995; Arnold,

"Skater Babes"; Maryellen Gordon, "It's Fitted Skaters vs. Baggy Ravers," *New York Times*, January 18, 1998; and Joseph Oppedisano, "Wheel Men," *New York Times*, March 21, 1999.

236. "With Money on the Line, Coast Skateboards Roll," *New York Times*, September 7, 1976, 104.

237. Karl Taro Greenfeld, "Life on the Edge," *Time*, September 6, 1999, 29.

238. Ibid.

239. Patricia Leigh Brown, "This Is Extremely Sporting," *New York Times*, August 13, 2000, 2.

240. See Dan Gordon, "Airborne," *Sport*, June 1999; Ellen Liberman, "Gravity Games: Hawk Is Skating's Chairman of the Board," *Providence Journal-Bulletin*, September 11, 1999, which notes "Like all parents, he is juggling late-night feedings with work the next day" (1A); and C. Luna, "Tony Hawk," *Current Biography* 61, no. 6 (2000): 22–25.

241. Gordon, "Airborne," 97.

242. Sean Mortimer, "Chairman of the Board," *Sports Illustrated for Kids*, July 1998, 62.

243. Liberman, "Gravity Games," 1A.

244. "With Money on the Line, Coast Skateboards Roll," 105.

245. Bill Donahue, "For New Sports, ESPN Rules as the X-Treme Gatekeeper," *New York Times*, March 11, 1998, G2.

246. Andrea Kannapell, "Taking Sports to the Limit," *New York Times*, October 11, 1998, NJ1.

247. Andrew McMains, "Call of the Wild: Saatchi Unveils Bourbon Effort," *Adweek*, January 18, 1999, 26.

248. Gordon, "Airborne," 97.

249. Donahue, "For New Sports, ESPN Rules as the X-Treme Gatekeeper," G2.

250. See Pinsker, "Personal Documentaries Are New Form of Marketing," 12.

251. Of course, I have noted already that Vans, Inc., sponsored the film, investing approximately 750,000 dollars. This investment is only evident in the logo for Vans Off the Wall Production Company in the opening credits and the frequent appearance of Vans shoes on the featured skateboarders. Still, Peralta suggests that Vans' sponsorship ensured that it could control the development and production of the film. See ibid.

252. Roger Ebert, "*Dogtown and Z-Boys* Review," http://rogerebert.suntimes.com/apps/pbcs.dll/ article?AID=/20020510/REVIEWS/205100301/1023.

253. Stephen Holden, "Skating on Top of the World during an Endless Summer," *New York Times*, April 26, 2002, 25. See also Neil Strauss, "Where the Wheel Was Reinvented," *New York Times*, April 28, 2002, 17.

254. Betts, "The Whoosh of What You'll Be Wearing," 6.

255. A. O. Scott, "When California Started Riding on Little Wheels," *New York Times*, June 3, 2005, 13.

256. O. Gleiberman, "You Say You Want a Skateboard Revolution? Then Hold On," *Entertainment Weekly*, June 10, 2005, 81–82.

257. Kusz, *Revolt of the White Athlete*, 110.

258. Bushmiller, "Nancy," 10.

259. Robbie Fraser, "Thrill Ride," *TV Guide*, August 10–16, 2002, 28.

260. Matt Higgins, "In Board Sports, Insiders' Status Makes Gear Sell," *New York Times*, November 24, 2006, 1.

261. Ibid.

262. Tim Layden, "What Is This 34-Year-Old Man Doing on a Skateboard? Making Millions," *Sports Illustrated*, June 10, 2002.

263. Ibid.

264. Goldman, "From Ramp to Riches."

265. Ibid.

266. Stuart Elliot, "Tony Hawk's New Trick: 2 Marketers in 1 Campaign," *New York Times*, October 23, 2006, 10. As I note later, this strategy seems to have been successful with at least one skateboarder, who excused Hawk's sponsorship of McDonald's as a true representation of his fondness for the chain.

267. Layden, "What Is This 34-Year-Old Man Doing on a Skateboard?"

268. J. Ressner, "10 Questions for Tony Hawk," *Time*, May 9, 2005, 8.

269. Tony Hawk and Sean Mortimer, *Hawk: Occupation, Skateboarder* (New York: Harper Entertainment, 2001).

270. Lola Ogunnaike, "A Skateboard King Who Fell to Earth," *New York Times*, August 21, 2003, 1.

271. Ibid.

272. Stephen Holden, Review of *Stoked: The Rise and Fall of Gator*, *New York Times*, August 22, 2003, 11.

273. Greenfeld, "Skate and Destroy."

274. Ibid.

275. Ibid.

276. Matt Higgins, "Champion Thanks a Legend of the Air Up There," *New York Times*, August 8, 2005, 3.

277. Joan Raymond, "Going to Extremes," *American Demographics*, June 1, 2002, n.p., accessed online, General BusinessFile ASAP, 28.

278. Ibid., 29.

279. Debbe Geiger, "Get Aerial," *Better Homes and Gardens*, June 2002, 112–19.

280. Abigail Sullivan Moore, "Skateboarding Heaven," *New York Times*, October 19, 2003, 1.

281. Bradford McKee, "Ramping Up the Suburbs," *New York Times*, November 27, 2003, 1. See also Robert Strauss, "Skaters Want a Better Image," *New York Times*, January 25, 2004.

282. Justin Porter, "A Skateboarder Gets a Voice in the Redesign of a Beloved Spot," *New York Times*, June 24, 2005.

"Freedom on four wheels"

1. Unfortunately, this study does not address skateboarding magazines, which, like many niche publications, serve as instructional documents about the norms of the culture. An analysis of these magazines would be a productive way to explore more fully the ways in which niche media interpellate their audiences and educate them in terms of cultural mores.

2. See, for example, Andrea L. Press, *Women Watching Television: Gender, Class, and Generation in the American Television Experience* (Philadelphia: University of Pennsylvania Press, 1991).

3. See, for example, Ien Ang, *Watching Dallas: Soap Opera and the Melodramatic Imagination*, translated by Della Couling (New York: Methuen, 1985).

4. Kimberle Crenshaw, "Mapping the Margins: Intersectionality, Identity Politics, and Violence against Women of Color," *Stanford Law Review* (1991); Valerie Smith, *Not Just Race, Not Just Gender: Black Feminist Readings* (New York: Routledge, 1998).

5. Barrie Thorne, *Gender Play: Girls and Boys in School* (New Brunswick, NJ: Rutgers University Press, 1993), 123.

6. Sunaina Maira and Elisabeth Soep, *Youthscapes: The Popular, the National, the Global* (Philadelphia: University of Pennsylvania Press, 2005).

7. See Tricia Rose, *Black Noise: Rap Music and Popular Culture in Contemporary America* (Hanover, NH: Wesleyan University Press, 1994). In her chapter "Prophets of Rage: Rap Music and the Politics of Black Cultural Expression," Rose offers a discussion of the "hidden transcripts" of rap music and its contradictory political stance (99–145).

8. Michel Foucault, *Discipline and Punish: The Birth of the Prison*, translated by Alan Sheridan (New York: Vintage, 1995).

9. Fred Pfeil, *White Guys: Studies in Postmodern Domination and Difference* (New York: Verso, 1995).

10. R. W. Connell, *Masculinities* (Berkeley: University of California Press, 1995).

11. Sean Brayton, "'Black-Lash': Revisiting the 'White Negro' through Skateboarding," *Sociology of Sport Journal* 22 (2005): 359.

12. Becky Beal and Charlene Wilson, "'Chicks Dig Scars': Commercialisation and the Transformation of Skateboarders' Identities," in *Understanding Lifestyle Sports: Consumption, Identity, and Difference*, edited by Belinda Wheaton (New York: Routledge, 2004), 32.

13. Belinda Wheaton, "Introduction: Mapping the Lifestyle Sport-Scape," in *Understanding Lifestyle Sports: Consumption, Identity, and Difference*, edited by Belinda Wheaton (New York: Routledge, 2004), 4.

14. David Savran, *Taking It Like a Man: White Masculinity, Masochism, and Contemporary American Culture* (Princeton: Princeton University Press, 1998).

15. Lynn Ta, "Hurt So Good: *Fight Club*, Masculine Violence, and the Crisis of Capitalism," *Journal of American Culture* 29, no. 3 (2006): 265–77.

16. Savran, *Taking It Like a Man*.

17. Stephen Lyng, *Edgework: The Sociology of Risk-Taking* (New York: Routledge, 2004).

18. Alana Young and Christine Dallaire, "Beware*#! Sk8 at Your Own Risk: The Discourses of Young Female Skateboarders," in *Tribal Play: Subcultural Journeys through Sport*, edited by Michael Atkinson and Kevin Young (Bingley, UK: JAI Press, 2008), 236.

19. George Lipsitz, *The Possessive Investment in Whiteness* (Chicago: University of Chicago Press, 2006).

20. See Robert N. Bellah, Richard Madsen, William M. Sullivan, Ann Swidler, and Steven M. Tipton, *Habits of the Heart: Individualism and Commitment in American Life* (Berkeley: University of California Press, 1985).

21. Not all skateboarders, of course, experienced such exclusion. Some did participate in traditional sporting activities and explained their love of skateboarding in descriptions that didn't reference being teased.

22. Matt Wray and Annalee Newitz, eds., *White Trash: Race and Class in America* (New York: Routledge, 1997).

23. Belinda Wheaton and Becky Beal, "'Keeping it Real': Subcultural Media and the Discourses of Authenticity in Alternative Sport," *International Review for the Sociology of Sport* 38, no. 2 (2003): 155–76.

24. The phrase is borrowed from Benedict Anderson, *Imagined Communities: Reflections on the Origin and Spread of Nationalism* (London: Verso, 1983).

25. Richard Dyer, *White* (London: Routledge, 1997).

26. Wheaton and Beal, "Keeping It Real," 169.

27. Skaters frequently located inauthenticity in skateboarders younger than themselves, espousing a lay theory of the current media culture that suggests that media texts such as *The X Games* have corrupted the latest generation of skateboarders. Becky Beal and Charlene Wilson's work echoes this finding. See Beal and Wilson, "Chicks Dig Scars." Exhibiting the "third-person effect," these claims also construct skateboarding as a culture that could be at risk. Although it is beyond the scope of this book to do so, these lay theories deserve further analysis.

28. Ibid.

"The things that make you a man"

The quotation in the chapter title is from Steve-O, *Wildboyz*, "Brazil," Season 2, Episode 2.

1. Sean Brayton, "MTV's *Jackass*: Transgression, Abjection, and the Economy of White Masculinity," *Journal of Gender Studies* 16, no. 1 (2007): 58.

2. Ibid., 63.

3. Although the show's portrayal of male initiation rituals in "faraway places" may suggest the universality of the process of becoming a man, the white, American Wildboyz are *always* mocking these rituals while the "natives" who guide them through the initiations appear to be taking them seriously. The show's main point, then, is not the cross-cultural existence of the rituals but that the rituals are inherently dumb—and thus unnecessary—in the eyes of the white Western heroes of the show.

4. bell hooks, "Eating the Other: Desire and Resistance," in *Black Looks: Race and Representation*, edited by bell hooks (Boston: South End, 1992); Eric Lott, *Love and Theft: Blackface Minstrelsy and the American Working Class* (New York: Oxford University Press, 1993).

5. David J. Leonard, "To the White Extreme in the Mainstream: Manhood and White Youth Culture in a Virtual Sports World," in *Youth Culture and Sport: Identity, Power and Politics*, edited by Michael D. Giardina and Michele K. Donnelly (New York: Routledge, 2008), 99.

6. David Savran, *Taking It Like a Man: White Masculinity, Masochism, and Contemporary American Culture* (Princeton: Princeton University Press, 1998), 38.

7. R. W. Connell, *Masculinities* (Berkeley: University of California Press, 1995).

8. Susan Fraiman, *Cool Men and the Second Sex* (New York: Columbia University Press, 2003), xi.

9. Savran, *Taking It Like a Man*, 38.

10. Gail Bederman, *Manliness and Civilization: A Cultural History of Gender and Race in the United States, 1880–1917* (Chicago: University of Chicago Press, 1995); John F. Kasson, *Houdini, Tarzan, and the Perfect Man: The White Male Body and the Challenge of Modernity in America* (New York: Hill and Wang, 2001).

11. Bederman, *Manliness and Civilization*, 220.

12. hooks, "Eating the Other."

13. Kasson, *Houdini, Tarzan, and the Perfect Man*.

14. Michael S. Kimmel, *Manhood in America: A Cultural History*, 2nd ed. (New York: Oxford University Press, 2006).

15. Susan Bordo, *The Male Body: A New Look at Men in Public and Private* (New York: Farrar, Straus and Giroux, 1999), 15–35.

16. Ibid., 32.

17. Ibid., 34.

18. Ibid., 21.

19. Ibid., 43.

20. Ibid., 44.

21. Brenton J. Malin, *American Masculinity under Clinton: Popular Media and the Nineties "Crisis of Masculinity"* (New York: Peter Lang, 2005).

22. Savran, *Taking It Like a Man*, 1–32.

23. Susan Jeffords, *Hard Bodies: Hollywood Masculinity in the Reagan Era* (New Brunswick, NJ: Rutgers University Press, 1994).

24. Peggy McIntosh, "White Privilege: Unpacking the Invisible Knapsack," in *White Privilege: Essential Readings on the Other Side of Racism*, edited by Paula S. Rothenberg (New York: Worth, 2002). McIntosh characterizes whiteness as an "invisible knapsack" of privilege, an identity perceived to be the norm. Although she does not discuss the ways in which it can open space for the critique of other identity norms, her notion of the "invisible knapsack" is useful for characterizing the privilege Steve-O and Chris Pontius enjoy in their travels to "faraway lands."

25. Eve Kosofsky Sedgwick, *Epistemology of the Closet* (Berkeley: University of California Press, 1990): 19–21.

26. In his late twenties, Margera is by conventional standards no adolescent. However, he operates in a moment when adolescence seems to be lengthening as more and more young people put off marriage, children, home ownership, and other traditional markers of adulthood. Furthermore, he performs adolescence, continuing to live with his parents and a host of roommates and reveling in childhood pranks. Although, as I have noted, his latest reality show depicts his wedding, the show makes it clear that Bam is reluctant to participate in marriage as an institution and will only do so on his arguably adolescent terms.

27. John Hartigan Jr., "Name Calling: Objectifying 'Poor Whites' and 'White Trash' in Detroit," in *White Trash: Race and Class in America*, edited by Matt Wray and Annalee Newitz (New York: Routledge, 1997), 47.

28. For a discussion of women's "civilizing" impact, see Garry Whannel, "From Pig's Bladders to Ferraris: Media Discourses of Masculinity and Morality in Obituaries of Stanley Matthews," in *Sport, Media, Culture: Global and Local Dimensions*, edited by Alina Bernstein and Neil Blain (Portland, OR: Frank Cass, 2003), 73–94.

29. Richard Dyer, *White* (London: Routledge, 1997).

30. Homi Bhabha, "The Other Question," in *Contemporary Postcolonial Theory: A Reader*, edited by Padmini Mongia (London: Arnold, 1997).

31. Dyer, *White*.

"It's just what's possible"

1. Skateboarders rely on the concrete and metal of urban and suburban spaces; thus, unlike surfers, they rarely venture into the so-called third world. They do, however, tour through the urban centers of North and South America, Europe, Asia, and Australia.

2. Women do, at times, appear as professional skateboarders in these videos, but their presence is rare. In response to both this reality and the present study's focus on masculinity, henceforth I use the male pronoun.

3. Michael Nevin Willard, "Séance, Tricknowlogy, Skateboarding, and the Space of Youth," in *Generations of Youth: Youth Cultures and History in Twentieth-Century America*, edited by Joe Austin and Michael Nevin Willard (New York: New York University Press, 1998), 327.

4. For the purposes of clarity, I use the term *sponsor-me tape* throughout this

chapter to refer to this kind of video despite the facts that most amateur recordings are never used to solicit a sponsorship and most are no longer on "tape," as they are recorded digitally.

5. Despite the fact that some of these videos are created in the hopes of national or international recognition, they are rarely seen by an audience outside the local "scene." It is, of course, difficult to define the boundaries of "local," particularly in the era of YouTube, MySpace, and other Internet sites that allow for simple and cheap worldwide distribution of video content. Nevertheless, local videos usually remain just that: shown mostly in venues where the participants know one another personally or distributed within a small skateboarding scene usually imagined at the regional level. For the purposes of this project, Ann Arbor, southeastern Michigan, and the state of Michigan comprise increasingly large but still regional points of identification for local skateboarders.

6. Sean Brayton, "'Black-Lash': Revisiting the 'White Negro' through Skateboarding," *Sociology of Sport Journal* 22 (2005): 357.

7. Ibid., 361–62.

8. In 1956, William H. Whyte published *The Organization Man*, which characterized middle-class white-collar workers as running a rat race in the service of organizations such as corporations. The organization man has lost his sense of self and works only to further the needs of the organization. See William H. Whyte, *The Organization Man* (1956; repr. with new foreword by Joseph Nocerd, Philadelphia: University of Pennsylvania Press, 2002). *Dilbert* is a comic strip developed by Scott Adams that pokes fun at the life of white-collar cubicle workers. *Office Space*, written and directed by Mike Judge (the creator of MTV's adolescent cartoon *Beavis and Butthead*) and released in 1999, satirizes cubicle life by telling the story of a white-collar worker who, for all intents and purposes, stops working but is still promoted. *The Office*, NBC's television show inspired by a British comedy of the same name, stars Steve Carell and satirizes white-collar work in its portrayal of a small paper supply company.

9. Brayton, "Black-Lash," 364.

10. Although there are exceptions, this individual is usually a white man. He is sometimes single, but he is always seeking heterosexual family life.

11. Sarah Thornton, "The Social Logic of Subcultural Capital," in *The Subcultures Reader*, edited by Ken Gelder and Sarah Thornton (New York: Routledge, 1997).

12. R. W. Connell, *Masculinities* (Berkeley: University of California Press, 1995).

13. The basketball industry, in particular, has found new success via a focus on individual players' personalities (think of Dennis Rodman or Michael Jordan). Despite the elevation of personality, the coverage of basketball and other mainstream sports continues to center on game play.

14. Indiana's sculpture graphically presents the word *love*. It is the inspiration for the nickname "Love Park," which is officially named John F. Kennedy Plaza. See

Ocean Howell, "The 'Creative Class' and the Gentrifying City: Skateboarding in Philadelphia's Love Park," *Journal of Architectural Education* 59, no. 2 (2005): 32–42.

15. Although I mean to neither conflate "black culture" with "hip-hop culture" nor essentialize either of these dynamic locations, the images deployed by DC are clearly meant to evoke both.

16. Brayton, "Black-Lash," 364.

17. This relationship, and MTV's spin-off show, require analysis that falls outside the scope of this study.

18. bell hooks, "Eating the Other: Desire and Resistance," in *Black Looks: Race and Representation*, edited by bell hooks (Boston: South End, 1992).

19. Martti Lahti, "As We Become Machines: Corporealized Pleasure in Video Games," in *The Video Game Theory Reader*, edited by Mark J. P. Wolf and Bernard Perron (New York: Routledge, 2003), 166. Although Lahti is discussing video games, her phrase aptly describes skateboarding videos.

20. George Yudice, "What's a Straight White Man to Do?" in *Constructing Masculinity*, edited by M. Berger, B. Wallis, and S. Watson (New York: Routledge, 1995).

21. Ibid., 272.

22. Robert Goldman and Stephen Papson, *Nike Culture: The Sign of the Swoosh* (Thousand Oaks: Sage, 1998), 104.

23. Adrienne Rich, "Compulsory Heterosexuality and Lesbian Existence," *Signs: Journal of Women in Culture and Society* 5, no. 4 (1980): 631–60.

24. The skateboard magazine *Big Brother*, famously purchased by porn king Larry Flynt in 1997, was decidedly more homophobic in its stance. In 2004, it published a "gay issue," *Bi Brother*, which operated to suggest "We're so secure in our masculinity that we can deal with homosexuality." The issue is decidedly ambivalent.

25. Whyte, *Organization Man*.

26. Henry Jenkins, *Textual Poachers: Television Fans and Participatory Cultures* (New York: Routledge, 1992), 12.

27. Ibid., 13.

28. Ibid., 19.

29. This discussion of sports fandom is not meant to essentialize the practice. Rather, I mean to delineate why images of sports fandom are valorized in popular culture while images of fans of fictional television are frequently negative. Although sports fans arguably identify with athletic stars via personality or stories of hardship, such identification does not mitigate the respect accorded sports fans in American culture.

30. Tania Modleski, *Loving with a Vengeance: Mass-Produced Fantasies for Women* (New York: Methuen, 1982), 88.

31. Janice Radway, *Reading the Romance: Women, Patriarchy, and Popular Literature* (1984; repr., Chapel Hill: University of North Carolina Press, 1991).

32. Bonnie J. Dow, *Prime-Time Feminism: Television, Media Culture, and the*

Women's Movement since 1970 (Philadelphia: University of Pennsylvania Press, 1996), 193–94.

33. Ien Ang, "Melodramatic Identifications: Television Fiction and Women's Fantasy," in *Feminist Television Criticism: A Reader,* edited by Charlotte Brunsdon, Julia D'Acci, and Lynn Spigel (New York: Oxford University Press, 1997), 162.

34. Radway, *Reading the Romance.*

35. Although I argue in the introductory chapter that the risks of skating are vastly overstated in popular accounts, skateboarding does present certain risks to joints and muscles, particularly for beginners.

36. Becky Beal, "Alternative Masculinity and Its Effects on Gender Relations in the Subculture of Skateboarding," *Journal of Sport Behavior* 19, no. 3 (1996): 204–20.

37. Natalie Porter, "Female Skateboarders and Their Negotiation of Space and Identity," *Journal for the Arts, Sciences, and Technology* 1, no. 2 (2003): 75–80.

38. Whannel, "From Pig's Bladders to Ferraris," 80.

39. There is an important point to be made here about young women, as well, though unfortunately it is not within the scope of this study to do so. I would argue that, in participating in what many of us would call "postfeminist" behavior—playing along with sexist jokes or participating as "one of the boys"—many young women actively reject the idea that all women play the civilizing role. That is, they are working against the stereotype of the fussy, rule-bound, civilizing woman (usually a mother) while at the same subscribing to or allowing sexist behavior.

40. Robert Hanke, "Redesigning Men: Hegemonic Masculinity in Transition," in *Men, Masculinity, and the Media,* edited by Steve Craig (Newbury Park, CA: Sage, 1992).

41. Quoted in Diana Saco, "Masculinity as Signs: Poststructuralist Feminist Approaches to the Study of Gender," in *Men, Masculinity, and the Media,* edited by Steve Craig (Newbury Park, CA: Sage, 1992), 31–32.

42. Though skateboarders never actually "film"—they use video—they frequently use the verb *film.* It is unclear whether or not this discrepancy results from linguistic norms or suggests an elevation of their practice from a practice akin to home videotaping to a professionalized art form.

43. Notably, Mark's use of the phrase "these kids" refers to younger skateboarders within the culture, and there is a perception that young skaters (those under the approximate age of 13) are skateboarding for recognition rather than out of an authentic love of the culture. The accuracy of this perception cannot be analyzed using the data I have collected and is outside the purview of this study.

"You do it together"

1. Stuart Hall, "Encoding/Decoding," in *Culture, Media, Language,* edited by Stuart Hall, Dorothy Hobson, Andrew Lowe, and Paul Willis (London: Hutchinson, 1980).

2. Dick Hebdige, *Subculture: The Meaning of Style* (London: Methuen, 1979).

3. Michel de Certeau, *The Practice of Everyday Life*, translated by Steven Rendall (Berkeley: University of California Press, 1984).

4. R. W. Connell, *Masculinities* (Berkeley: University of California Press, 1995).

5. Matt Higgins, "Riders of the World, Unite! Skateboarding Sprouts as Team Sport," *New York Times*, June 6, 2007.

6. On mediascapes, see Arjun Appadurai, "Disjuncture and Difference in the Global Cultural Economy," in *The Phantom Public Sphere*, edited by Bruce Robbins (Minneapolis: University of Minnesota Press, 1993), 269–95.

7. Jennie Yabroff, "Betas Rule," *Newsweek*, June 4, 2007.

8. Jeff Zeleny, "Daschle Ends Bid for Post; Obama Concedes Mistake," *New York Times*, February 6, 2009.

9. Adam B. Ellick, "Skateboarding in Afghanistan Provides a Diversion from Desolation," *New York Times*, January 26, 2009.

Bibliography

Scholarly Sources

Anderson, Benedict. *Imagined Communities: Reflections on the Origin and Spread of Nationalism*. London: Verso, 1983.

Ang, Ien. "Melodramatic Identifications: Television Fiction and Women's Fantasy." In *Feminist Television Criticism: A Reader*, edited by Charlotte Brunsdon, Julie D'Acci, and Lynn Spigel, 155–66. New York: Oxford University Press, 1997.

Ang, Ien. *Watching Dallas: Soap Opera and the Melodramatic Imagination*. Translated by Della Couling. New York: Methuen, 1985.

Appadurai, Arjun. "Disjuncture and Difference in the Global Cultural Economy." In *The Phantom Public Sphere*, edited by Bruce Robbins, 269–95. Minneapolis: University of Minnesota Press, 1993.

Atkinson, Michael, and Kevin Young. *Tribal Play: Subcultural Journeys through Sport*. Bingley, UK: JAI Press, 2008.

Austin, Joe, and Michael Nevin Willard, eds. *Generations of Youth: Youth Cultures and History in Twentieth-Century America*. New York: New York University Press, 1998.

Beal, Becky. "Alternative Masculinity and Its Effects on Gender Relations in the Subculture of Skateboarding." *Journal of Sport Behavior* 19, no. 3 (1996): 204–20.

Beal, Becky, and Charlene Wilson. "'Chicks Dig Scars': Commercialisation and the Transformation of Skateboarders' Identities." In *Understanding Lifestyle Sports: Consumption, Identity, and Difference*, edited by Belinda Wheaton, 31–54. New York: Routledge, 2004.

Bederman, Gail. *Manliness and Civilization: A Cultural History of Gender and Race in the United States, 1880–1917*. Chicago: University of Chicago Press, 1995.

Bellah, Robert N., Richard Madsen, William M. Sullivan, Ann Swidler, and Steven M. Tipton. *Habits of the Heart: Individualism and Commitment in American Life*. Berkeley: University of California Press, 1985.

Berger, John. *Ways of Seeing*. London: Penguin, 1972.

Bernstein, Alina, and Neil Blain. *Sport, Media, Culture: Global and Local Dimensions*. Portland, OR: Frank Cass, 2003.

Bhabha, Homi. "The Other Question." In *Contemporary Postcolonial Theory: A Reader*, edited by Padmini Mongia, 37–54. London: Arnold, 1997.

Borden, Iain. *Skateboarding, Space, and the City: Architecture and the Body*. New York: Berg, 2001.

Bordo, Susan. *The Male Body: A New Look at Men in Public and Private*. New York: Farrar, Straus and Giroux, 1999.

Brayton, Sean. "'Black-Lash': Revisiting the "White Negro" through Skateboarding." *Sociology of Sport Journal* 22 (2005): 356–72.

Brayton, Sean. "MTV's *Jackass:* Transgression, Abjection, and the Economy of White Masculinity." *Journal of Gender Studies* 16, no. 1 (2007): 57–72.

Brunsdon, Charlotte, Julia D'Acci, and Lynn Spigel. *Feminist Television Criticism: A Reader*. New York: Oxford University Press, 1997.

Campbell, Neil. *American Youth Cultures*. New York: Routledge, 2004.

Canclini, Néstor García. *Consumers and Citizens: Globalization and Multicultural Conflicts*. Minneapolis: University of Minnesota Press, 2001.

Clarke, John, Stuart Hall, Tony Jefferson, and Brian Roberts. "Subcultures, Cultures, and Class: A Theoretical Overview." In *Resistance through Rituals: Youth Subcultures in Post-War Britain*, edited by Stuart Hall and Tony Jefferson, 9–74. London: Hutchinson, 1976. Reprint, New York: Routledge, 2000. Page references are to the Routledge edition.

Connell, R. W. *Masculinities*. Berkeley: University of California Press, 1995.

Craig, Steve, ed. *Men, Masculinity, and the Media*. Newbury Park, CA: Sage, 1992.

Crenshaw, Kimberle. "Mapping the Margins: Intersectionality, Identity Politics, and Violence against Women of Color." *Stanford Law Review* (1991): 1241–99.

de Certeau, Michel. *The Practice of Everyday Life*. Translated by Steven Rendall. Berkeley: University of California Press, 1984.

Donnelly, Michele K. "Alternative *and* Mainstream: Revisiting the Sociological Analysis of Skateboarding." In *Tribal Play: Subcultural Journeys through Sport*, edited by Michael Atkinson and Kevin Young, 197–214. Bingley, UK: JAI Press, 2008.

Donnelly, Michele K. "'Take the Slam and Get Back Up': *Hardcore Candy* and the Politics of Representation in Girls' and Women's Skateboarding and Snowboarding on Television." In *Youth Culture and Sport: Identity, Power, and Politics*, edited by Michael D. Giardina and Michele K. Donnelly, 127–43. New York: Routledge, 2008.

Douglas, Susan J. *Listening In: Radio and the American Imagination*. New York: Times Books, 1999.

Dow, Bonnie J. *Prime-Time Feminism: Television, Media Culture, and the Women's Movement since 1970*. Philadelphia: University of Pennsylvania Press, 1996.

Dyer, Richard. *White*. London: Routledge, 1997.

Faludi, Susan. *Backlash: The Undeclared War against American Women*. New York: Crown, 1991.

Foucault, Michel. *Discipline and Punish: The Birth of the Prison*. Translated by Alan Sheridan. New York: Vintage, 1995.

Fraiman, Susan. *Cool Men and the Second Sex*. New York: Columbia University Press, 2003.

Frank, Thomas. *The Conquest of Cool: Business Culture, Counterculture, and the Rise of Hip Consumerism*. Chicago: University of Chicago Press, 1998.

Gelder, Ken. "Introduction to Part Two." In *The Subcultures Reader*, edited by Ken Gelder and Sarah Thornton, 83–89. New York: Routledge, 1997.

Gelder, Ken, and Sarah Thornton, eds. *The Subcultures Reader*. New York: Routledge, 1997.

Giardina, Michael D., and Michele K. Donnelly. "Introduction." In *Youth Culture and Sport: Identity, Power, and Politics*, edited by Michael D. Giardina and Michele K. Donnelly, 1–12. New York: Routledge, 2008.

Goldman, Robert, and Stephen Papson. *Nike Culture: The Sign of the Swoosh*. Thousand Oaks: Sage, 1998.

Gunn, Joshua. "Marilyn Manson Is Not Goth: Memorial Struggle and the Rhetoric of Subcultural Identity." *Journal of Communication Inquiry* 23, no. 4 (1999): 408–31.

Hall, Stuart. "Encoding/Decoding." In *Culture, Media, Language*, edited by Stuart Hall, Dorothy Hobson, Andrew Lowe, and Paul Willis, 128–38. London: Hutchinson, 1980.

Hall, Stuart, Dorothy Hobson, Andrew Lowe, and Paul Willis, eds., *Culture, Media, Language*. London: Hutchinson, 1980.

Hall, Stuart, and Tony Jefferson, eds. *Resistance through Rituals: Youth Subcultures in Post-War Britain*. London: Hutchinson, 1976. Reprint, New York: Routledge, 2000.

Hanke, Robert. "Redesigning Men: Hegemonic Masculinity in Transition." In *Men, Masculinity, and the Media*, edited by Steve Craig, 185–98. Newbury Park, CA: Sage, 1992.

Hartigan, John, Jr. "Name Calling: Objectifying "Poor Whites" and "White Trash" in Detroit." In *White Trash: Race and Class in America*, edited by Matt Wray and Annalee Newitz, 41–56. New York: Routledge, 1997.

Hebdige, Dick. *Subculture: The Meaning of Style*. London: Methuen, 1979.

hooks, bell. "Eating the Other: Desire and Resistance." In *Black Looks: Race and Representation*, edited by bell hooks. Boston: South End, 1992.

Howell, Ocean. "The 'Creative Class' and the Gentrifying City: Skateboarding in Philadelphia's Love Park." *Journal of Architectural Education* 59, no. 2 (2003): 32–42.

Jeffords, Susan. *Hard Bodies: Hollywood Masculinity in the Reagan Era*. New Brunswick, NJ: Rutgers University Press, 1994.

Jenkins, Henry. *Textual Poachers: Television Fans and Participatory Cultures*. New York: Routledge, 1992.

Kasson, John F. *Houdini, Tarzan, and the Perfect Man: The White Male Body and the Challenge of Modernity in America*. New York: Hill and Wang, 2001.

Kay, Joanne, and Suzanne Laberge. "Mapping the Field of "AR": Adventure Racing and Bourdieu's Concept of Field." *Sociology of Sport Journal* 19, no. 1 (2002): 25–46.

Kelly, Deirdre M., Shauna Pomerantz, and Dawn H. Currie. "'You Can Break So Many More Rules': The Identity Work and Play of Becoming Skater Girls." In *Youth Culture and Sport: Identity, Power, and Politics*, edited by Michael D. Giardina and Michele K. Donnelly, 113–26. New York: Routledge, 2008.

Kimmel, Michael S. *Manhood in America: A Cultural History.* 2nd ed. New York: Oxford University Press, 2006.

Kusz, Kyle. "Extreme America: The Cultural Politics of Extreme Sports in 1990s America." In *Understanding Lifestyle Sports: Consumption, Identity, and Difference*, edited by Belinda Wheaton, 197–213. New York: Routledge, 2004.

Kusz, Kyle. *Revolt of the White Athlete: Race, Media and the Emergence of Extreme Athletes in America.* New York: Peter Lang, 2007.

Lahti, Martti. "As We Become Machines: Corporealized Pleasure in Video Games." In *The Video Game Theory Reader*, edited by Mark J. P. Wolf and Bernard Perron, 157–70. New York: Routledge, 2003.

Leonard, David J. "To the White Extreme in the Mainstream: Manhood and White Youth Culture in a Virtual Sports World." In *Youth Culture and Sport: Identity, Power, and Politics*, edited by Michael D. Giardina and Michele K. Donnelly, 91–112. New York: Routledge, 2008.

Lipsitz, George. *The Possessive Investment in Whiteness.* Chicago: University of Chicago Press, 2006.

Lott, Eric. *Love and Theft: Blackface Minstrelsy and the American Working Class.* New York: Oxford University Press, 1993.

Lyng, Stephen. *Edgework: The Sociology of Risk-Taking.* New York: Routledge, 2004.

Maira, Sunaina, and Elisabeth Soep. *Youthscapes: The Popular, the National, the Global.* Philadelphia: University of Pennsylvania Press, 2005.

Malin, Brenton J. *American Masculinity under Clinton: Popular Media and the Nineties "Crisis of Masculinity."* New York: Peter Lang, 2005.

Marchart, Oliver. "Bridging the Micro-Macro Gap: Is There Such a Thing as a Post-subcultural Politics?" In *The Post-subcultures Reader*, edited by David Muggleton and Rupert Weinzierl, 83–97. New York: Berg, 2003.

McIntosh, Peggy. "White Privilege: Unpacking the Invisible Knapsack." In *White Privilege: Essential Readings on the Other Side of Racism*, edited by Paula S. Rothenberg, 97–101. New York: Worth, 2002.

McRobbie, Angela. "Second-Hand Dresses and the Role of the Ragmarket." In *The Subcultures Reader*, edited by Ken Gelder and Sarah Thornton, 191–99. New York: Routledge, 1997.

McRobbie, Angela, and Jenny Garber. "Girls and Subcultures." In Angela McRobbie, *Feminism and Youth Culture: From "Jackie" to "Just Seventeen,"* 1–15. London: Macmillan Education, 1991.

Medovoi, Leerom. *Rebels: Youth and the Cold War Origins of Identity.* Durham: Duke University Press, 2005.

Modleski, Tania. *Loving with a Vengeance: Mass-Produced Fantasies for Women.* New York: Methuen, 1982.

Mongia, Padmini, ed. *Contemporary Postcolonial Theory: A Reader.* London: Arnold, 1997.

Muggleton, David. *Inside Subculture: The Postmodern Meaning of Style.* New York: Berg, 2000.

Muggleton, David, and Rupert Weinzierl, eds. *The Post-subcultures Reader.* New York: Berg, 2003.

Pfeil, Fred. *White Guys: Studies in Postmodern Domination and Difference.* New York: Verso, 1995.

Piano, Doreen. "Resisting Subjects: DIY Feminism and the Politics of Style in Subcultural Production." In *The Post-subcultures Reader,* edited by David Muggleton and Rupert Weinzierl, 253–65. New York: Berg, 2003.

Porter, Natalie. "Female Skateboarders and Their Negotiation of Space and Identity." *Journal for the Arts, Sciences, and Technology* 1, no. 2 (2003): 75–80.

Press, Andrea L. *Women Watching Television: Gender, Class, and Generation in the American Television Experience.* Philadelphia: University of Pennsylvania Press, 1991.

Radway, Janice. *Reading the Romance: Women, Patriarchy, and Popular Literature.* 1984. Reprinted with a new introduction by the author. Chapel Hill: University of North Carolina Press, 1991.

Rich, Adrienne. "Compulsory Heterosexuality and Lesbian Existence." *Signs: Journal of Women in Culture and Society* 5, no. 4 (1980): 631–60.

Rinehart, Robert E. "ESPN's X Games: Contests of Opposition, Resistance, Co-option, and Negotiation." In *Tribal Play: Subcultural Journeys through Sport,* edited by Michael Atkinson and Kevin Young, 175–95. Bingley, UK: JAI Press, 2008.

Rinehart, Robert E. "Exploiting a New Generation: Corporate Branding and the Co-optation of Action Sport." In *Youth Culture and Sport: Identity, Power, and Politics,* edited by Michael D. Giardina and Michele K. Donnelly, 71–90. New York: Routledge, 2008.

Robbins, Bruce, ed. *The Phantom Public Sphere.* Minneapolis: University of Minnesota Press, 1993.

Rose, Tricia. *Black Noise: Rap Music and Popular Culture in Contemporary America.* Hanover, NH: Wesleyan University Press, 1994.

Rothenberg, Paula S., ed. *White Privilege: Essential Readings on the Other Side of Racism.* New York: Worth Publishers, 2002.

Saco, Diana. "Masculinity as Signs: Poststructuralist Feminist Approaches to the Study of Gender." In *Men, Masculinity, and the Media,* edited by Steve Craig, 23–39. Newbury Park, CA: Sage, 1992.

Savran, David. *Taking It Like a Man: White Masculinity, Masochism, and Contemporary American Culture.* Princeton: Princeton University Press, 1998.

Sedgwick, Eve Kosofsky. *Epistemology of the Closet.* Berkeley: University of California Press, 1990.

Smith, Valerie. *Not Just Race, Not Just Gender: Black Feminist Readings.* New York: Routledge, 1998.

Stahl, Geoff. "Tastefully Renovating Subcultural Theory: Making Space for a New Model." In *The Post-subcultures Reader,* edited by David Muggleton and Rupert Weinzierl, 27–40. New York: Berg, 2003.

Ta, Lynn. "Hurt So Good: *Fight Club,* Masculine Violence, and the Crisis of Capitalism." *Journal of American Culture* 29, no. 3 (2006): 265–77.

Thorne, Barrie. *Gender Play: Girls and Boys in School.* New Brunswick, NJ: Rutgers University Press, 1993.

Thornton, Sarah. *Club Cultures: Music, Media, and Subcultural Capital.* Cambridge, UK: Polity, 1995.

Thornton, Sarah. "The Social Logic of Subcultural Capital." In *The Subcultures Reader,* edited by Ken Gelder and Sarah Thornton, 200–209. New York: Routledge, 1997.

Wheaton, Belinda. "After Sport Culture: Rethinking Sport and Post-Subcultural Theory." *Journal of Sport and Social Issues* 31, no. 3 (2007): 283–307.

Wheaton, Belinda. "Introduction: Mapping the Lifestyle Sport-Scape." In *Understanding Lifestyle Sports: Consumption, Identity, and Difference,* edited by Belinda Wheaton, 1–28. New York: Routledge, 2004.

Wheaton, Belinda, ed. *Understanding Lifestyle Sports: Consumption, Identity, and Difference.* New York: Routledge, 2004.

Wheaton, Belinda, and Becky Beal. "'Keeping It Real': Subcultural Media and the Discourses of Authenticity in Alternative Sport." *International Review for the Sociology of Sport* 38, no. 2 (2003): 155–76.

Whannel, Garry. "From Pig's Bladders to Ferraris: Media Discourses of Masculinity and Morality in Obituaries of Stanley Matthews." In *Sport, Media, Culture: Global and Local Dimensions,* edited by Alina Bernstein and Neil Blain, 73–94. Portland, OR: Frank Cass, 2003.

Whyte, William H. *The Organization Man.* 1956. Reprinted with new foreword by Joseph Nocerd. Philadelphia: University of Pennsylvania Press, 2002.

Willard, Michael Nevin. "Seance, Tricknowlogy, Skateboarding, and the Space of Youth." In *Generations of Youth: Youth Cultures and History in Twentieth-Century America,* edited by Joe Austin and Michael Nevin Willard, 327–46. New York: New York University Press, 1998.

Willis, Paul E. "Culture, Institution, Differentiation." In *The Subcultures Reader,* edited by Ken Gelder and Sarah Thornton, 121–29. New York: Routledge, 1997.

Winge, Theresa M. "Constructing 'Neo-tribal' Identities through Dress: Modern Primitives and Body Modifications." In *The Post-subcultures Reader,* edited by David Muggleton and Rupert Weinzierl, 119–32. New York: Berg, 2003.

Wolf, Mark J. P., and Bernard Perron, eds. *The Video Game Theory Reader.* New York: Routledge, 2003.

Wray, Matt, and Annalee Newitz, eds. *White Trash: Race and Class in America.* New York: Routledge, 1997.

Young, Alana, and Christine Dallaire. "Beware*#! Sk8 at Your Own Risk: The Discourses of Young Female Skateboarders." In *Tribal Play: Subcultural Journeys through Sport,* edited by Michael Atkinson and Kevin Young, 235–55. Bingley, UK: JAI Press, 2008.

Yudice, George. "What's a Straight White Man to Do?" In *Constructing Masculinity,* edited by M. Berger, B. Wallis, and S. Watson, 267–83. New York: Routledge, 1995.

Popular Press

"All-Day Safety Program Slated at Laurel Plaza." *Los Angeles Times,* November 13, 1975, SF14.

Allen, Henry. "The New Fad Afoot." *Washington Post,* March 29, 1979, D1.

Allen, Philip T. "Letter to the Editor: Dangerous Sport." *Los Angeles Times,* December 1, 1964, A14.

Almond, Elliott. "Skateboarder Means Business." *Los Angeles Times,* August 13, 1976, D8.

Almond, Elliott. "Skateboarding's New Young Pros." *Los Angeles Times,* September 18, 1977, OC1.

Appleman, Marc. "Celebrations, Color Will Mark Easter." *Los Angeles Times,* April 1, 1983, SDA1.

Arnold, Mary-Kate. "Skater Babes: Asexual or Not?" *Sassy,* December 1992, 46–47.

Baker, Al. "Law Requires Children to Wear Helmets While Skateboarding." *New York Times,* November 25, 2004, B9.

"Ban on Skateboards Enacted 'Reluctantly.'" *Los Angeles Times,* June 22, 1965, 23.

Barker, Mayerene. "Law, Order Become Part of Curriculum." *Los Angeles Times,* June 4, 1981, SG8.

Barnes, George. "Althol Bans Skateboards Downtown." *Worcester Telegram and Gazette* (MA), May 16, 2000, B2.

Bayley, Patricia A. "Letter to the Editor: Skateboards." *Los Angeles Times,* July 7, 1975, C6.

Beck, Joan. "Transfusion New Aid for Unborn Rh Babies." *Washington Post,* June 17, 1966, D6.

Belcher, Jerry. "Georgia's 'Colonial Dream' Wins Top Prize for Floats." *Los Angeles Times,* January 2, 1975, A1, 4.

Bender, Marylin. "Advertising Heeds the Eloquent Call of Fashion." *New York Times,* August 16, 1966, 30.

Berkman, Leslie. "Swap Meet at Fairgrounds Raided by 130 Law Officers." *Los Angeles Times,* February 3, 1975, 6A.

Betts, Kate. "The Whoosh of What You'll Be Wearing." *New York Times,* May 5, 2002, 6.

Bienvenue, Richard. "A Little Bit of Noise but a Whole Lot of Fun." *Washington Post,* July 28, 1990, A18.

"Blood Transfusion Ordered for Youth." *Los Angeles Times*, June 12, 1975, OC5.

Blum, David J. "U.S. Makers Confident of Victory in Trade Battle with Cheap Skates." *Wall Street Journal*, April 6, 1981, 25.

"Boy Avoids Bad Injuries as Car Runs over Chest." *Los Angeles Times*, September 21, 1964, E7.

Brooke, Michael. *The Concrete Wave: The History of Skateboarding*. Los Angeles: Warwick, 1999.

Brown, Patricia Leigh. "This Is Extremely Sporting." *New York Times*, August 13, 2000, 2.

Burchard, Hank. "Riding the Skateboard Wave." *Washington Post*, August 5, 1976, D7.

Burgi, Michael. "Don't Try This at Home." *Mediaweek*, June 12, 1995, 24.

Bushmiller, Ernie. "Nancy." *Los Angeles Times*, July 27, 1965, A7.

"Business Bulletin." *Wall Street Journal*, May 27, 1965, 1.

Carlson, Peter. "Ragin' on the Ramp." *Washington Post Magazine*, February 25, 1990, W22.

Cavanaugh, Jack. "Towns Cite Safety Cares as Skateboarding Gains." *New York Times*, May 10, 1987, CN1, CN14, CN15.

Cave, Damien. "Dogtown, U.S.A." *New York Times*, June 12, 2005, ST1.

Chirls, Stuart. "Extreme Gear." *Popular Mechanics*, May 1996, 62.

"CHP to Ticket Skateboarders for Speeding." *Los Angeles Times*, March 30, 1975, SE2.

"Christmas Eve a Time of Fear for Young Burglar." *Los Angeles Times*, December 26, 1975, 3.

Chunovic, Louis. "X Games Score Big with Advertisers." *Electronic Media*, August 13, 2001, 2.

"City Will Study Skateboarding." *Los Angeles Times*, June 5, 1975, OCA10.

Cleland, Kim. "Action Sports Form Fabric of Generation." *Advertising Age*, April 16, 2001, 22. Accessed online, GeneralBusinessFile ASAP.

Cocks, Jay. "The Irresistible Lure of Grabbing Air: Skateboarding, Once a Fad, Is Now a National Turn-On." *Time*, June 6, 1988, 90.

Coyne, Catherine. "Family Guide to Weekend Events." *Los Angeles Times*, May 8, 1975.

Crowther, Bosley. "Who Says There Is No Talent?" *New York Times*, December 4, 1966, X5.

D'Amico, Esther, and L. Maxine Sanford. "Pint-Size Purchasers." *Home Office Computing*, October 1994, 98.

Darling, Lynn. "Skateboard: Status Symbol for the Young in Suburbia." *Washington Post*, November 13, 1977, 36.

Davis Fishman, Katharine. "Danger: Children at Play." *New York Times*, September 25, 1966, 286.

Davis, James. *Skateboarding Is Not a Crime: 50 Years of Street Culture*. Buffalo: Firefly, 1999.

DeCaro, Frank. "Forgotten but Not Yet Gone: French Blue, Platforms, and Pierced Navels." *New York Times*, July 19, 1998, ST2.

Deford, Frank. "Promo Wiz in Kidvid Biz." *Sports Illustrated*, February 7, 1977, 30–33.

Doernberg, Jerry. "Skateboarders Near Thin Ice." *Los Angeles Times*, May 24, 1965, SG8.

Donahue, Bill. "For New Sports, ESPN Rules as the X-Treme Gatekeeper." *New York Times*, March 11, 1998, G2.

Donaldson, Charles R. "Few Youths Entering Skateboard Contests." *Los Angeles Times*, August 14, 1966, C8.

Early, Gene. "Skateboard Ban Drive Growing." *Los Angeles Times*, April 29, 1962, SG14.

Ebert, Roger. "Dogtown and Z-Boys Review." http://rogerebert.suntimes.com/apps/pbcs.dll/ article?ID=/20020510/REVIEWS/205100301/1023.

"84 Compete in Skateboard Tournament." *Los Angeles Times*, January 3, 1965, WS13.

Ellick, Adam B. "Skateboarding in Afghanistan Provides a Diversion from Desolation." *New York Times*, January 26, 2009, D1.

Elliott, Stuart. "Tony Hawk's New Trick: 2 Marketers in 1 Campaign." *New York Times*, October 23, 2006, 10.

Elliott, Stuart. "The X Games: Going to Extremes in an Effort to Tap a Growing Segment of Sports." *New York Times*, June 21, 1996, 6.

Enfield, S. "Boy Talk." *Gentlemen's Quarterly*, September 1991, 142, 146, 148.

"5,266 Raised for MS." *Los Angeles Times*, April 17, 1975, SG4.

"Fortune 100 Best Companies to Work For, 2006." *Fortune*, http://money.cnn.com/magazines/ fortune/bestcompanies/snapshots/637.html.

"41 Groups Plan Safety Exhibits." *Los Angeles Times*, September 4, 1975, SE5.

Fowler, Brenda. "Teen Taste: Like, Trendy." *New York Times*, November 6, 1988, EDUC7.

Fraser, Robbie. "Thrill Ride." *TV Guide*, August 10–16, 2002, 26–28, 30.

Fry, Kathie, ed. "1995 Summer X Games." Skatelog.com, http://www.skatelog.com/x-games/1995/summer.

Funding Universe. "Hot Topic, Inc." http://www.fundinguniverse.com/company-histories/Hot-Topic-Inc-Company-History.html.

Fuse Marketing. http://www.fusemarketing.com/fuse.php (accessed December 1, 2005).

Garrigues, George. "Skateboard Ban Plea Puts Burbank in Spin." *Los Angeles Times*, May 21, 1964, G1.

Geiger, Debbe. "Get Aerial." *Better Homes and Gardens*, June 2002, 112–19.

Givens, Rob. "Skateboarding's Best Seller." *New York Times Upfront*, December 11, 2000, 20–21.

Gleiberman, O. "You Say You Want a Skateboard Revolution? Then Hold On." *Entertainment Weekly*, June 10, 2005, 81–82.

"Glendale Police Chief's Edict Bans Skateboarders." *Los Angeles Times*, June 23, 1965, SG9.

"Glendora Will Prohibit Skateboards Downtown." *Los Angeles Times*, April 27, 1975, SG5.

"Going to Extremes." *American Demographics*, June 1, 2001, 26. Accessed online, GeneralBusinessFile ASAP.

Gold, Bill. "The District Line." *Washington Post*, November 8, 1965, B12.

Goldman, Lea. "From Ramp to Riches." *Forbes*, July 5, 2004, 98–99, 101.

Goldman, Lea. "Going to Xtremes." *Forbes*, April 3, 2000, 140.

"A 'Good Skate' Competes Above Board." *Los Angeles Times*, October 19, 1964, 3.

"Good Skates." *Los Angeles Times*, August 26, 1966, A1.

Gordon, Dan. "Airborne." *Sport*, June 1999, 97.

Gordon, Dan, Brannan Johnson, Dennis McCoy, Carey Hart, and Chris Edwards. "Future Shock." *Sport*, September 1999, 93.

Gordon, Maryellen. "It's Fitted Skaters vs. Baggy Ravers." *New York Times*, January 18, 1998, ST2.

Gorman, Tom. "Playing Santa Can Be Tough Sledding." *Los Angeles Times*, December 14, 1975, SE7.

Granberry, Mike. "At 21, Top S.D. Skateboarder Is Sport's Old Man." *Los Angeles Times*, April 25, 1985, SDC1.

Green, Penelope. "Absolute Necessities." *New York Times*, October 18, 1992, SMA94.

Greenfeld, Karl Taro. "Life on the Edge." *Time*, September 6, 1999, 28–36.

Greenfeld, Karl Taro. "Skate and Destroy." *Sports Illustrated*, June 7, 2004, 66–68, 70, 72, 74, 76, 80.

Greenfeld, Karl Taro. "A Wider World of Sports." *Time*, November 9, 1998, 80–81.

Gross, Michael. "A Club Scene Just for Teen-Agers." *New York Times*, August 1, 1987, 56.

Gustkey, Earl. "Skateboarding May Be Kids' Stuff but It Pays." *Los Angeles Times*, September 22, 1977, E1.

Hawk, Tony, and Sean Mortimer. *Hawk: Occupation, Skateboarder.* New York: Harper Entertainment, 2001.

Helberger, Joe. "Skateboards Scoot Up in Popularity." *Washington Post*, October 5, 1975, 9–10.

Hevesi, Dennis. "Parents Vow to Protest AIDS Student." *New York Times*, September 16, 1990, 34.

Hiestand, Michael. "Going to Extremes." *TV Guide*, June 24–30, 1995, 32–35.

Higgins, Matt. "Champion Thanks a Legend of the Air Up There." *New York Times*, August 8, 2005, 3.

Higgins, Matt. "In Board Sports, Insiders' Status Makes Gear Sell." *New York Times*, November 24, 2006, 1.

Higgins, Matt. "Riders of the World, Unite! Skateboarding Sprouts as Team Sport." *New York Times*, June 6, 2007, D7.

Hill, Jean Laquidara. "Skateboards at Town Hall Mean Trouble." *Worcester Telegram and Gazette* (MA), August 16, 2000, B1.

Hiss, Tony, and Sheldon Bart. "Free as a Board." *New York Times*, September 12, 1976, 40.

Hochman, Paul. "Street Lugers, Stunt Bikers, and—Colgate Palmolive! Spokesmen with Nose Rings." *Fortune*, November 22, 1999, 60. Accessed online, GeneralBusinessFile ASAP.

Hofmann, Deborah. "Clothes for Beach (or Mall or Main Street)." *New York Times*, August 6, 1989, 44.

Holden, Stephen. Review of *Stoked: The Rise and Fall of Gator. New York Times*, August 22, 2003, 11.

Holden, Stephen. "Skating on Top of the World during an Endless Summer." *New York Times*, April 26, 2002, 25.

Holt, Janet L. "Letter to the Editor: Sidewalk Surfers." *Los Angeles Times*, November 14, 1964, A14.

Horstman, Barry M. "Shrinking Territory Upsets S.D. Skaters." *Los Angeles Times*, March 8, 1982, SDA1.

Howard, Theresa. "Being True to Dew." *Brandweek*, April 24, 2000, 28.

Hume, Ellen. "'Sharks Circling,' Hayakawa Concedes." *Los Angeles Times*, July 5, 1981, A8.

Jensen, Jeff. "Vans Readies $25 Mil Brand Blitz." *Advertising Age*, March 3, 1997. http://search.epnet.com/login.aspx?direct=true&db=ufh&an= 9703134485.

J. M.C. "'Peanuts' on TV." *Christian Science Monitor*, June 10, 1966, 4.

Jones, Carolyn. "Supes Ponder Plan for Greater Access for Sport on Sidewalks." *San Francisco Chronicle*, April 1, 2005, F1.

Kannapell, Andrea. "Taking Sports to the Limit." *New York Times*, October 11, 1998, NJ1.

Kellogg, Mary Alice. "Rebirth of the Boards." *Newsweek*, June 21, 1976, 56–57.

Kesselman, Judi R. "The Skateboard Menace." *Family Health*, August 1976, 34–35, 76.

Keteyian, Armen. "Chairman of the Board." *Sports Illustrated*, November 24, 1986, 46–50.

Kirk, C. W. "Around the Beltway." *Washington Post*, March 28, 1968, F2.

Knoedelseder, William K., Jr. "Skateboarding: A Story." *Los Angeles Times*, October 16, 1977, T99.

Koncius, Jura. "Video Games: Regulating America's Latest Craze." *Washington Post*, October 8, 1981, VA1.

Kornheiser, Tony. "Whoosh! Skateboards Zip Back into Big Time." *New York Times*, June 19, 1976, 35.

Launer, Sharon. "Ah, the Sounds of Summer." *New York Times*, July 12, 1981, LI20.

Laurent, Lawrence. "Johnny Carson Knows His Job." *Washington Post*, May 4, 1966, B17.

Layden, Tim. "What Is This 34-Year-Old Man Doing on a Skateboard? Making Millions." *Sports Illustrated*, June 10, 2002, 80.

Lefton, Terry. "Alt-Sports: Popular, Yes, but No Salvation for Licensing." *Brandweek*, February 7, 2000, 32.

Levine, Rich. "Curbing Teen Violence." *American Health*, April 1989, 108.

Lewin, Tamar. "Hey There, Dudes, the Kids Have Grabbed a Network." *New York Times*, October 21, 1990, H35.

Liberman, Ellen. "Gravity Games: Hawk Is Skating's Chairman of the Board." *Providence Journal-Bulletin*, September 11, 1999, 1A.

Louie, Elaine. "In Schools, Fashion Is Whatever Is 'Fresh.'" *New York Times*, September 22, 1987, C11.

Luna, C. "Tony Hawk." *Current Biography* 61, no. 6 (2000): 22–25.

"Manhattan Will Apply Brakes to Skateboarding." *Los Angeles Times*, January 19, 1975, CS4.

Mann, Judy. "Skateboard Fever." *Washington Post*, May 25, 1979, B1–9.

Martin, Judith. "Tagging Toy Prices." *Washington Post*, December 5, 1975, D1.

McCormick, Lynde. "Skateboards Come Back with Fresh Set of Antics." *Christian Science Monitor*, August 27, 1975, 19.

McDowell, Edwin. "Roller Skates: 300,000 Pairs a Month." *New York Times*, May 13, 1979, F13.

McGuinness, Liz. "Cities Ponder What's in a Game." *Los Angeles Times*, August 16, 1981, D1, 16–17.

McHugh, Mary. "Skateboards Are the Hottest Thing on Wheels." *New York Times*, June 6, 1976, 101.

McKee, Bradford. "Ramping Up the Suburbs." *New York Times*, November 27, 2003, 1.

McMains, Andrew. "Call of the Wild: Saatchi Unveils Bourbon Effort." *Adweek*, January 18, 1999, 26.

McMillan, Penelope. "Top Skateboarders Spin Their Slicks." *Los Angeles Times*, September 26, 1977, B3.

Moore, Scott. "Skateboarding Industry Rolling to Success." *Los Angeles Times*, September 18, 1977, OC1.

Mortimer, Sean. "Chairman of the Board." *Sports Illustrated for Kids*, July 1998, 62.

Moukheiber, Zina. "Later, Skater." *Forbes*, November 29, 1999, 108.

"Movies." *New York Times*. http://movies2.nytimes.com/gst/movies/movie.html?v_id=138604.

Myking, Lynn. "New Wheels Help Spur Revival." *Los Angeles Times*, February 6, 1979, SDA4.

National Sporting Goods Manufacturing Association. *Pediatrics* 105, no. 3 (2000): 659.

"New Skateboarder." *Los Angeles Times*, June 14, 1965, 27.

"A New Sport or a New Menace?" *Consumer Reports*, June 1965, 273–74.

Newton, Tom. "104 Arrested in Tujunga after Street Melee." *Los Angeles Times*, June 10, 1975, A3.

". . . No List." *Washington Post*, November 16, 1975, 75.

Nordhiemer, Jon. "Skateboards Make Comeback as Older Boys and Girls Join In." *New York Times*, October 9, 1975, 46.

Ogunnaike, Lola. "A Skateboard King Who Fell to Earth." *New York Times*, August 21, 2003, 1.

O'Hara, Jane. "Trouble in Paradise." *Maclean's*, April 6, 1987, 48.

Oppedisano, Joseph. "Wheel Men." *New York Times*, March 21, 1999, 371.

O'Reilly, Richard. "Skateboard: Personal Rapid Transit, Southern California Style." *Los Angeles Times*, June 2, 1975, OCA1.

Ostler, Scott. "Some Things Will Just Never Be the Same." *Los Angeles Times*, October 5, 1983, D3.

Packaged Facts. "The New Teens Market." April 1, 1995.

Pearsall, Susan. "Soaring Teen-Agers at the Skate Park." *New York Times*, October 11, 1998, CT1.

"Peninsula Cities Get Tough on Skateboards in Streets." *Los Angeles Times*, August 7, 1975, CS2.

"Pepper . . . and Salt." *Wall Street Journal*, November 2, 1965, 18.

Petrecca, Laura. "Going to Extremes." *Advertising Age*, October 11, 1999, 36.

Petrecca, Laura. "Going to Extremes." *Advertising Age*, July 24, 2000, 16. http://search. epnet.com/loginaspx?direct=true&db=ufh&an=3357939.

Phillips, McCandlish. "Family Visit Is Happy Day in Life of a Plebe." *New York Times*, May 26, 1966, 31.

Phillips, Patrick. "Boy Wonder Gets the Purple Crayon." *New York Times*, May 7, 1995, 59.

Pileggi, Sarah. "Wheeling and Dealing." *Sports Illustrated*, September 1, 1975, 22.

Pinsker, Beth. "Personal Documentaries Are New Form of Marketing." *New York Times*, April 15, 2002, 12.

Plate, Thomas. "Snap Goes the Skater." *Washington Post*, September 1, 1965, A3.

Porter, Justin. "A Skateboarder Gets a Voice in the Redesign of a Beloved Spot." *New York Times*, June 24, 2005, B1.

Raser, Derek, and John McCoy. "Over Board." *Los Angeles Times*, July 31, 1985.

Ray, Nancy. "Scouts to Save Skateboard Park." *Los Angeles Times*, October 27, 1985, SDA1.

Raymond, Joan. "Going to Extremes." *American Demographics*, June 2002, 28–30.

Reed, Susan. "From Homemade Chutes to Steep Streets, San Francisco's Thrashers Just Love Riding for a Fall." *People Weekly*, December 3, 1984, 130.

Ressner, J. "10 Questions for Tony Hawk." *Time*, May 9, 2005, 8.

"Retailer Doubles Earnings," *New York Times*, May 11, 2004. http://query.nytimes.com/gst/ fullpage.html?res=9907EEDD133CF932A25756C0A9629C8B63.

Richman, Phyllis C. "Try It!" *Washington Post*, September 26, 1976, 276.

Rick, Annette. "Fifty-Four Hours." *Los Angeles Times*, July 21, 1983, G8.

"Robbers Flee on Skateboards." *Los Angeles Times*, August 3, 1975, SFA2.

Robinson, Debora. "Good Scouts Get Together to Show Off Their Skills." *Los Angeles Times*, November 15, 1982, OC4.

Rugoff, R. "Get Big! Fashions Worn by Skateboarders." *Vogue*, September 1992, 191, 194, 207, 212.

"Safety Series on Skateboards." *Los Angeles Times*, July 13, 1975, WS5.

Salisbury, David F. "Skateboarding: From Fad to Sport." *Christian Science Monitor*, September 3, 1976, 6.

"Santa Monica Civic Shows Surfing Movie." *Los Angeles Times*, May 19, 1964, B4.

Schaefers, Jim. "Why Boys Have More Fun." *Seventeen*, July 1989, 68–69.

Scheiber, Dave. "Science Comes to Skateboards and the Sport Is Booming." *Washington Post*, August 11, 1977, D9.

Scott, A. O. "When California Started Riding on Little Wheels." *New York Times*, June 3, 2005, 13.

Seabrook, J. "Tackling the Competition." *New Yorker*, August 18, 1997, 42–51.

"Sidewalk Plan Hits Obstacle." *Los Angeles Times*, October 21, 1965, SG1.

"Sidewalk Surfin.'" *Washington Post*, June 8, 1975, 160.

"Sierra Madre Plans Skateboard School." *Los Angeles Times*, July 5, 1965, SG8.

"Skate-Board Rider Dies after Crash." *Los Angeles Times*, September 1, 1964, C8.

"Skateboard Award." *Los Angeles Times*, July 22, 1965, WS2.

"Skateboard Fall Fatal to Youth." *Los Angeles Times*, May 6, 1975, OC1.

"Skateboard Skiddoo." *Newsweek*, May 10, 1965, 45.

"Skateboarders in Action." *Los Angeles Times*, August 25, 1966, WS2.

"Skateboarders Wheel around in City Finals." *Los Angeles Times*, August 27, 1965, SF8.

"Skateboarding: Hazardous New Fad for Kids." *Good Housekeeping*, August 1965, 137.

"Skateboarding Ordinance Ok'd." *Los Angeles Times*, December 15, 1975, D2.

"Skateboards: Fun but Dangerous." *Consumer Bulletin*, August 1965, 13.

"Skateboards on the Way Out? Not in This Generation." *Los Angeles Times*, August 29, 1966, SF9.

"Skating Dog." *Los Angeles Times*, August 15, 1964, B8.

Smith, Doug. "Lorenzen Seeks Law to Regulate Skateboard Use." *Los Angeles Times*, May 11, 1975, SFA1.

Snyder, Don. "Skateboarder Plunges Feet First into Routines." *Los Angeles Times*, April 15, 1979, GB1.

Spiegel, Peter. "Gen-X-Tremist Pitchmen." *Forbes*, December 14, 1998, 188.

Spindler, Amy M. "Flip-Flop: The Runway Leads the Street." *New York Times*, September 19, 1995, B9.

Steinhauer, Jennifer. "Feet First into the Clubs." *New York Times*, May 22, 1994, V1.

Steinhauer, Jennifer. "Lulu and Her Friends Are, Therefore They Shop." *New York Times*, April 29, 1998, G6.

Stern Brothers advertisement. *New York Times*, August 29, 1965, 101.

Stonesifer, Jene. "Kids' Fashion Cuts." *Washington Post*, April 23, 1992, 15.

Strauss, Neil. "Where the Wheel Was Reinvented." *New York Times*, April 28, 2002, 17.

Strauss, Robert. "Skaters Want a Better Image." *New York Times*, January 25, 2004, 1.

Sullivan Moore, Abigail. "Skateboarding Heaven." *New York Times*, October 19, 2003, 1.

Surf Crazy Advertisement. *Los Angeles Times*, May 19, 1964, B3.

"The WWD List: Going to Extremes." *Women's Wear Daily*, December 13, 2004, 110S. Accessed online, GeneralBusinessFile ASAP.

Thomas, Kevin. "Film Short Is Long on Artistry." *Los Angeles Times*, March 15, 1966, C11.

Thrasher: Insane Terrain. New York: Universe, 2001.

"Vacation Events Set for Children." *Los Angeles Times*, December 19, 1975, U16.

"Views and News." *Los Angeles Times*, November 26, 1963, 31.

Wagner, Dick. "Hanging 10 at 36." *Los Angeles Times*, October 31, 1985, LB8.

Watrous, Peter. "Pop Turns the Tables—with Beefcake." *New York Times*, February 10, 1991, H1.

"The Week in Review." *Los Angeles Times*, June 14, 1959, SG2.

"The Week in Review." *Los Angeles Times*, July 12, 1959.

Weintraub, Arlene. "Chairman of the Board." *Business Week*, May 28, 2001, 96.

"Wheel Crazy." *Time*, October 27, 1975, 46.

Wilkinson, Alec. "Bob Burnquist." *Rolling Stone*, June 10, 1999, 105.

"Winning Form." *Los Angeles Times*, August 29, 1965, WS2.

Winzelberg, David. "Skateboarding, a Big Business, Seeks More Venues on L.I." *New York Times*, October 27, 1996, LI1.

"With Money on the Line, Coast Skateboards Roll." *New York Times*, September 7, 1976, 14.

Wolinsky, Leo C. "Skateboarding the Next Pro Sport?" *Los Angeles Times*, June 23, 1977, CS1.

Yabroff, Jennie. "Betas Rule." *Newsweek*, June 4, 2007, 64–65.

Zeleny, Jeff. "Daschle Ends Bid for Post; Obama Concedes Mistake." *New York Times*, February 6, 2009.

Zinsser, William Knowlton. "Super Rad Means O.K., Dad." *Sports Illustrated*, April 24, 1978, 36.